D1391151

Tunnel 29

Tunnel 29

*Love, Espionage and Betrayal: the True Story of
an Extraordinary Escape Beneath the Berlin Wall*

Helena Merriman

HODDER &
STOUGHTON

First published in Great Britain in 2021 by Hodder & Stoughton
An Hachette UK company

2

A CIP catalogue record for this title is available from the British Library

Hardback ISBN 978 1 529 33401 2
Trade Paperback ISBN 978 1 529 33396 1
eBook ISBN 978 1 529 33398 5

Typeset in Bembo MT Pro by Palimpsest Book Production Ltd, Falkirk, Stirlingshire

Printed and bound in Great Britain by Clays Ltd, Elcograf S.p.A.

Hodder & Stoughton policy is to use papers that are natural, renewable
and recyclable products and made from wood grown in sustainable forests.
The logging and manufacturing processes are expected to conform to
the environmental regulations of the country of origin.

Hodder & Stoughton Ltd
Carmelite House
50 Victoria Embankment
London EC4Y 0DZ

www.hodder.co.uk

For Henry, Matilda and Sam
Mum and Dad
Rosie, Livy, Sas and Seb

'Like all walls it was ambiguous, two-faced. What was inside it and what was outside it depended upon which side you were on.' Ursula K. Le Guin, *The Dispossessed*

Contents

Foreword

———◆———

WHEN I FIRST meet him, I can barely talk. It's eight flights up to Joachim's apartment and by the time I'm up there, holding my microphone to record our first meeting, I'm puffed out.

Joachim laughs and invites me in. I'd phoned him a week earlier (in October 2018), said I wanted to come to Berlin to ask some questions about something he'd done almost sixty years ago. The phone call was short, his English was limited, my German was even more limited, but in that conversation one thing struck me. Most of the people I've interviewed in my career as a journalist tend to generalise, summing up their experiences through their emotions. Joachim was different: he spoke in details, remembered smells, sounds, measurements, colours. I was intrigued and asked if I could come and meet him the following week. He said yes.

We walk round his apartment. It's light and airy, full of plants, and his shelves are dotted with puppets, buddha statues and porcelain cats. Above the door to the bathroom there's a white enamel plate with the number seven on, wrenched off the wall by Joachim in the middle of the night, he tells me, from an apartment block on the other side of the city. The apartment block where it all happened.

We walk over to the full-length windows and I admire the panoramic view, the city coming to life below us in the winter sun. Joachim's flat is on the edge of things, where the apartment blocks and high-rises of inner-city Berlin meet the conifers and pines of Grunewald forest. We stand there a moment and Joachim gestures in front of us, pointing into the distance where the Berlin Wall once stood. I think of those images from 1989, the night when people climbed on top of the Wall, danced on the concrete, then hacked into it with hammers, pulling it down. Every year that ends in a nine, we replay that moment, but I've always been more interested in the other end of the Berlin Wall story: 1961. The year it was built.

What happens when a government builds a barrier that cuts a city or country in half? That question was in the back of my mind when I was working as a journalist in Egypt and the police built a ten-foot-wall in front of the Ministry of Interior and protesters pulled it down. It was in my mind when I was living in Jerusalem and spent hours queueing at checkpoints to cross into Gaza or the West Bank. People talk about the fall of the Berlin Wall as the end of an era, and in one way it was: it marked the end of the Cold War. But a new era soon began: the age of walls. Right now, walls are in fashion – over seventy countries (a third of the world) have some kind of barrier or fence. Some run along borders, others separate areas *within* countries, or even within cities. Whatever their scale, with their guard-towers, death strips and alarm systems, many draw inspiration from the Wall of all walls – the one built in Berlin in the summer of 1961.

Joachim gestures to a table where the two of us sit. I clip a microphone onto Joachim's navy fleece and ask what he ate for breakfast, the standard radio question to check his levels. As he tells me about his smoothie and scrambled egg, I jack the microphone right up. His voice is quiet, modest. Up close I notice his elfin ears, his bright blue eyes that squint closed when he smiles. I calculate his age: eighty. Then I press record.

That day we talked for three hours. I returned the next day and we talked for five. It went on like this for over a week, me asking questions, Joachim answering them with breathtaking detail, his wife bringing cups of tea, gently squeezing his shoulder as she set them down. Over the following three years, I tracked down others involved in this story, interviewed them and read their letters and diaries, then discovered thousands of Stasi files that give you the kind of minute-by-minute detail that, as a journalist, you usually only dream of. I discovered a replica tunnel, the same dimensions as Tunnel 29, and recorded inside it; I wanted to know what it felt like to be underground, digging in the space the width of a coffin, and wondered why someone would choose to spend so long down here.

This research changed what I thought I knew about many things: the end of the Second World War, the beginning of the Cold War, the building of the Berlin Wall, the birth of TV news, and what it means to become a spy and betray the people around you. The result is this book.

Any dialogue that appears comes directly from those interviews as well as from Stasi meeting reports and interrogations, and I've drawn on oral histories, maps, memoirs, court-papers, declassified CIA and State Department files, and print, TV and radio reports to fact-check names and dates as well as for additional research. Any errors are mine.

Joachim

*T*HE FIRST THING *that hits him is the smell. Coal-dust. Then he feels it. It pours out, onto his head, his shoulders and into his eyes until he's blind with it. But he keeps going, hacking into the floor above with an axe, the ceiling shaking, everything shaking, the noise so deafening he can feel it in his bones. Then, suddenly: fresh air. He's made a hole, one big enough to climb through. He puts the axe down and picks up his gun: if they find him, he's not going alive. Smearing the coal-dust from one eye with the back of his sleeve, Joachim prepares to climb into the room, no idea what's up there. He pauses and in the silence he finds himself thinking, not for the first time, how had it all come to this?*

I

The Beach

—•—

JOACHIM PULLS HIS foot back from the water. It's cold, even in August. His friends are splashing in the sea, teasing him, calling him to come in, but he hates cold water and they know he won't.

He thinks back to last night. Workers beer. Sweat. Bodies tightly packed in against each other. Fumbling and kissing in the corner. He's never had a holiday like this, not once in his twenty-two years and he doesn't want it to end. Bright green forest covers the chalk cliffs behind him, white-tailed eagles wheel overhead and the sea is so clear he can see tiny fish flitting through the water.

Just one week left, then it's back to East Berlin. Three hundred kilometres south, it's a different world. Grey. Edgy. Even more so over the past few months. They've all noticed the changes: more border guards on the streets, the soaring numbers of people escaping to West Germany, as though they know something. There's electricity in the air, that hum before a storm.

Joachim looks up to see his best friend Manfred wading out of the water. They've known each other since they were six, smoked their first cigarettes together, dreamt up elaborate tricks at school. Manfred always got into arguments, but Joachim was that child at school who never got caught, always knew where the line was – never crossed it.

That night, Joachim and Manfred change into jeans and T-shirts, comb their hair and set out across the sand to the beer tent. Another evening in this beach-side paradise on the edge of East Germany, a couple of twenty-two-year-olds in that weightlessness of a long summer with nowhere they have to be.

What they don't know is that, right now, they're exactly where the government want young men like them: young men who might make trouble if they knew what was about to happen. For dozens of tanks are rumbling towards East Berlin and tens of thousands of soldiers are creeping into trucks, armed with Kalashnikovs, machine-guns and anti-tank missiles. Any minute they'll receive their orders and then it will begin.

The next morning it's the sound that wakes him – the whine of a loudspeaker crackling into action. As he hears the efficient sound of tents being zipped open, Joachim climbs out into the campsite and walks towards the loudspeaker, now blaring out the brassy pomp of military music. Then, a man's staccato voice: '*Das Ministerium des Innern der Deutschen Demokratischen Republik veröffentlicht folgende Bekanntmachung . . .*'

Joachim can tell straight away. It's a government announcement and he tunes out, bored. But then the voice changes, becomes more urgent: 'Wollankstrasse, Bornholmer Strasse, Brunnenstrasse, Chausseestrasse . . .' The man is listing streets in Berlin, streets Joachim has run around in since he was little, and now he's interested. He can't work out why the man is talking about them, but then he hears it – the voice says: 'The border between East and West Berlin is closed.'

Joachim's stomach registers adrenaline, but his head is catching up, trying to work out what's happened: if the border between East and West Berlin has been closed, that would mean the city has been cut in half, but how can you split a city overnight? It would mean severing everything – electricity, trams, trains, sewage – and it's such an obscene notion that Joachim and his friends ignore the announcement and go to the beach.

The following morning, the campsite buzzes with rumours: barbed wire; soldiers on the streets; tanks; machine-guns. Suddenly, Joachim feels a long way from home, and, like a storm chaser, he wants to be in the middle of whatever is happening. After breakfast, Joachim and his friends pack up their old Citroën, zooming back to East Berlin in one stint, arriving at dusk.

As the car weaves through the streets, something doesn't feel right. It's quiet. Too quiet. Hardly any people on the roads, few other cars. Eventually, after zigzagging down streets lined with linden trees and functional concrete buildings, they reach Bernauer Strasse, the mile-long road that straddles the border. Climbing out of the car, Joachim and his friends walk towards a sign, a sign they've passed hundreds of times crossing the border from East to West Berlin:

YOU ARE NOW LEAVING THE
DEMOCRATIC SECTOR OF BERLIN

It's always made them laugh, that word, *democratic*. *Nothing that democratic about East Berlin*, Joachim would say. Usually there'd be a couple of policemen standing by that sign, but now, silhouetted in the glare of a single street-lamp, Joachim sees a group of men in green uniforms and steel helmets. But it's not their uniforms that scares him. It's what they're holding across their chests: machine-guns. Barely breathing, Joachim watches as one man turns and strides over: 'What are you doing? Get out of here! If you don't . . .' The man gestures with his machine-gun.

Joachim turns to leave and that's when he sees it: a twist of barbed wire glinting in the streetlight. He has no idea what's happened, what these men are guarding, but somehow he knows that in one night, everything has changed.

2

The First Escape

February 1945 – East Germany

JOACHIM WAKES TO find his mother stuffing photographs, jewellery and clothes into a suitcase, his one-year-old sister perched on her hip. Downstairs, Joachim's father is ransacking cupboards, piling fruit and tins into bags, hauling mattresses off beds and taking it all outside where everything is soon coated in snow.

Joachim doesn't know why they're leaving; he knows something is wrong but there's no time to ask questions. His parents pack everything onto their cart, two horses tethered in front puffing out white smoke-clouds of condensation into the cold air. Joachim clambers up, burrowing under a woollen blanket alongside his grandmother, baby sister and mother. Then his father climbs onto the coachman's seat, nudging the horses into a trot.

Joachim listens to the wheels as they squeak through the ice, watches the snow sift through the trees, dappling their horses white. The farm recedes behind them and Joachim has no idea if he'll ever see it again, if he'll ever do those morning walks with his father, racing to keep up on his tiny legs as they checked on the cows, horses, pigs and geese. At the end of a gravel lane, past the fruit trees, where the farm turned into forest, Joachim and his father would watch the stags rutting, their burnt-red fur glinting in the dawn light. He can't understand why they're leaving it all behind.

What Joachim's father can't tell him – because how do you tell a six-year-old any of this – is that they're on the run from the Red Army. He'd heard about them last night on the radio, the Russian soldiers coming from the East, raping women and torching farms, and he's desperate to get his family to Berlin before the Russians find them.

What he doesn't know is just how close the Russians are already. Only a day's ride behind, the first troops of the Red Army are marching, leading a column that stretches hundreds of miles. Underneath their feet, the ground shakes, like the first stir of an avalanche, for there are an obscene number of men: six million soldiers. There are soldiers with padded leather helmets driving monstrous T-34 tanks that flatten the snow; there are commanders driving Chevrolet trucks with mortars on the back; there are cavalrymen on long-haired ponies and camels; then, on foot, a million criminals released from gulags, spurred on by rousing Russian war music that blasts from loudspeakers.

And they are fast.

The Russians are veterans of winter battles, and this weather – averaging minus twenty Celsius – is to their advantage. While German soldiers in thin socks lose toes to frostbite, the Russians know to bandage their feet in linen to protect them from the cold. At night, Russian sappers clear minefields; during the day, their tanks blast across snowdrifts, and these tanks are so enormous that when they come across escaping families in carts, they crush them under their huge metal tracks.

These are the final months of the Second World War and Josef Stalin, leader of the Soviet Union, has sent his soldiers to take what is now his. A few weeks ago, on the 4 February 1945, Stalin had met British prime minister Winston Churchill and American president Franklin Roosevelt in a palace on the coast of Yalta to discuss what to do with Germany. For years, the US, Britain and the Soviet Union had been allies, fighting against Germany, but now, with victory in sight, like vultures they were scrapping over the spoils. After long negotiations over champagne and caviar, they'd agreed to share Germany. The Soviet Union would take one half: the East. Britain, the US and France would share the West. Berlin, 100 miles inside the Soviet zone, would be divided too.

But Stalin is playing dirty. He wants his soldiers to reach Berlin first, before the British and the Americans, so they can strip the city of whatever is left. Money. Machinery. Uranium – for Russia's first atomic bomb.

But it is also about pride. Stalin is still recovering from the shock of being invaded by Germany in 1941, over twenty million Russians killed, and killed in horrific ways. Following Hitler's orders 'to close their hearts to pity and act brutally', German soldiers had burnt Russian houses, murdered mothers and babies and sent survivors to labour camps where most starved. Now, it is payback. As Stalin's troops race through East Germany, they are taking revenge. Scrawny Soviet soldiers, many of them survivors of the horrors of the German invasion, others who'd been brutalised by years of fighting under the command of generals who saw them as expendable, are now tearing into villages and farmhouses, stealing jewellery and china and stuffing it into their tanks, slaughtering animals, raping and mutilating women and setting everything on fire.

Joachim's father drives the horses on, past frozen lakes and leafless copses, their hooves scudding and sliding on the icy road. They've been going for a day without a break, but he knows he can't stop, because as well as the soldiers, there's the problem of the river. The River Oder. It's a day's ride away and they must cross it to reach Berlin. Though it's bitterly cold, the first thaw is arriving and the river will soon melt: if he doesn't get there soon, the ice will crack under the weight of the cart.

But as they draw closer to the river, they are slowed by others on the road, millions of refugees like them, all desperate to escape the Russians. Pregnant women lie on mattresses in carts pulled by oxen, children fix broken axles on overloaded wagons, mothers walk carrying their babies, having abandoned their prams to the snow. Already there are some who've not made it – small bundles in the snow, stiff and frozen.

There are hardly any men around, most have been drafted to the German army in a desperate attempt to save the country, though there are a few German platoons on the roads, sent here to cut off the Russians before they reach Berlin. Joachim's father is relieved to see the soldiers. He feels safer, though most look like teenagers with enormous helmets that almost cover their eyes.

As daylight fades, in the back of the cart, something wakes Joachim: a low hum. Just as he registers that it's the sound of an engine, he hears a plane tear through the sky, the staccato rattle of gunfire, then a sound much closer – his grandmother screaming as she clutches her foot, writhing in pain.

The cart stops.

German soldiers are now shooting in all directions and with all the smoke from the gunfire Joachim can't see what's happening so he hides under the blanket, his whole body shaking. Eventually, the gunfire ends and, as the smoke clears, Joachim peers over the cart. There are dozens of green lumps in the snow. The German soldiers are motionless, the snow around them turning red.

That's when the Russians come.

A group of soldiers surrounds the cart and drag Joachim and his family into an abandoned house. Inside, the soldiers shove Joachim's father into a cupboard to restrain him, then finish their rations of vodka and things happen that Joachim will struggle to ever talk about.

By dusk, the soldiers pass out and Joachim creeps from the corner where he's been hiding to the cupboard where his father sits, powerless to do anything. Joachim crawls into his lap, nestles in his arms and they sleep.

Next morning, Joachim climbs out of the cupboard to see the Russians packing. For a brief moment he feels relief that they've survived, but it is followed by dread when the soldiers drag his father out of the house, marching him down the snow-covered road until they all disappear into the white.

There are no goodbyes. No final words.

Joachim sits in the house with his mother, sister and grandmother for a moment, the wind and snow whooping around them, all of them lost in their own grief. But there is no time for tears, for they must leave the house before the next wave of Russian soldiers find them, before it all happens again. His mother knows they can't make it to Berlin; she must take them all home, back to the farm.

Joachim runs after his mother as she scours the roads for a cart, for the soldiers have taken their horses and his grandmother has a bullet lodged in her foot and cannot walk. A few miles away, Joachim and his mother reach an abandoned village where they spot a hand-cart, small but still intact; they pull it back to the house, hoisting his grandmother and baby sister on top. His mother then lifts the cart from the front and Joachim pushes from behind as they begin the slow walk home.

As they trudge back along the icy roads, Joachim discovers that despite his stick-thin arms and legs, he is strong. He doesn't complain about the cold that grips his bones or the pain that sits in his back. Instead, hour after hour, he pushes the cart steadily through the snow, this six-year-old who is too young to understand about war and soldiers and borders but old enough to know that his father has disappeared and he may never see him again.

3

The Long Walk

JOACHIM'S MOTHER LADLES stew into bowls and brings them to the
table. Sitting there, a group of Russian officers who now live in the
house. *Their* house. Joachim's mother is now their servant, Joachim and
his sister confined to bedrooms upstairs.

They'd arrived back in the middle of the night after walking two days
only to discover their village had been taken by the Russians. Not all
of them turned out to be violent rapists; the officers now living in their
house are polite, well behaved. Every day Joachim hopes his father might
return, but he never comes.

Meanwhile, the Russian soldiers continue their race to Berlin,
rampaging through villages and dragging artillery across rivers on skis
just before the ice melts.

Two months later, by late April 1945, carrying flags and banners,
armed with aircraft, tanks, field guns, mortars and flame-throwers, two
million Red Army soldiers are just outside Berlin. Over the next two
weeks, the Russians fire a war's worth of artillery shells onto the city.
Fire flows down Berlin's streets, into its buildings; it finds people hiding
in shelters, animals in the zoo, anything that can burn, burns. The sky
above the city is red with ash and, underneath, Russian soldiers fight
for the city street by street, house by house.

Defending the city are the remains of the German army, bolstered
by recently drafted women, wrinkled old men in straw-filled shoes and
terrified schoolboys in baggy uniforms incentivised with bags of sweets.
The better-equipped German Gestapo spend most of their time hanging
deserters from their own side, often while plotting their own escape.
And so Berliners are largely defenceless.

Women have drawn crimson-red lipstick-crosses on bedsheets, hoping
the Russians will respect the international sign for the Red Cross and

spare them, but instead the soldiers come for them. As the soldiers take the city, they take its women, raping over a hundred thousand – grandmothers, mothers, children. The lucky ones are only raped once or twice. Others are gang-raped multiple times, horribly mutilated, and thousands of women kill themselves – for fear of being raped, or shame after it happens. (These mass rapes are still denied by many in Russia, even by veterans of the war.)

On 2 May 1945, the Red Army takes the city and their soldiers climb onto the Reichstag – the parliament building – where they hoist their hammer-and-sickle flag high into the sky. Below them, fires burn, fuelled by petrol in abandoned equipment; buildings are splayed open, their twisted metal insides spread across the streets; and the stench of chlorine, gunpowder and rotting corpses fills the air. Most of the city is destroyed, buried under seventy million cubic metres of rubble, and the streets churn with mud, blood, sewage and even alligators – escapees from the zoo. Then there are the bodies: bodies buried under debris that will never be matched with a name, bodies of the Nazi elite who committed suicide after alcohol-fuelled orgies, bodies of children who drowned in Berlin's tunnels while trying to escape, and then, unearthed by Russian soldiers, the charred body of Hitler, a single shot wound on his skull.

But somehow, though a hundred thousand had been killed in the fight for the city, somehow, there are survivors. Amid the May sunshine, as the oak and maple trees come into bloom, those survivors wander the streets, zombies in torn clothes, scavenging for food, trying to exist in a city where there are no hospitals, buses, trains, fuel or drinking water.

Yet it's to Berlin that Joachim and his family are now walking, for they have been thrown out of their farm. This time, it's not the cold they're up against, but the heat. It's the hottest summer in years, and every day is framed by the search for water. They become experts at spotting farms where they place tin buckets under spigots and the swollen udders of abandoned cows, pull plums and apples off fruit trees, and search kitchen cupboards for processed cheese and tinned meat. They walk through bombed-out villages and ghost towns, the roads scarred with black scorch marks from shells shot by Katyusha rockets. Everywhere, the earth is dry and cracked – a lunar landscape of craters.

Walking among them, the human detritus of war – limbless soldiers, dazed commanders, Nazis, communists and war criminals. Then there are the other refugees – fathers carrying injured children on stretchers and mothers pushing prams stuffed with squawking chickens wedged next to babies with newspapers for nappies. Joachim keeps his eyes down, away from all of them and away from the swollen, staring bodies in the ditches. Once you've seen them, you can't un-see them.

They walk for days, weeks, so long that Joachim, his skin now caked with mud, has stopped asking his mother when they might reach Berlin. At night, they sleep where they can, in pine forests, ditches or, best of all, barns – straw tucked around them to keep warm. The farms remind Joachim of home and memories flash up: the radio in the kitchen that spewed out boring speeches that Joachim ignored, but when marching songs were played he'd turn up the volume and dance, feet drumming on the floor, hips thrust out, his mother laughing as she watched. Then there was the day the new mechanical grain thresher arrived at the farm. Joachim stood there mesmerised as the motor thrummed into action, the belt zipping along, cylinders whirring, threshed corn sifting through the grates. Eventually, lost in memories, sleep comes and by dawn they're on the road again.

They arrive in Berlin on a bright autumnal morning in November – five months after they began walking. Joachim has never seen anything like it. The rubble he expected, but not the trams that screech out of nowhere, or the cars that roar past, flooding the streets with their headlights. Berlin's overground train network – the S-Bahn – is now operating again and they take a train to Greifswalder Strasse in the north-east of the city, where a relative has found them somewhere to stay – a two-bedroom flat that only really counts as one since the front-room window has been blown out by a bomb. None of that matters though. After months sleeping in barns and ditches, never feeling safe, finally, they have a home.

4

The Rebrand

November 1945

J OACHIM STANDS IN the room, shivering. Arms outstretched, all joints and bones, he waits patiently as a man in a white coat points a large wooden syringe at him, coating him in a fine, white powder. *To get the lice off*, he says.

And so the business of living in Berlin begins. It's winter, their flat with its bombed-out window is freezing and they have nothing to eat. His mother goes out every day, looking for food and anything to burn to heat the house. She walks to the shops that Russian soldiers hang out in, begs them for cigarettes (Berlin's post-war currency), which she trades for bread. Other days she cleans houses or works in a nearby cowshed, bringing home money and buckets of fresh milk. Sometimes she takes Joachim and his sister Sigrid to the forests on the edge of the city. They're bare; most of the trees – the oaks, conifers, maples, elms and chestnuts – have been chopped down for firewood. But they're not here for wood – instead, they scrabble in the shrubbery, looking for the silky brown and white skins of mushrooms, remembering what they'd learnt at their farm back home about which are safe to eat. And then there are the offerings that appear on their doorsteps from generous neighbours – herring heads wrapped in newspaper, which his mother brews into fish soup, Joachim repulsed by the black, shiny eyes that float on top.

While his mother is working, Joachim is meant to stay at home with his grandmother, but instead he explores the adventure playground that is post-war Berlin. With a gang of boys, he runs in and out of bombed-out-buildings, leaping over charred beams and iron girders, playing hide-and-seek to the sound of the chip-chip-chip of the *trümmerfrau* –

'rubble-women' – who probe into the masonry with small hammers, prising away bricks, placing them in buckets ready to exchange for potatoes. Sometimes, when he's hiding, the floor collapses and Joachim crashes to the ground, twisting an ankle, laughing as he gets up again to hide. And then there are the prized discoveries, what the boys call 'bangers and crackers' – small explosives used in the war to ignite grenades. Excavating the explosives with delicate fingers, they lay them on tram tracks, jumping and shrieking when they explode. Long after the sun goes down, Joachim arrives home, hungry, happy and exhausted, streaked in ash.

Meanwhile, around them, Berlin is changing. Hardly anyone notices at first. A clock above the S-Bahn changes to Soviet time. Then a Cyrillic street sign appears. Soviet newspapers are sold at street-stalls, posters advertise Russian plays and concerts are performed by Soviet musicians flown in from Moscow. The Russians are turning Berlin into a new city: *their* city. It's part of Stalin's new massive post-war empire, stretching all the way from Moscow, through Bulgaria, Romania, Hungary and Poland, and on to Berlin and the border with Western Europe. Twenty million Russians had been killed during the Second World War and Stalin never wanted to be invaded again. All this land, these villages between the West and Moscow, gives Stalin a huge protective buffer behind which he feels safe.

And though Stalin has agreed to share Berlin with the British, French and Americans, since they're not here yet, he can do what he wants: his soldiers steal money and gold from Berlin's banks, rip paintings off museum walls and take millions of books from the city's libraries, flying it all back to Moscow. They steal uranium from atomic research labs for the Soviet Union's first atomic bomb and dismantle thousands of factories, putting the brass, metal and machinery on trains for Moscow. After the last train leaves, they pull up the track and take that too.

Finally, Stalin turns to politics. For there is one important difference between Germany and other parts of his new empire. Elsewhere – in Ukraine or Poland – if people don't do what he wants, Stalin can just send out his tanks. He doesn't need to worry about public opinion or elections. But since Germany is to be split down the middle, with the West insisting on inconvenient things like elections, Stalin can't rely on tanks. He needs to get Germans onside, win them over to communism.

But how? After the horrific way in which Soviet soldiers forced their ways into German homes, and onto women's bodies, many Germans now hate everything about the Russians, including their politics.

Stalin needs to rebrand, find a way of selling communism without calling it that, and he needs a group of people who can sell it for him, speaking in German, not Russian. Luckily for him, he has the perfect group of people for the job – a handful of German communists who'd fled Nazi Germany and sat out the war in expensive Moscow hotels. They were part of a German communist movement that stretched back to 1836 when Karl Marx arrived in Berlin on a yellow postal coach. German communists had made links with communists in Moscow, the Soviets teaching them how to fight back against a succession of German leaders who arrested and imprisoned them, until Berlin was the largest communist city outside of Moscow.

But Germany's working-class movement was bitterly divided; there were moderates who wanted gradual change; and radicals who wanted revolution. In 1933, this infighting had a catastrophic result – it gave Hitler a clear path to power and he went after both communists and socialists, throwing them in prison camps where most were tortured and killed. A lucky few escaped to European capitals, such as Moscow, and now, a world war later, the survivors were standing on the other side of the Nazi horror, with Hitler dead and everything to play for. As Stalin cast his eye over these German communist exiles in Moscow, there was one who stood out. Someone Stalin thought he could rely on: Walter Ulbricht.

Short, with a squeaky high-pitched voice (a result of childhood illness), Walter Ulbricht was known for his lack of charisma and humour, and his shrewd opportunism. He'd trained as a carpenter, fought in the First World War, then joined the Communist Party, styling his facial hair into a Lenin-like-goatee beard. He rose fast, went to Moscow where he met senior Soviet communists (including Lenin – which he would dine out on for the rest of his life), then made a name for himself by ruthlessly killing Stalin's opponents in the Spanish Civil War. And it was this ruthlessness that Stalin so admired – Walter Ulbricht's dedication to pursuing communism at any cost.

A few weeks before the end of the war, Walter Ulbricht and nine other German communists had sat around a table in an art-deco room at the Hotel Lux in Moscow, hatching a plan to return to Germany and build a new Stalinist-state. Walter Ulbricht had experience of this kind of thing – trying to persuade people of the merits of Stalinist communism. And he'd been terrible at it. During the war, he'd visited prisoner-of-war camps in Russia, delivering long speeches about communism to bored German soldiers. At one point he'd even driven a truck to the Russian front, shouting propaganda over loudspeakers for the benefit of German soldiers nearby. Ulbricht had since learnt that there were better ways of doing things. That the best propaganda was invisible.

On 30 April 1945, the day Hitler shot himself, two Soviet planes landed on a makeshift runway, a few miles from Berlin. On board, Walter Ulbricht and nine other German communists. With the fires of war still burning, they got to work, enacting the plan they'd hatched in Moscow. Underpinning it were two principles: because of the hatred of Russia in Germany, they would never talk openly of their time in Moscow. Second, they wouldn't refer to themselves as communists. From now on, they would be known as socialists.

With financial and political support from Moscow, they began creating a new Stalinist government, careful not to make it look like a communist takeover. The strategy was simple: staff local government with competent administrators while putting their most trusted communist leaders in the most powerful positions – in finance departments and the police. As Ulbricht put it: 'It has to look democratic, but we have to hold everything in our hands.' After just a few weeks, they'd created something that looked like a government, filled with people from a range of backgrounds and parties, with all the power in the hands of communists.

Only a few months ago, the communists had been the little people, the vermin, crushed under the black boots of the National Socialists. Now, they were the powerful ones, with the full weight of the Soviet Union and its tanks behind them. In 1848, Marx wrote that communism was the inevitable successor to capitalism. During the darkest days of the Second World War, to his disciples, the fulfilment of Marx's prophecy had seemed unimaginable. Finally, a hundred years after Marx's prediction, their time had come.

5

The Smuggler

—◆—

1949

JOACHIM SPRINTS THROUGH the street. The ball is just ahead of him, bumping along the road. It will be his any minute – his legs are almost buckling with the effort – but as he closes in, a foot swipes in from the right and takes it. It's a familiar feeling. He's the smallest of all his friends. It's why they call him *Der Kleine* – 'Little One'.

'Joachim!' shouts his grandmother. 'Get over here!'

He runs over to her, sees something in her hands. It reeks. A bag of coffee, freshly ground.

His grandmother waves it in front of him. 'You need to take this to Wilmersdorf.'

Joachim blinks back at her. He doesn't know much about Wilmersdorf. What he does know is that it isn't in East Berlin where they live, but on the other side of the border in West Berlin.

Joachim's grandmother explains that he has to get on the train, cross the border into West Berlin and meet a man who'll give him money in return for the coffee. It won't be easy – if border guards smell the coffee, they'll arrest him. His grandmother puts the coffee in a rubber sack to disguise the smell. The sack goes into a briefcase. Then off he goes, not suspicious at all: a scrawny eleven-year-old carrying a briefcase.

Joachim walks to the station, the smell of metal and oil filling the air. Hopping up to the train, he finds somewhere to sit and looks up at the passengers around him. A few, like him, are holding bags and cases. He wonders if they're hiding secrets too. Out of the window he watches trees give way to buildings as they draw closer to the border. There, border guards will appear and he knows they're looking for smugglers like him.

By now, four years after the war, East and West Berlin are two separate zones. Berliners can go between them – by train, car or just by walking over the border – but going from East to West, they're often searched by border guards looking for smuggled coffee, cigarettes and sausages. It's an easy way for East Berliners to make money – buy something cheap on the black market in their half of the city, sell it for a profit in West Berlin. Almost everyone is at it, exploiting the massive economic gap between the communist East and capitalist West.

That gap began straight after the war, when the Russians stripped East Germany of its gold, metal and machinery. For a country recovering from a war, this was disastrous – like beating up someone already in a coma. Then its new socialist government introduced its new socialist economy, going further than even Stalin had expected.

Walter Ulbricht nationalised banks, businesses and factories – now called *People's Own Factories*. Then he turned to the farms, throwing out landowners and forcing small-scale farmers to join communal farms, pooling their crops. The technical term is 'forced collectivisation', one of those phrases that somehow takes the sting out of things. Anguished letters written by farmers describe watching their wheat and potatoes rotting in the fields, their 'beautiful horses' taken away to be slaughtered.

Next, Walter Ulbricht turned to shops and supermarkets, taking them for the state. The government would now decide what they'd sell and for how much. Everything would have a set price: a potato from one shop would cost the same as a potato in another, and ration cards allocated weekly allowances of food and clothes. Tiny *HO* letters soon appeared on every government-controlled shop representing the state trade organisation that decided what they could sell.

Behind all of this were inspiring ideals: life would improve. No more poverty. No more unemployment. Free healthcare and education for everyone. And these ideas fell on eager ears: many were hungry for change, and the promise of a new system that would share wealth equally, give everyone free education and somewhere to live was intoxicating. But the shelves in the shops got emptier.

Walter Ulbricht promised it would be worth it in the end – that the economy would soar and people would be better off than their neigh-bours in West Germany. But the economy never took off. Worse, it was becoming clear how far the government would go to keep East Germany under control.

Stalin and Ulbricht created a new political party, the Socialist Unity Party (SED). Stalin hoped the SED would win enough votes to take power without violence, but in the first post-war elections, the SED did terribly. And so Stalin and Ulbricht decided it was time to play dirty: if they couldn't win votes through love, they would win them through fear.

They created police units that dragged anti-Soviet workers and activ-ists off the streets and took them to repurposed Nazi concentration camps. In a horrific irony, while in one breath the Soviets proudly announced that they were arresting and executing ex-Nazis, at the same time, they sent at least a hundred and fifty thousand people to Bautzen, Hohenschönhausen and other prisons, re-using Nazi torture instruments that had once been used on them.

By 1948, three years after the Second World War ended, the relation-ship between the Soviet Union and the West had broken down. It was clear that Stalin wanted the whole of Germany, not just the East, and it was only a matter of time before he would try to take it.

In June that year, he made his move: Stalin switched off the electricity supplying West Berlin, then blocked British and American access. Since Berlin lay a hundred miles inside the Eastern Soviet zone of Germany, the Western half of the city relied entirely on trucks, canal boats and trains from West Germany for its food and coal. With access blocked, Stalin knew that two and half million people in West Berlin would starve.

After just one month, West Berliners began to run out of food. What saved them was one of the most ambitious operations in history: the Berlin airlift. For a year, British and American pilots flew food, clothes, medicine and cigarettes into West Berlin. In the busiest period, a plane landed at Tempelhof airport in West Berlin every *sixty-two seconds*. What made this even more extraordinary was that the American planes that brought food were the same planes that a few years earlier had dropped bombs. Now, instead of bombs, as they approached Tempelhof airport, American pilots threw hand-made parcels of sweets and chocolates down to children, who watched the planes from the edges of the airfield. *Rosinenbomber* – 'the raisin bombers' – the pilots were called.

A year later, after 300,000 air-drops, Stalin gave up. The Red Army pulled down the barriers to the city, allowing British and American trucks back into West Berlin. Tens of thousands of West Berliners cheered the British and American soldiers as they drove in, throwing flowers onto their tanks and holding up posters that read:

HURRAH! WE'RE STILL ALIVE!

If you're looking for the moment the Cold War began, this was it. East and West Germany were now two separate countries with two irreconcilable ideologies: capitalism and communism. That year, West Germany was officially created, its occupying powers – the US, Britain and France – introducing a Western model of democracy, with free elections, free media and private ownership. Six months later, the Soviets declared the creation of the German Democratic Republic (GDR); a communist one-party system with a state-run economy under Soviet control.

Only a few years earlier, the West and the Soviet Union had come together to defeat Hitler. Now, the two were bitter enemies, limbering up for a new war that would soon spread to every corner of the world, dividing it in two, Berlin their battleground.

Yet an eleven-year-old boy could still take a train from one political system to another in the hope of making easy money. At the penultimate station before the border, Joachim scrunches his nose. In a flash of terror, he realises he can smell the coffee. His heart thumps. Pulling his briefcase closer, Joachim tries not to think about what could happen when border guards enter the train, if they smell the coffee. He tries not to imagine what the prison cell would be like, how long he might be kept there.

Joachim eyes the door, knowing it will open any moment. And that's when the idea hits him. Running to the doors, he stands next to them, and when they eventually open and two border guards board the train, all they see is a scrawny boy holding something, the smell obscured by fumes from the platform.

Joachim's body slumps with relief, and when he reaches his stop in the West, he skips off the train and takes the coffee to the address his grandmother gave him, where he is rewarded with a handful of coins.

That afternoon, *little one* is his family's hero and eleven-year-old Joachim learns that though tiny, he is tough, with a mind that finds solutions just when he needs them.

6

The Radio

1952

JOACHIM IS SINGING. It's 8.30 in the morning, and he's at school, a building sliced in half by a bomb where girls are taught in one wing, boys in the other. Every day begins with a song, usually 'High on the Yellow Wagon'. To keep it fresh, his teacher tells them all to sing it slowly some days, fast on others. It gets his pupils laughing. Wholesome state-sanctioned humour.

> Flutes I hear and violins
> Happy sounds
> Young people in a roundel
> Dancing around the lime tree
> Circling like leaves in the wind
> Cheering and laughing and romping
> I'd love to stay at the lime tree
> But the wagon, it rolls on.

The song, when you listen to it now, feels nostalgic, a throwback to a rose-tinted version of Germany where everything is horse-drawn carriages, green fields and happy families. The irony is that here, at Joachim's school, there's not much looking back: school in the new East Germany is the place where the future is created, where the party creates model socialist citizens for its model socialist country. As East Germany's new national anthem puts it, 'Resurrected from the ruins, faces towards the future turned . . .'

If communism is East Germany's new religion, then the school is its church, its pupil-congregation sitting in pews, learning at the feet of priest-teachers who often have a stronger influence on their lives than their parents. Six days a week, children are in the care of its party-appointed teachers, right from kindergarten where two-year-olds are taught the principles of socialism through communal potty breaks.

Joachim learns through repetition, his teachers discouraging questions or critical thinking, rebuking pupils who ask challenging questions, threatening to exclude them. In severe cases, children who display 'anti-social behaviour' (stealing, for example) are sent to *Jugendwerkhöfe* – juvenile correction facilities – where they carry out factory-style work, and are 're-educated', sometimes spending days in solitary confinement.

One afternoon, a man visits Joachim's class and tells the children about a special after-school youth group that runs arts and crafts, games, even camping in the countryside. Whoever wants to join should put their name on a list. Like most of the children, Joachim is excited, writes down his name.

When he tells his mother that evening, she's furious. She tells him this man is from the *Junge Pioniere*, a scout-like youth group sponsored by the party where children in red neckties and blue bowl hats (reminiscent of the Hitler Youth) are introduced to communist principles and encouraged to report anti-socialist behaviour by their friends and teachers, even their parents.

At eleven, Joachim is learning that the party presents itself in all kinds of ways. Like a shape-shifter, it's not always easy to spot. At school the next day, Joachim crosses his name off the list. He's never part of the *Junge Pioniere*, or the Free German Youth, which the pioneers graduate to aged fourteen, where they're given Marx's *Das Kapital* and taught Ulbricht's 'Ten Commandments of Socialist Morale'.

But there's one subject Joachim loves: physics. Sitting at his desk, legs dangling above the floor, Joachim watches as his teacher – a double amputee from the war – chalks up equations on the board. Here, there is no talk about the party or socialist values. There are just numbers, which Joachim finds he can understand as easily as a child's puzzle. In the school library, Joachim pulls thick books down from the shelves and spends hours studying long lines of numbers cradled between parentheses, spotting patterns.

Soon, his teacher introduces the class to electronics and Joachim is entranced by machines that seem to work like magic. He thinks back to the grain thresher in the barn back home, these new inventions like new tunes that riff on a theme he's beginning to understand because the basics are the same. Circuits. Motors. Conduction. Induction.

He puzzles over diagrams of radios in electronics manuals, reverse engineering them in his mind, trekking off to specialist shops where he buys wires and cogs and batteries to experiment at home. Aged fourteen, he decides he will build a radio. At an electrical shop Joachim buys wire, a rectifier circuit and a capacitor, and with a soldering iron he joins them around a cardboard tube. Finally, he attaches headphones. There's a crackle of static and his heart leaps as he realises he's tuned into a nearby transmitter in East Berlin. Lying in bed, he listens to the East German radio station, and for a few weeks this is enough, but soon he becomes curious and wants to find out what else is out there.

One night, Joachim makes a bigger radio, with two aluminium capacitors, which means it can receive more than one transmitter. Connecting the ground wire to a radiator in his bedroom, he stretches the ten-metre antenna wire back and forth under his mattress, then, sitting in his bedroom, he hunts through the ionosphere, past the transmitter in East Berlin, searching for sounds from worlds beyond his own, until, eventually, he finds something, something he knows comes from beyond the East. It's a song, 'Rock around the Clock', and Joachim loses himself in the steel guitar, the saxophone and Bill Haley's voice, the announcer coming off the back of it to tell his listeners that they are listening to *Schlager der Woche* – 'Hit of the Week'.

Joachim has stumbled across RIAS radio in West Berlin. Built on high ground near the border between East and West Berlin, Radio in the American Sector (RIAS) is funded by the US and described by diplomats as one of the most powerful weapons of the Cold War. For through the transmitter of RIAS radio, Americans can reach into East German homes, dripping music and dramas into people's ears, giving them a sonic version of life beyond the Iron Curtain. Night after night, Joachim listens to comedies and political satire such as *Die Insulaner* – 'The Islanders' – a programme that pokes fun at communism and East Germany. At the end of the night, Joachim switches the channel back to an East German station in case anyone comes round and discovers he's been listening to the enemy.

As a teenager, Joachim is now learning how far he can push things – both at home and at school. As one of the school's top science students, he is in charge of the chemistry cupboard, a place of wonder crammed with jars of white powder and bottles containing liquids of every colour. Joachim soon has a favourite chemical – potassium, because of how it fizzes and bangs when he adds it to water. One New Year's Eve, Joachim blends potassium chlorate and red phosphorus to make firecrackers, lighting them with friends in his backyard after dark. Sometimes he concocts potions at school, decanting them into plastic bottles and throwing them out of the window into the playground, where he watches them blow up. Somehow, he never gets caught.

One afternoon, at school, his amputee physics teacher tells him about the world above the earth's atmosphere, where nations and borders and politics don't mean anything. Joachim starts dreaming about space and decides that when he is older, he will become an astronaut.

Then, a few weeks later, a man comes to the house and tells Joachim and his mother that he has something to tell them. He was a prisoner-of-war in a Russian camp, the man says, and he was there with Joachim's father. He died a few years ago.

Joachim listens, his eyes glazing over. He finds himself back at the farm where he grew up. It's a Sunday morning in spring, bright sunshine, and he's walking through the forest with his father when a hunter comes running, asks if they've seen a stag he shot. They shake their heads, the hunter walks on and Joachim's father takes his hand.

Joachim blinks himself back to Berlin, the memory over. He has only a few fragments like these to remember his father by. And so Joachim joins the ranks of fatherless German children and a seed of anger blooms in his stomach that he doesn't yet know what to do with.

7

The Tank

June 1953

I F THEY'D KNOWN what would happen that day, maybe they wouldn't have gone. Or maybe they would. Because that's when they learn how far the party will go to protect itself.

It began in March 1953 when Stalin died. In East Germany, there was a surge of hope as people thought things might be different, that the most Stalinist country in the world might be forced to change now the man behind its politics was gone.

But they were wrong. The secret police still came for people in the middle of the night, the economy stayed stagnant. Then, in June, Walter Ulbricht, now leader of East Germany, announced that work quotas were to go up. Again. He'd raised them before, many times, everyone ordered to work harder without being paid more, but this time, something in the souls of East German workers snapped. After eight years of debilitating factory work, long hours, horrific accidents, the constant fear of a Soviet prison, it was all too much.

On 16 June, eighty workers on a building site in East Berlin put down their hammers and walked out onto the streets. Hundreds joined until there were thousands marching, chanting for free elections and an end to Soviet domination. That evening, news of the protests and a plan for a general strike spread, and made it into Joachim's home. He wanted to be part of it.

The next day, on 17 June, Joachim and his friends meet on a street corner and set off to find the protesters.

They hear them before they see them – tens of thousands of people singing old workers' songs as they march to Marx-Engels Square in the centre of East Berlin. Normally you'd only see this many people on parade days, when the Stalinallee was flooded with people waving flags and flaming torches, celebrating a political party that somehow always won elections with results that never added up. But today, for the first time since its creation, people have come out to bring that party down.

Joachim weaves through the protesters, excited to march alongside grown men and women. He hears that the protests have spread beyond Berlin, that workers in other cities in East Germany are marching too, and he begins to hope that this will be the day the party falls. As they march, people sidle in – from shops, bakeries, schools. At a shoe factory, a group of women lean out of windows, cheering them on.

Joachim waves up to them. 'Come join us!'

The women shake their heads, pointing to the door. 'We can't! We've been locked in!'

Joachim ducks out of the march and helps the aproned-women climb out of the windows, over the steel gates. Soon, Joachim is at the front, helping lead the way to a government building at Rosenthaler Platz where the protesters hope that someone will come out to address them. But the windows and doors are locked – terrified party members have barricaded themselves in. Joachim runs up the stairs, banging on the shutters. Then he sees a man with one leg hobbling up to a window with his crutches. An ex-soldier, Joachim guesses. The man's face is twisted with anger; he screams at the politicians inside, lift his crutch and starts pounding the glass: stab, stab, stab, stab, stab, stab—

Smash!

The glass shatters, revealing a huddle of petrified officials inside.

Buoyed by their success, the protesters keep marching, shouting: 'We are workers not slaves!' until they reach the wide tree-lined avenue of Unter den Linden, where they break into another old workers' song:

> Brothers, to the sun, to the freedom,
> Brothers get up to the light,
> Brightly out of the dark past
> The future is shining through.

Joachim is entranced. He's never known anything like it, the sound of that singing, the banners streaming high into the air, the feeling that this is the start of something.

But suddenly the mood changes. As the protesters wait for someone to appear, anyone from the government to answer their demands, they get restless. Groups of men break off from the march, setting cars on fire, tearing down Soviet flags and breaking into prisons.

From the government, still nothing.

Then, Joachim hears it before he sees it: a low rumble coming from the East. Whispers fly through the crowd, '*Die Panzer kommen! Die Panzer kommen!*' – 'The tanks are coming! The tanks are coming!'

In the distance Joachim sees a cloud of blue smoke from which a tank emerges, a Soviet commander standing on the turret, a steel helmet on his head, his cape billowing. His fists are clenched, his mouth contorting as he spits angry words into the smoke, words that are lost in the noise of the tank and now the screaming. For his tank has ploughed into protesters, teenaged limbs turned to powder under the tread of the tracks. Two men start climbing up the tank, but they fall back, hit by sniper's bullets. As the tank mows through the square, the protesters hurl bricks, stones, even push cars into its path to stop it, but it's pointless. Like a malfunctioning robot, the tank keeps going.

Joachim doesn't want to leave, he's not ready to accept it's all over, but then behind the tank, he sees eight more. In the footage of this moment you see protesters throwing stones at the tanks, which drive forwards then pull back, as if taunting the protesters, before ploughing straight into them.

Joachim races home and doesn't look back.

That evening, he watches from his window as tanks drive up and down empty streets, monitoring the newly announced curfew. Tuning his radio to the West, Joachim discovers what had happened at the square after he left: dozens of people killed. The following week, thousands are thrown into secret prisons and hundreds executed after show trials.

And so ends the first anti-Soviet uprising in Eastern Europe. There won't be another in East Germany for thirty years. People have learnt the limits of what they can do.

8

A Thousand Little Things

――•――

February 1960

J OACHIM IS ON the train to West Berlin. This time there is no smuggled coffee in a briefcase. He's out with his friends; he's been saving
up for tonight for months.

The journey to West Berlin is familiar; he comes here with friends
every weekend. Usually, they head straight for the Kufürstendamm – or
the Ku'damm, as they call it – a boulevard in the heart of West Berlin
where they buy Coca-Cola and sweets from Woolworths, watch glamorous women in sheer stockings and moleskin fur coats wander in and
out of jewellery shops, and lust after the gadgets in department store
windows: washing machines, hair-dryers, vacuum cleaners. Joachim
always brings his camera so he can take photos of the cars on the streets
– the VW Beetles, the Borgwards and then, best of all, the American
road cruisers, their freshly painted doors glinting in the sun. At home
he develops the photos in home-made chemical solutions in his bathtub,
pinning them on his wall. A homage to a life he can visit but not live.

Unlike East Berlin, where the buildings are all functional concrete
and linoleum, West Berlin is glitzy and over-the-top. The city had had
a makeover in the 1950s – old Prussian buildings were pulled down in
an attempt to shake off its violent past and begin again from *Stunde Null*
– 'Zero Hour'. Now it is full of American-style high-rises, like the new
thirteen-storey, black and white Hilton Hotel. In every way they could,
West Berliners were saying we're different to East Berlin: yes, we're the
same city, but we're a different country.

For Joachim, coming to West Berlin is like taking a plane to the US.
Stuffed with department stores, hamburger joints and all-night jazz bars,

West Berlin is now the most American city outside America. It's partly down to that airlift, the American pilots who'd saved West Berlin from starvation. Like someone who falls in love with the person who rescues them, West Berliners became infatuated with everything American, and all East Berliners had to do to get a taste of mini-America was hop over the border.

Some nights, Joachim and his friends come to West Berlin to watch a film at the cinema that sells tickets to East Berliners at a discount. American rom-coms and cowboy movies play out on the screen in front of them, a world away from the Soviet films in East Berlin cinemas. But tonight they're off to West Berlin's biggest music arena, the Deutschlandhalle, for an evening they will remember for the rest of their lives.

Joachim leads the way. He's no longer the runt of the pack, ever since a growth spurt when he was sixteen. On a school trip into the country-side, picking potatoes for farmers who couldn't keep up with work quotas, Joachim had caught typhus and was put in a hospital isolation chamber. Four weeks he'd lain there – some days delirious with fever, other days listening to Western music on an illicit radio made by a friend, hidden in a cigar box. When Joachim left hospital, the world looked smaller, and when his mother stood him against the pencil-line she'd last drawn over his head on their kitchen wall, she laughed as she saw his head wobbling above it. They guessed it was a freak growth spurt, and no longer was Joachim *Der Kleine* – 'Little One'. Yet his nickname stuck.

At the arena in West Berlin, Joachim and his friends weave through thousands of people to the front and they watch her as she comes out and everyone goes wild.

Ella Fitzgerald.

The drums begin, then the piano – the three-note-refrain of 'Black Magic', the first song in tonight's set. Ella gives them romance in 'Love is Here to Stay', she gives them swagger in 'The Lady is a Tramp', she brings them all down to silence with a slow version of 'Summertime', then, with a nervous voice, she sings 'Mack the Knife' for the first time. 'I hope I remember all the words,' she jokes, but she doesn't and she freestyles from halfway through until everyone is delirious with excitement and love for her, and Joachim leaves, walking on air, until he's back on the train home and he thumps down to reality, along with everyone else on the carriage.

He looks around the train. Most of the people on it are *Grenzgänger* – 'border-crossers' – people who live in East Berlin but work in West Berlin for jobs that pay better. Crossing into the West in the morning, they come home in the evening, but there are always fewer workers on the return journey. Bewitched by West Berlin, many decide that instead of coming home at the end of their shift, they'll stay in West Berlin. It's like a gateway drug: once people get a taste for West Berlin, it's hard to go back. From West Berlin, if you have the money, you can buy a plane ticket and fly anywhere.

Joachim arrives home and flops into bed. By now, Joachim, his mother and sister are living in a new apartment with an oven, TV, even a bath. Once a week, Joachim runs down four flights of stairs with a zinc bucket to collect coal to heat the water. Each time he tries to beat his record, taking up heavier and heavier bucket-loads, after which he climbs into the bath, his skin pulsing as he lowers himself into the burning water and basks.

Some nights, he creeps out to meet his friends, sitting under carpets that are hanging out to air, a Chesterfield hanging from his lower lip, feeling all grown up as he watches the smoke rise into the night.

They've come a long way since those days in their bombed-out flat, begging for food and living off fish heads. Like most in East Germany, they're living far better than before. The party had invested heavily in the plastics industry, so people now cook with plastic spoons, eat off plastic plates and sit on plastic chairs on Sprelacart floors. People who can afford it fill their homes with Bauhaus-inspired furniture – glossy yellow stools and red table lamps. It's a colourful new plastic world that Walter Ulbricht and his party hope will smell and feel like the future. Give people enough of these shiny, bright new things, their thinking goes, and maybe they won't leave the East.

The party is always looking for ways to make people stay, to persuade them that the East has everything they need. They produce TV adverts, showing grinning shoppers in East German supermarkets buying hard-to-find things like bottle openers and hoses. '*Tausend kleine dinge!*' goes the jingle at the end – 'a thousand little things!' But people rarely find those little things, and even if they can, they never work as well as things in the West.

The party fills magazines with photos of sausages, sweets, biscuits and fruit, but they are in such short supply that when they do appear, *Sozialistische Wartegemeinschaften* – 'socialist waiting communities' – made up of friends and family, phone each other to spread the news and they race to the shops, joining queues that snake down the street. Then there are the car adverts for cute pastel-coloured Trabants – or Trabis, as East Germans call them. The cars look great, but the average waiting time is seven years, sometimes fourteen, and in any case most can't afford one. And though holidays are permitted (trips to Hungary or Prague, or even Black Sea cruises on a ship named *Völkerfreundschaft* – 'Friendship between nations'), the party only issues holiday permits to people it considers model socialist citizens.

And so by 1960, though most East Germans are living far better than in the years after the war, though there is free education, free healthcare and subsidised rent, the comparison with the West makes them *feel* poor. When people watch TV, soap operas from West Berlin remind them how people over the border live – the supermarkets that not only sell fruit, but twenty kinds of fruit. And while there is almost no unemployment in the East, many people work long hours in jobs they don't like, for not much money. And people have heard the rumours about government ministers: how they live in idyllic walled-off woodland retreats with boathouses, private chefs, swimming pools and cinemas; how they shop at special supermarkets stuffed with imported products and holiday in luxury resorts.

While there are some who share the Stalinist ideals of the party – those who believe the struggle is worth it for the promise of creating a socialist utopia that will one day bloom – most feel frustration and bitterness at their lives and how little they control. And though there is camaraderie in youth groups and factory sports-teams, as Joachim puts it: 'what kind of camaraderie is enforced?'

Then, behind it all, ever since that day when the tanks crushed the protesters, there's the backdrop of fear. People who criticise the government lose jobs, disappear in the night. Never seen again. There are whispers about the organisation behind these disappearances, these arrests. No one knows much about it or the people who run it. Just the name.

Stasi.

9

The House of One Thousand Eyes

———

THERE ARE VARIOUS ways of describing the Stasi. East Germany's 'internal army'. Or 'the Firm', as some called it. But perhaps the best way to explain it is to start with the man who ran it for thirty-two years, a man whose name came to be synonymous with the Stasi: Erich Mielke.

Like Walter Ulbricht, Erich Mielke was surprisingly short. Unlike Ulbricht, he was muscular and charismatic. With his squat frame and the rolls of neck that spilled over tight white shirts, he looked like a bulldog and in many ways he was. In 1931, aged twenty-four, the Communist Party he was a member of set Erich Mielke on two Berlin policemen, giving him a mission to kill them. Shooting the policemen with a nine-millimetre Luger pistol at point-blank range, Erich Mielke fled to Moscow, where he proved his loyalty to the party, learning Russian and becoming one of the top students in the International Lenin School. Things go murky at that point. Mielke was in Spain during the civil war, then in France, but what he was doing there is unclear, as was his role during the Second World War, which remains a closely guarded secret. He must have done something impressive though, as after it ended, Erich Mielke was awarded a string of medals with grand communist titles – the Order of the Red Banner, the Order of the Great Patriotic War First Class and the Order of Lenin, twice. By the time he returned to Germany, with his faultless Russian and passion for singing Prussian marching songs, Erich Mielke was a trusted member of the Soviet secret police and they had big plans for him.

Within months, Erich Mielke was working for the Soviet secret police in Berlin in a secret unit called K-5. It was stuffed with German communists like him; people who'd survived the concentration camps of the Nazi years, or escaped to the Soviet Union and were now returning after exile. Their circle of trust was small and they arrested anyone they didn't like – not only former Nazis but communists too, sending hundreds of thousands to former concentration camps.

Over the next five years, Eric Mielke worked his way up K-5, until, in 1950, a new organisation was created: the Ministry for State Security (MfS). No one really called it that though. Instead, it was known as the 'Stasi', and within a few years Erich Mielke was running it, recruiting thousands of young men (only one-fifth were women). Poorly educated, often fatherless from the war, they looked up to Mielke and other veteran communists as father figures.

In just a few years, Erich Mielke turned the Stasi into one of the most powerful secret police forces in history and he became the most feared person in the country, the very mention of his name instilling terror. The Stasi's job was simple in purpose: to keep the party, the SED, in power, or, as Mielke put it, the Stasi was to become the 'sword and shield of the party', a phrase he'd copied from the Soviet secret police, the KGB, which the Stasi was modelled on. It was the Stasi's job to protect the government from underground organisations and opposition activists; for example, people linked to the Battle Group Against Inhumanity (the KgU), a group based in West Berlin that encouraged resistance in the East, at one point sending thousands of helium balloons over the border, dropping leaflets with anti-communist messages. As well as throwing stink bombs into Communist Party offices, KgU activists in East Germany burnt Communist Party banners, and even bombed a bridge. The Stasi arrested hundreds of them, sentencing them to hard labour, even beheading two.

Like the Soviet KGB, the point of East Germany's secret police was to protect the party *from* the people, and the party desperately felt it needed protecting – not just from bridge-bombing activists, but from ordinary people too. The party never recovered from the shock of the 1953 uprising that Joachim had been part of. They blamed the secret police for not predicting it and were determined that nothing like that ever happen again.

In the early days, East Germany's secret police had been a crude, brutal operation; if you made trouble, they'd arrest you, there might be a show trial with forced confessions, possibly a death sentence. But when Erich Mielke took over, he wanted to do things differently. Instead of coming for you *after* you'd committed a crime, his police would come for you the moment you started plotting. It was the same philosophy behind the machines in the Tom Cruise sci-fi film, *Minority Report*, where police use futuristic technology to catch criminals before they committed a crime. In 1950s East Germany though, without that technology, there was only one way to anticipate crimes: through information.

And so began the most ambitious project in state surveillance. The Stasi wanted to know everything about everyone: where you worked, what you read, what you worried about, who you were married to, who you were sleeping with, what you dreamt of, even what you smelt like.

There's an old East German joke: why do Stasi officers make such good taxi drivers? Because you get in the car and they already know your name and where you live. Information was everything to the Stasi and they became the best information hunters around, buying equipment from the West and reverse engineering it so they could make listening devices and spy cameras. The Stasi would come up with a reason for you to be out of your apartment – a doctor's appointment perhaps – then they would break in with a small team, taking polaroid pictures so that they could recreate your flat afterwards, searching your home, looking for anything incriminating: letters, foreign money, dissident poetry. They'd hide cameras and microphones in your telephones and light fittings so they could record every hour of your waking and sleeping life. Thousands of those recordings still exist in the archives today: you can hear children's parties, lovers' arguments, sex, loo visits, all of life in its beauty, mundanity and absurdity recorded, catalogued and filed.

A word was soon invented to describe this mass surveillance: *flächendeckend*. It translates as 'covering all areas'. And all areas *were* covered, as the Stasi soon had a network of spies monitoring the entire country. There were the Stasi 'mailmen' from Department M who'd sit in secret rooms in every post office in the country, X-raying and steaming open thousands of letters. There were the officials in Department 26 who eavesdropped on phone calls. Find enough dirt and they'd come for you at work, arresting you in front of colleagues to remind people they were watching. Once arrested, you would be taken to the Stasi headquarters in the district of Lichtenberg in East Berlin. *The House of One Thousand Eyes* – that's what people called it.

At first, the Stasi headquarters was just a small collection of offices on Magdalenenstrasse, somewhere to house the fledgling secret police force. Then, over the years, it grew into a concrete fortress, swallowing up the streets and houses around it like a black hole. The windows all had shutters, the concrete walls bristled with security cameras and the entrance was obscured by thick steel so that no one could see in. Inside, the compound housed every activity of secret policing imaginable – not only interrogation rooms, prisons, a training academy and thousands of offices, but also cafes, shops with luxury products imported from the West, a hospital and even a hairdressing salon, so that, once at work, Stasi employees would never have to leave. No popping out for a sandwich in your lunch-break.

Right at the heart of it, through the maze of linoleum corridors, sat Erich Mielke, the Stasi's Wizard of Oz, masterminding everything from his study, a bust of Lenin watching over him. From here, Erich Mielke ran the Stasi's operations, as well as its universities, even its football team, BFC Dynamo, which he was obsessed with, rigging matches with Stasi-referees.

Of course, anyone brought here to be questioned did not see any of this. They were taken straight down to the *Hundekeller* – 'the dogs' cellar'. It's the name prisoners gave to the interrogation rooms where people would disappear, never seen again. There are horrifying stories of the physical and sexual torture that went on there in the 1950s – prisoners kept in solitary confinement in cells with no windows before secret trials in which they might be sentenced to death, or hard labour in prisons like Bautzen, where the conditions were so appalling that around sixteen thousand died.

But the Stasi were also pioneering more sophisticated tactics, such as *zersetzung* – 'decomposition'. This was a subtle art the Stasi perfected and taught at the Stasi Academy, of applying continuous pressure to people they didn't like, so they would feel as though their lives were falling apart. The Stasi had oversight over most jobs, not just in the army or government, but in universities or factories. If they didn't like you, a simple phone call to your boss or partner would end your career, break your marriage, until you felt completely powerless, leading some to commit suicide. The Stasi pursued this strategy of *zersetzung* so effectively that it became impossible to trust anyone: you never knew who was one of *them*, so you would imagine the Stasi were everywhere, listening in on every phone call (when, of course, they didn't have the manpower for that), opening every letter. And so East Germany became a country of hushed voices, suspicious looks and self-censorship.

Stasi agents had been out on the streets, shooting protesters during the 1953 uprising that Joachim had been part of. And that year, for those who'd had enough of feeling afraid, who were no longer brave enough to sing songs in the street and march, there was only one option: to leave.

In 1953, the year of the uprising, 330,000 people left East Germany. And every year people kept leaving. Soon, Walter Ulbricht was so worried that he made leaving East Germany a crime, inventing a new word to describe it: *Republikflucht* – 'flight from the republic'. Anyone caught crossing the border unauthorised was arrested, put on trial, thrown in prison.

Still, they kept leaving.

Bus drivers leave, nurses leave, engineers, dentists and lawyers all leave. Soon, there are towns in East Germany without a single doctor or teacher. Then there are the more embarrassing defections: the Soviet soldiers, the government officials, and then, in 1961, in a particularly high-profile humiliation, Marlene Schmidt, a beautiful, blonde engineer who'd escaped out of the East – described in a West German newspaper as having an 'engineer's brain on a Botticelli figure' – became Miss Universe. After she'd minced down a catwalk in Miami Beach in her Miss Universe crown, in an event broadcast all over the world, including East Germany, *Time* magazine published a piece expressing surprise that 'the East German border guards failed to spot lissome, 5-ft. 8-in. Marlene . . . The West had no difficulty.'

Walter Ulbricht discovers that there is something worse than his country being an international pariah: East Germany is becoming a joke.

By 1961, East Germany has lost three million people – around a fifth of its population. That year, each month, the numbers increase: in June, 20,000 leave; 30,000 in July. Soon, the deluge of people leaving becomes so great that East Germans describe it as *Torschlusspanik* – 'the rush to get out before the door slams shut'.

And that now is Walter Ulbricht's dilemma: how can he not only slam that door, but bolt it so that no one else can escape? There is already a 900-mile barbed-wire fence running the length of East Germany to stop people escaping into the West, but all they have to do is travel to East Berlin and, from there, they can hop on a train into West Berlin. The problem, he knows, is East Berlin. It's an escape hatch.

And so Walter Ulbricht comes up with a plan: if he can't persuade people to stay in the East, he will build a wall and lock them in. But when Walter Ulbricht puts his wall-plan to his Soviet commissars, they are appalled: it will be a PR disaster! How can they persuade the world that communism is better than capitalism if East Germany has to build a wall to stop people escaping the so-called communist paradise? Instead, the Soviet government's instructions to Walter Ulbricht are surprising: if you want to stop people leaving, make their lives better. After all, the Soviet Union was now opening up, beginning to reform, yet here was East Germany continuing down the Stalinist path more obsessively than any other country in the Soviet empire.

But Walter Ulbricht does not introduce reforms or change direction. And later that year, as East Germany continues to haemorrhage its youngest and brightest, and as Walter Ulbricht badgers the Soviet government, sending maps outlining the route of the wall, the Soviet Union caves in.

Walter Ulbricht will get his wall.

10

Operation Rose

———◆———

Saturday 12 August 1961

I T'S DUSK IN East Berlin. The streets are covered in streamers and pastel splodges of ice-cream after the annual children's fair. High on sugar, children have been allowed to stay out late and they crane their necks to the sky, watching fireworks.

As the rockets whizz and pop above them, further east, in the People's Army headquarters, the country's most senior military commanders are gorging on a luxurious buffet. It's all the food you can't usually get in East Germany – sausage, veal, smoked salmon, caviar. The commanders have no idea what's brought this on, what's about to happen. All they've heard is that there's a secret operation happening that night. At 8 p.m. exactly, the commanders open sealed envelopes and read detailed instructions, setting out what must happen every hour of the night ahead.

Meanwhile, the mastermind of all this, Walter Ulbricht, is hosting a garden party. It's out of character – he's serious, terrible at small talk and doesn't have friends, but here he is, surrounded by his ministers in his woodland retreat. There's music, a Soviet comedy film plays in the background – an attempt at light entertainment – but it's awkward. No one knows why they're here and they can see soldiers skulking in the birch trees.

After supper, at around 10 p.m., as hundreds of tanks and armoured personnel carriers rumble towards East Berlin, ready to catch anyone who might escape, Walter Ulbricht directs his guests into a room and that's when he tells them: he's about to close the border between East and West Berlin. If anyone wanted to stop him, warn friends or even escape, it's too late. They're locked in. Everything is set.

Operation Rose can begin.

It starts with the street lights.

At 1 a.m. they switch them off. They don't want anyone to see what's about to happen. Tens of thousands of soldiers then move into position, forming a circle around West Berlin so there can be no last-minute escapes. It takes half an hour.

Now the construction starts. Walter Ulbricht has delegated that to his most trusted units: his border police, the riot police, ordinary police, secret police, and, finally, 12,000 members of the *Betriebskampfgruppen* – a militia of specially trained factory workers. Ulbricht has thought of every detail: how many men to have at each crossing point, how much ammunition each gets – enough to scare people off but not so much that things spin out of control.

Trucks drive towards the crossing points, depositing soldiers armed with machine-guns who crouch on the streets, weapons pointing towards the West. Behind them, a second group of soldiers creep down from the trucks, pulling out giant coils of barbed wire.

There's 150 tons of it, bought secretly over the past few weeks from manufacturers in West Germany and even Britain, stockpiled by police units who had no idea what they were keeping it for. Next, the soldiers bring out wooden posts and then, using steel rods, they unfurl the barbed wire, stringing it between those posts, sealing the crossing points at the border.

They begin at Potsdamer Platz, the busiest crossing between East and West Berlin. From there, the soldiers move to other checkpoints, ensuring the barbed-wire fence follows the border exactly, not edging a millimetre into the West: they don't want to provoke war. And so the barbed wire cuts through parks, playgrounds, cemeteries, squares, not stopping for anything. There are no nasty surprises, nothing the soldiers can't handle. Every inch of the twenty-seven-mile-long internal border and the sixty-nine-mile border separating West Berlin from the East German countryside has been mapped. They know exactly what's required.

At 1.30 a.m., armed units shut down all public transport that leads to the West. They split train tracks and seal train stations, under and above ground. It's hard work, but the night is quiet. Walter Ulbricht has chosen the perfect time for this operation – a Sunday morning in the height of summer when many East Berliners, like Joachim, are on holiday. Ulbricht knew the success of his operation depended on surprise. He didn't want messiness, anyone trying to stop them as they sealed the city.

By 6 a.m. on Sunday 13 August, the soldiers have closed off 193 streets, 68 crossing points and 12 train stations.

Their work is done.

II

Mousetrap

———

DAWN ON SUNDAY 13 August and it's the city's workers who are up first. Straight away they know something's happened. In the half-light they see men in uniforms on the streets – soldiers, police, border guards and, looming behind them, the hulking outline of tanks. Then, at the border, they see it: the barbed wire.

At first, they don't know what to think. Wandering along the barbed wire, they try to work out where it's come from, where it's going. As others wake and stumble towards the border, a group of men gathers, shouting at the border guards, asking what's happened, getting angrier and angrier until the border guards turn and shoot tear gas. Coughing and spluttering in the chemical smoke, their eyes streaming, the men run away.

Then the vans appear. Weaving through the streets, East German officials inside broadcast over loudspeakers the news that the border is closed.

Panic sets in.

Parents pack suitcases and drag children to railway stations, hoping that trains might still be running to West Berlin. Cramming on trains, they take the same journey that Joachim had done many times as a boy, but at Friedrichstrasse station, instead of passing through the border, they hear a new announcement: '*Der Zug endet hier*' – 'The train ends here'. Then, onto the trains come the VoPos (short for *Volkspolizei* – 'People's Police', referring to the East German armed forces who defend the border). The VoPos herd everyone off the train and onto the platform, which is now heaving with people. Sitting on suitcases, women, children and grown men are crying at the unreality of it all. One elderly lady walks up to a VoPo and asks when the next train will go to West Berlin. He turns and laughs. 'That is all over now,' he tells her, with a sneer. 'You are all sitting in a mousetrap.'

43

Back at the barbed wire, thousands of East Berliners are standing in a daze – mothers with babies perched on their hips, children holding teddies, groups of lanky teenagers. Some ask about the Americans; surely they'll do something – bulldoze the barbed wire with their tanks? But American tanks never come. At one point, a few British jeeps show up, watch for a while, then go home.

On the other side of the border, in West Berlin, young men on motorbikes tear through the city to the Brandenburg Gate where East German soldiers are breaking up the road with jackhammers and pounding in concrete posts. 'Ulbricht! Murderer!' they chant, more men joining until there are hundreds, screaming and shouting at the soldiers. Eventually, just as their protest threatens to spiral out of control, West German riot police pull them back.

And it's then that Berliners realise what the barrier means.

Mothers in East Berlin are now separated from their new-born babies in West Berlin, brothers from sisters; friends, lovers, grandparents, all divided by the barbed wire. Those in East Berlin with telephones at home try calling children or friends in West Berlin, they dial the numbers but—

Nothing.

The phone lines between East and West Berlin have been cut. Walter Ulbricht has thought of everything.

And so, as evening draws in, East Berliners are reduced to waving: waving from the tops of cars, waving out of apartment windows, white handkerchiefs in their hands. They have no idea if they'll ever see their parents, their children again.

There are lots of photos from that day, but there's one that stands out. It's a mother with her baby, and they're standing behind the barbed wire in East Berlin. The rest of her family are on the other side and the mother holds her baby high up in outstretched arms so they can see her child, as the barrier between them gets higher and higher.

That night, as the sun goes down, the full horror of it all sets in.

And now, as Joachim and his friends stare at that barbed wire, having driven back from their camping holiday at the beach, a single question presents itself.

Will you try to escape?

12

Snow

—◆—

FOR JOACHIM, THIS is difficult. He knows all about escapes, how easily they can go wrong. Memories flash up: the horse and cart. The sound of the Red Army. Sitting in the cupboard with his father, feeling safe in his arms. The sight of his father being dragged away. The feeling that his life had become unhinged from something.

Now, fifteen years later, Joachim must decide whether to risk everything again. Standing at the barbed wire, the houses and cars and streetlights of West Berlin just a few metres away, tantalising him with their proximity, Joachim knows he must stay this side of the border. He's learnt how to function in East Berlin, how to keep his head down and never risk too much. Now, he must just keep going.

And so Joachim, who loves equations, who loves numbers that always behave as they're meant to, Joachim turns his back to the border and the barbed wire and returns home, his first night sleeping in the newly divided city.

13

The Escapes

15 August 1961 (two days after the Wall), 3 p.m.

THE BORDER GUARD patrols the barbed wire, looking just like any other border guard, except he isn't. He has something on his mind. Hans Conrad Schumann is just nineteen years old; he only arrived in East Berlin a few months ago from the countryside. There are lots of VoPos like him here, out-of-towners who don't know the city. Walter Ulbricht thinks border guards from outside East Berlin are less likely to be soft on anyone who tries to escape – less chance they'll sympathise with people they don't know.

Standing in front of the barbed wire, Hans feels a long way from home. He comes from a family of sheep farmers and he is not a born-soldier or socialist, yet here he is, in a strange city, guarding a barrier he doesn't believe in. His orders are to stop people escaping, because all along the barbed wire, people are trying to get over it. The day it went up, 800 people escaped. There were the construction workers building the barrier at gunpoint who – when left unguarded – took their chance, and jumped over. There were the brave teenagers who sidled up to the barrier looking for a weak spot in the fence, a hole perhaps, or an unguarded section, and wriggled through the barbed wire. And then there were the families who crept up to the barbed wire, threw suitcases over it, then leapt into West Berlin.

Hans knows his job is to stop escapees, but he finds himself rooting for them. Yesterday, he'd seen a little girl in East Berlin trying to squeeze through the barbed wire to be with her parents. They were standing a few metres away on the other side of the barrier, calling to their daughter with outstretched arms. VoPos had pulled the girl back, stopped her going to them. Now she might end up in an orphanage or with a foster family. Hans can't bear to be part of it.

As Hans reaches the end of his section of barbed wire, he edges towards it, puts out his hand and pushes. *To see if it's rusting,* he tells the other border guard on duty.

In West Berlin, a photographer is watching. The news networks in the West pay good money for photos of escapes and the photographer watches as Hans tests the barbed wire again, watches for an hour as Hans wanders towards the wire, then away again, playing out his indecision.

Then, at 4 p.m. exactly, Hans makes up his mind: flicking away his cigarette, he runs forward and leaps onto the barbed wire, arms outstretched as though in flight and—

SNAP

The photographer takes his shot, freezing Hans forever in mid-air as he hovers over the barbed wire, somewhere between East and West, creating one of the most iconic images of the Berlin Wall. Within hours, the photo is on the front pages of newspapers around the world, one caption reading:

THE GDR'S OWN TROOPS ARE RUNNING AWAY

Hans is the first border guard to escape, but not the last. Sixty-seven more will escape over the coming days. All along the barbed wire, people are squirming through, jumping to freedom, and they are the lucky ones, for right now, unknown to anyone except his closest advisors, Walter Ulbricht has a plan to turn this barbed wire into something else, something that will be almost impossible to escape over.

14

The Boy in Short Pants

—◆—

PRESIDENT KENNEDY SITS back on the *Marlin*, the cabin cruiser gliding through the water at Hyannis Port in Cape Cod. The water is calm and so is he. Kennedy is here with his family to get away from everything, to revive himself after his first six months in Washington as president.

Around noon, the radio on the boat crackles into life: it's Kennedy's military advisor with an urgent message. It's about Berlin, he tells Kennedy – the border has been sealed, you've got to come back.

Kennedy had been dreading something like this. When he became president seven months earlier, he was told by his advisors that Berlin was the place to watch, the place where a new world war could break out at any moment. The US and the Soviet Union were now locked into a new Cold War, each of them with nuclear weapons that could obliterate each other's cities. Berlin was the flashpoint, the only place in the world where soldiers from each side faced one another, nuzzle to nuzzle. One wrong move could spark nuclear war.

Ten years ago, the world had seen how easily a divided country could fall into war. In 1950, North Korean soldiers (backed by the Soviet Union) began firing into South Korea (backed by the US.) It led to a three-year war with millions killed. The fear was that Germany could be next.

Despite those warnings, in his first months in office, President Kennedy had mostly ignored Berlin, partly because he felt it was an unsolvable problem. The Soviet Union was now led by Nikita Khrushchev, who'd made it clear that he wanted British, American and French soldiers out of West Berlin. If Khrushchev sent Soviet soldiers into West Berlin to take it, Kennedy's options were terrible: if he ordered Western forces to fight back, they would lose – there were only 12,000 of them in Germany, compared to 350,000 Soviet soldiers. The only war Kennedy could win was a nuclear one, but he did not want to start a nuclear war over Berlin. Kennedy's choice was defeat or global destruction.

And so, in June 1961, Kennedy had gone to Vienna to meet Khrushchev, hoping he could charm him into dropping talk of nuclear war. The two men could not have been more different.

President Kennedy, or 'the boy in short pants' as his staff called him, was charismatic and well educated, but young and inexperienced. That summer, he'd been humiliated after approving an operation for a group of Cuban exiles to land at the Bay of Pigs in Cuba and overthrow Fidel Castro. The operation was a disaster: Castro's army killed some, captured the rest, and Kennedy looked out of his depth.

Khrushchev, twenty years older than Kennedy, was his opposite. With no proper education, he'd worked his way up from coal mining into the Communist Party, bulldozing his way to the top. Pug-faced and gap-toothed, he was impulsive and unpredictable, with a mischievous sense of humour. Khrushchev knew how terrified the West was about what could happen in Berlin and he loved to rub it in. As he put it, Berlin was the 'testicles of the West. Every time I want to make the West scream, I squeeze on Berlin.' At cocktail parties and ballets, Khrushchev would sidle up to European diplomats and remind them how many missiles it would take to destroy their capitals. Then he'd watch them squirm as he described how Russia was churning out long-range missiles 'like sausages on an assembly line'. Since testing their first atomic bomb in 1949, the Soviets had built up a huge nuclear arsenal, including twelve missiles in East Germany. At a push of the finger, Khrushchev could take out Paris and London; it was only a matter of time before Soviet missiles could reach New York.

Before Kennedy's meeting with Khrushchev in Vienna, American intelligence agencies had commissioned psychiatrists to write a report about Khrushchev: just how crazy *was* this man with his nuclear weapons? The psychiatrists studied footage of Khrushchev, even analysed photos of his arteries to see if they could determine his blood pressure. In a classified report, the psychiatrists described Khrushchev's mood swings, his depression and excessive drinking, concluding that he was a 'chronic opportunist', with good political timing, showmanship and a 'touch of the gambler's instinct'. Not the kind of man you'd want in charge of nuclear weapons.

The pressure was on Kennedy to talk Khrushchev down, come to some kind of agreement. In Vienna, Kennedy went straight to the point, talked about the dangers of slipping into nuclear war. They were just one hour in when Khrushchev 'went berserk' (Kennedy's words). Shouting at Kennedy, Khrushchev jumped up and down, slamming his hands on the table, threatening Kennedy with war. The Soviet leader clearly felt invincible with his growing stockpile of nuclear weapons; he wasn't going to be constrained by this new boy-president.

Kennedy was shocked. It was the first time a Soviet leader had threatened an American president like this. Reeling, he pushed back, told Khrushchev that he would not abandon Berlin. But then, Kennedy added something that gave Khrushchev the edge: Kennedy told him that he didn't want to go to war over Berlin, that Khrushchev must not meddle in West Berlin, but – and this was the crucial part – he could do what he liked in East Berlin. At the climax of this game of poker, Kennedy had lowered his cards and shown Khrushchev his hand.

Some historians say Kennedy gave in too easily, others say he was cornered and didn't have a choice. Either way, Kennedy himself thought he'd done badly. As he later put it, Khrushchev 'beat the hell out of' me, it was the 'roughest thing in my life'. The young president felt humiliated, and worse, he came away convinced that Khrushchev might just be mad enough to start a nuclear war. When he returned to Washington, Kennedy even wept on his brother Bobby's shoulder at the thought of it. He was no longer bored by Berlin. He was obsessed by it.

Like a newly infatuated lover, Kennedy doodled the word 'Berlin' repeatedly during White House meetings on a yellow notepad. He read every Berlin report he could find (earning him a new nickname, the 'Berlin Desk Officer'), and he'd invite White House staff to boating weekends where they'd discuss Berlin as they splashed in the sea.

All that work culminated in a speech, given by Kennedy on 25 July, less than three weeks before Walter Ulbricht installed the barbed wire. In that speech, the president restated his controversial position: if Khrushchev meddled in West Berlin, the US would retaliate, but he could do what he liked in the East. A few days later, one of Kennedy's most senior officials went on American radio, questioning why the Soviet Union hadn't already closed the border to stop people leaving East Germany. 'I think they have the right to do it at any time,' he said.

It seems that Khrushchev was listening. For a long time he'd been undecided about this wall idea that Walter Ulbricht had been pestering him about. With Kennedy making it clear that he could do what he wanted in East Berlin, Khrushchev gave Ulbricht the green light.

Now, sitting on the boat as it takes him back to his family cottage at Hyannis Port, Kennedy has to make a decision. How does he respond to the barbed-wire barrier? Neither he nor his advisors had any idea that the East Germans were about to build it; they're already thirteen hours behind the information that has been speeding through the news wires.

And Kennedy's allies aren't much help: British prime minister Harold MacMillan was shooting grouse in Yorkshire when he found out about the barbed wire, and the French president, General Charles de Gaulle, was on holiday at his country house. Despite the mass of informants in Berlin, the spy capital of the world, no one in the West (not even the West Germans) knew that East Germany was about to build the barrier. It was one of the biggest intelligence failures of the Cold War.

This was partly down to the meticulous planning of Walter Ulbricht. He'd made sure there were no telephone calls or cables about the barrier. Photos had emerged of concrete and barbed wire stockpiled near the border, but American intelligence agents didn't know what it meant. Some suggested it could be building material for a wall, but analysts dismissed the idea – it was just too far-fetched.

Now the barbed wire had gone up, the British, French and Americans were caught off guard and none of them knew what to do.

Back at his house on Cape Cod, President Kennedy talks to his Secretary of State, Dean Rusk. The two men are calm. After all, the Russians haven't interfered in West Berlin. No need for a dramatic response.

In Berlin, everyone is waiting for a reaction from the West. Berliners know their best hopes lie with the US, the only country that can take on the Soviet Union. But so far—

Silence.

Walter Ulbricht is watching too, waiting to see if American tanks will show up. They don't. But he can't begin the next stage of his plan just yet. It is too dangerous. He must wait.

The next day, there is still no response from Kennedy, nor the day after that. Three days later, West Berlin newspapers run headlines saying: 'THE WEST DOES NOTHING!' From Kennedy – still nothing. That day, three-quarters of a million West Berliners gather at City Hall holding posters saying:

'WHERE ARE THE AMERICANS?'

It is a good question. Now back in Washington, Kennedy is still working out what to do. The barbed wire had taken him by surprise, but in meetings with advisors, instead of being concerned, he's relieved. Kennedy's biggest fear over Berlin was being forced into a decision that could lead to nuclear war. The barbed wire is provocative, but it has followed the border exactly, not straying into West Berlin, which means Kennedy doesn't have to retaliate. He'd made it clear to Khrushchev where the red line was and he is grateful that the Soviet leader hadn't crossed it – for a president worrying about nuclear war, a barbed-wire fence was small fry. Or, as Kennedy put it, 'a wall is a hell of a lot better than a war'. Plus, argued some of his advisors, the barbed wire was a propaganda victory for the capitalist West – it showed better than anything how desperate people were to escape communism.

But in Berlin, people see it differently. The deafening silence from the US smells of defeat. Defeat for the *West*.

Willy Brandt, mayor of West Berlin, writes an angry letter to Kennedy, criticising him for undermining morale and boosting the East German government with his silence. Then, at City Hall, Willy Brandt delivers a powerful speech to thousands of West Berliners, describing the wall as *die Schandmauer* – 'the Wall of Shame' – saying 'Berlin expects more than words. Berlin expects political action!'

Some Berliners even send black umbrellas to the White House, a reference to the umbrella that Chamberlain carried after appeasing Hitler – a symbol of weakness.

Eventually, Kennedy asks an advisor to trawl through State Department files to look for ideas. His advisor finds a promising-looking file with the title 'Division of Berlin'. It's empty. 'Why,' President Kennedy asks, 'with all those contingency plans, do you never have one for what actually happens?'

Back in Berlin, Walter Ulbricht is still waiting. By Thursday 17 August, five days after what Berliners now call 'barbed-wire Sunday', Ulbricht knows he's waited long enough. If Kennedy hasn't done anything by now, he never will.

Late that evening, Walter Ulbricht sends construction crews to the border with tens of thousands of concrete slabs. Using giant cranes, the workers hoist ten-foot-prefabricated concrete blocks from trucks, then lower them to the border, where builders plaster them together with mortar that slowly drips down the sides.

Watching them build this new concrete wall are thousands of American soldiers. They stand there, silently, impotently, under orders to do nothing. The construction workers lay slab after slab, many of them horrified by what they're doing. For they are building the walls of their own prison.

Eventually, one of the East German construction workers takes a risk and calls over to an American Military Police Officer. 'Lieutenant!' he says, 'Look how slowly I'm working! What are you waiting for?' An East German police officer joins in, telling the American that his gun isn't loaded. The two East Germans *want* the Americans to stop them. The American soldier passes this information on to his superiors.

The answer returns: do nothing.

As the builders mould the slabs together, in Washington, Kennedy is still deliberating. If he sends tanks to the barrier, he could start a ground war he knows the West will lose. And he isn't prepared to threaten nuclear war over what's described in his presidential daily briefing as just 'new travel restrictions in Berlin'. As he dithers, Edward R. Murrow, the veteran American reporter who Kennedy admires, who was in Berlin the day the barbed wire went up, writes to Kennedy. He compares Ulbricht's barrier to Hitler's conquest of the Rhineland in 1935, telling Kennedy he has to do *something*.

Six days after the barbed wire goes up, Kennedy finally does something. He sends his vice-president, Lyndon B. Johnson, to Berlin. But it's too little, too late.

Johnson arrives to find a huge concrete wall running through the city. It is obvious to everyone who sees it: Berlin is now divided.

It is one of the biggest 'what ifs' of the twentieth century: what if Kennedy and the West had done more? After all, in building this barrier, Walter Ulbricht had broken the post-war agreement that the US had signed with the Soviet Union. Kennedy had every right to retaliate.

What if Kennedy had at least sent tanks to that barbed-wire fence? The British sent troops? Would Walter Ulbricht have built his concrete wall? Kennedy's most experienced diplomat in Berlin, General Clay, thought not. 'I do not believe we should have gone to war to stop the creation of the wall,' he wrote in a letter to Kennedy after the concrete wall appeared, but 'we could have moved back and forth across selected places on the border with unarmed military trucks and this limited action might well have prevented the wall.'

Now, though, it is too late. For an enormous grey wall runs through most of Berlin, encircling the old city in the East, then running past the districts of Wedding, Moabit and Tiergarten in the West, all the way down to the River Spree. Compared to other walls in history, the Berlin Wall in its early stages is shoddy, an embarrassment of engineering. One onlooker says it looks as though it's been put together by 'a band of stonemasons when drunk'. But it is unique in one respect: most walls in history have been built to keep enemies out. This is one of the only walls built to keep people in.

When the barbed wire first appeared, most described it as a barrier. From now on, it would be called 'the Wall'. And anyone who wants to escape has to work out how to get over it.

15

Valley of the Clueless

———•———

September 1961

J OACHIM OPENS HIS window and looks out. The River Elbe stretches below, the bright morning sun glistening on the water, luscious green trees covering its banks. It's been a month since Joachim drove back from the campsite and saw the barbed wire. Now he's back at university in Dresden, two hour's drive south of Berlin.

Looking out over the rooftops, Joachim feels a long way from Berlin and its new concrete Wall, far enough that he can almost ignore it. *Almost.* Though he's seen photos of the new Wall, knows how hard it would be to escape over it, now and then Joachim finds himself imagining living on the other side. He could study what he wanted – engineering – rather than Transportation Studies, which he had no interest in. Though he'd got brilliant marks at school, because of his patchy socialist record – in particular, not being part of the Free German Youth – he wasn't allowed to study what he wanted. He knows he will never amount to much in East Germany. People like him never did.

And he's heard the rumours, how the party was going after people who'd spent time in West Berlin before the Wall went up. Like a jealous lover punishing an unfaithful partner, the party sent *Grenzgänger* – people who lived in the East but worked in the West – to work in factories, told teachers who'd worked in West Berlin's schools they could never teach again, and they barred students who'd studied in West Berlin from universities in the East, forcing them to do grunt work in factories. Now that the Wall was there to cage people in, the party didn't have to try so hard to win people's love. Though the party had always taken a tough line with anyone who criticised it, after building the Wall the number of political activists arrested sky-rocketed. In the first half of 1961, 1,500 East Germans were arrested for political crimes. In the second half of that year, after the Wall went up, that number quadrupled to 7,200.

As well as the arrests, the party was spinning the narrative about the Wall. First, they never called it that – a Wall. Instead, in articles that appeared in the party newspaper, *Neues Deutschland*, Ulbricht called it the *antifaschistischer Schutzwall* – 'the anti-fascist protection barrier'. This wasn't a Wall to keep people *in*, Ulbricht wrote; it was a Wall to keep people *out*, to protect East Germans from the 'vermin, spies, saboteurs, human traffickers, prostitutes, spoiled teenage hooligans [who] have been sucking on our . . . republic like leeches on a healthy body'.

In Ulbricht's alternative story, he was the protector of East Germany, for it was under constant threat of invasion from the West. The party even funded a film that they released shortly after building the Wall, a film with a title suspiciously similar to a book that came out the year before, written by Ian Fleming – *For Your Eyes Only*. In the East German film – *For Eyes Only* – an East German spy discovers an American plot to invade his country. The message in state newspapers, TV and film was clear: West Germany is full of bad people and only the Wall can protect you.

While a few party faithfuls bought this alternative story, felt protected by the new Wall, most didn't. They had seen the VoPos patrolling the border in their helmets and knee-high black boots, and they'd noticed that their Kalashnikovs didn't point towards the 'hooligans and saboteurs' in the West. They pointed back at them.

Things were changing. Fast. In this newly divided city, everyone was choosing sides, and though Joachim had chosen to stay, he wasn't sure it was the right decision. He'd just heard that the party had introduced forced conscription: with such a long Wall to protect, they needed more VoPos, and he'd been told he would have to sign up soon. Joachim imagines patrolling the Wall, Kalashnikov at the ready, under orders to shoot anyone who tries to escape. The idea horrifies him.

Until now, his only military experience was two compulsory stints in the reserves during the last two summers, when Joachim spent hours marching in drill practice and running around in field exercises. As the technology whizz-kid, Joachim was put in the communications group, his backpack stuffed with radios. Dressed in a khaki-green uniform, steel helmet wobbling on his head, gas mask strapped to his face, Joachim ran away from imaginary foreign soldiers, threw himself onto the ground to avoid imaginary aircraft, up and down, up and down, until all the bones in his body ached. He'd hated it and found himself getting into heated arguments with senior officers. Until then he'd always been good at toeing the line, but he was finding it harder to bite his tongue. His best friend Manfred was becoming even more belligerent: a few weeks ago he'd refused to swear the oath of allegiance and he'd been kicked out of university.

Joachim looks out over Dresden. *Tal der Ahnungslosen* they call it – 'the valley of the clueless'. For in Dresden, unlike East Berlin, it is almost impossible to get a TV or radio signal from West Germany. People who live there are stuck with Deutsche Fernsehfunk, East Germany's only TV station, famous for its weekly show, *Der Schwarze Kanal* – '*The Black Channel*'. It begins with an electro-pop theme tune that sounds like the 1990s internet dial-up tone; then, after a title sequence involving an eagle, a plump man with thick-lensed, oversized glasses wearing a dull suit and tie appears. His name is Karl-Eduard von Schnitzler and he is here to warn people about the poisonous sewage streaming out of the West through its TV stations. Hence the title – *The Black Channel* – which is what German plumbers call the sewers. Selecting clips from West German TV, Karl-Eduard von Schnitzler explains in an avuncular tone why it is all filth. With so much air-time, he is now the face of the party, and anyone who hates the party now hates him as much as Walter Ulbricht.

The only way people in Dresden could get away from von Schnitzler and East German TV was by climbing onto their roof and turning their aerial towards the West. But this was dangerous. Ulbricht was determined to stop people in East Germany tuning into news from the West; he knew TV was powerful propaganda. His party tried jamming the signal, but people found it. And so he'd made it a criminal offence to consume Western news: anyone caught doing so could be fined or arrested. And the party always had ways of finding out. If pupils doodled logos of Western TV news stations, teachers would report them and their parents could be arrested. In Dresden, Stasi informants stood at windows with binoculars, scanning the skyline for aerials pointing west. Looking at those aerials, thinking about the people risking jail to watch TV from over the border, Joachim thinks about the years ahead, wondering whether he can keep his head down as the party becomes ever more controlling, taking away his choices, one by one.

Picking up his bag, Joachim sets off for his first class of the day, first walking to the kiosk, where he picks up a newspaper. And there on the front page, he sees it: the article that changes everything. It's a list of names of everyone in Dresden who'd been caught pointing their aerials towards West Germany, along with photos of their apartments. It's the first time Joachim has seen anything like it, and as he holds the newspaper, he feels an anger rise up within him. Suddenly he sees himself, a twenty-two-year-old with his whole life ahead of him, living in a country where you can't say what you want, think what you want or watch what you want. All the things he'd got used to – the compromises, the unwritten rules – now flash up before him, and seeing his life afresh, Joachim doesn't like what he sees. It's like one of his home-developed photographs suddenly drained of colour.

Everyone has different breaking points and this is his. And so the Wall forces a decision upon Joachim, as it has for others: people who thought they could cope if they just kept their head down make new calculations. Across East Germany, in the shadow of the Wall, there are awakenings: teenage boys who know the army will soon call on them, daughters who want to feel their mother's arms around them again, farmers who want to be able to live off their own land, doctors who want a proper career – they express the same fears, and come to the same conclusions that people all over the world have reached time and again, whenever the place they're living in becomes too much to bear.

They decide to escape.

16

Binoculars

———•———

J OACHIM HEARS FOOTSTEPS on the stairs. It's Manfred, here for their morning's planning, for the two of them have decided to escape together and they need to find a way out that won't get them killed. They've heard about the escapes at the border, they know people have been jumping the barbed wire, but getting over the new concrete Wall is a different prospect.

They read about the ones who've succeeded: the delivery driver who smashed his van through the Wall, the couple with their baby who broke through the Wall in a seven-tonne dump truck full of gravel. But with every escape, the VoPos had got smarter: they sealed holes in the Wall, added lookout posts, dog runs, anti-vehicle ditches, then created a no-man's-land, a strip that ran along the eastern side of the Wall. It was under the cover of darkness that most tried their luck; searchlights would rake the Wall, then there were screams and shouts from people who disappeared into the night.

Some of the most extraordinary escapes happened on a mile-long street called Bernauer Strasse, a street now famous all over the world as the Berlin Wall ran right down the middle of it. The living areas of the houses were in the East, pavements in the West. To escape, all residents had to do was walk out of their front door. Then the VoPos came, forced thousands out of these houses at gunpoint and bricked up the windows and doors.

Only a handful of residents were allowed to stay – those on the top floors. Their windows looked out into West Berlin and they would wave down to friends and family on the pavement, throwing out handwritten notes and presents. One afternoon, a bride in a white lace dress and her groom came to the pavement in the West to get married, the parents of the bride watching from the window above, lowering flowers in a basket. Then there were the teenagers who appeared at the windows, holding up signs for their girlfriends in West Berlin; and parents who held up two-day-old babies for their grandparents.

But soon all these things were forbidden. Walter Ulbricht released new rules criminalising any kind of contact over the Wall, including chatting and waving, and life in those wall-side apartments got bleaker. As border guards patrolled the buildings, monitoring what people were doing at their windows, those inside became more desperate, so desperate that some decided if they couldn't escape through the front door, they would take a different route.

Windows on the third and fourth floors would open, windows that hadn't been bricked up as the border guards thought no one would be crazy enough to escape out of them, and from those windows people would emerge. Tottering on window ledges, some slid down bedsheets, others leapt into the air, hoping that people on the pavement in the West would catch them. Sometimes, pieces of paper would flutter down from the windows onto which were scrawled floor numbers, window numbers and a date and time. At the appointed hour, on the appointed day, firemen in West Berlin would huddle under the window, holding heavy-duty fire-nets ready to catch whoever jumped.

Seventy-seven-year-old Frieda Schulze decided to jump on 24 September. That day, she threw a few precious things – including her cat – out of the window, then climbed onto the window sill. News crews from the West were filming, and in the footage you see Frieda wearing a long black dress, hovering out of her window, her short white hair glinting in the sun.

Then suddenly you see them – a pair of arms grabbing her from the inside. Border guards have broken into Frieda's apartment and they yank her arms, trying to pull her back in, while people on the street below jump up and grab her legs.

The East and the West are fighting over one woman.

After a few minutes, Frieda's shoe falls off and she dangles by one arm, looking as though she might snap. A border guard throws a tear gas canister out of the window, but the people below don't give up. Choking on smoke, throats burning, they pull on Frieda's legs, harder and harder, until suddenly, her arm comes loose and she falls into the net to the sound of cheering and whooping. The border guards pull back from the window. They'd lost this one.

It was also on Bernauer Strasse that the first death at the Wall was recorded. Ida Siekmann lived in one of the apartments there; she was fifty-eight years old and before the Wall went up, she'd go into the West every week to see her sister. Photos show a woman with a soft, plump face, no hard edges. After the Wall was built, Ida was cut off from her sister and she knew she might never see her again. The day VoPos bricked up the door to her building, it all became too much. Ida threw her bedding and a few belongings out of the window of her third-floor apartment and jumped.

There was no net.

She died on the way to hospital one day before her birthday. An East German police report noted her death in a couple of lines, adding, 'the blood stain was covered up with sand'. A few days later, a makeshift memorial appeared at the spot where Ida died, her name carved into a piece of wood. Next to it, a garland of flowers.

Though the police wrote meticulous reports of escape attempts, they tried to keep deaths out of the news. They didn't want the bad publicity, particularly once the killings began. On 22 August, the party gave new orders to border guards: from now on, anyone 'violating the laws of the GDR could be called to order, if necessary by the use of weapons'. If you were caught trying to escape, you could be shot. Two days later, the border guards showed they were following orders.

Günter Litfin was a twenty-four-year-old tailor with brown eyes and a mass of dark, curly hair. He lived in East Berlin, but worked in the West as a costume maker for the theatre. He was doing well; he'd made beautiful costumes for some of the greatest actresses of the time and he planned to move to West Berlin. When the Wall went up, Günter lost not only his job, but the whole life he'd created.

Just after 4 p.m. on 24 August, Günter crept onto the bank of the River Spree. The river was a popular escape route; it was only thirty metres to the other side – hundreds had escaped this way, including a couple who'd swum across, pushing their three-year-old in a bathtub.

But Günter wasn't as lucky. TraPos – (transport police) – spotted him before he even got into the water, shouting at him to stop, but he carried on, running towards a jetty as the TraPos fired warning shots. Leaping into the water, Günter swam frantically towards the West as the TraPos fired their machine-guns, bullets peppering the water, yet still he kept going, and he'd almost made it to the other side when a bullet found him. Ducking under the water, Günter tried to hide, but he had to come up for air eventually, and when he did, gasping a panicked breath and raising his hands in a kind of surrender, the police fired their final shot, the bullet piercing the back of his head.

Günter sank. His body was pulled out three hours later, by which time hundreds of West Berliners had heard what was happening and had raced down to the river, watching and screaming as his body was fished out. The next day, the story appeared in West Berlin's newspapers:

ULBRICHT'S HUMAN HUNTERS HAVE BECOME MURDERERS

The party knew they couldn't keep this story out of the news in the East, but they could spin it. They ran an article in their party newspaper, *Neues Deutschland*, describing Günter as a homosexual criminal, then used their favourite propagandist, Karl-Eduard von Schnitzler, host of *The Black Channel*, to disparage Günter on air. A few days later, secret police searched Günter's mother's apartment and interrogated his brother, but didn't tell them what had happened. His family only found out he'd been killed from West Berlin TV. At the funeral, hundreds of people turned up, people who didn't even know Günter, and they watched as his brother, Jürgen, leapt into his grave and broke open the coffin to see Günter one last time.

The party followed the same procedure for most deaths at the Wall. They never admitted their shoot-to-kill policy, so these deaths were awkward events that had to be managed. They rarely allowed families to see the bodies, though sometimes the party would fund a funeral, using money they'd found in the dead escapee's pocket. This wasn't out of charity, but because funerals were good opportunities for intelligence gathering. While the family mourned at the graveside, secret police would lurk in the background, making notes of future trouble-makers. VoPos killed on duty were treated very differently: they were given funerals with full military honours, streets and schools named after them. But the families of those killed while trying to escape soon found their own way to mark their grief: they wrote the names of their dead on pieces of paper, wrapped them onto the barbed wire and erected small white crosses where they'd been killed.

Joachim and Manfred had seen those small white crosses, knew that if their escape went wrong, there could be a wooden cross for them. They had to find a way out, fast. It was already mid-September, one month and four killings since the barbed wire went up. Every week they waited, it would get harder.

Joachim walks over to the TV and turns it on. There's a programme on West Berlin TV that shows different sections of the border, updating viewers on the latest places to be closed off. This is how Joachim and Manfred begin each morning's research: sitting up close to the TV, they watch the programme closely, looking for places they might sneak over. When they see something promising, they circle street names or squares on maps in front of them. But every day, the number of places is whittled down as new barriers appear, new parts of the border sealed off.

The following day, Joachim and Manfred jump on bicycles and cycle to the places they've identified to check them out: quiet spots in corners of East Berlin, places they think they might sneak through. But none look safe, too many VoPos around. And they can't swim through the river, as VoPos have strung barbed wire under the water.

Back home, they puzzle over the maps again. Joachim follows streets and squares and train lines with his eyes, looking for inspiration. Then it comes to him: so far they've been looking for escape routes *inside* East Berlin, but maybe there's a better chance of escaping *outside* the city.

For their next recce, they cycle right out of East Berlin, into the countryside, until they reach a small village with a cluster of houses. At the far edge there's a sign:

GRENZGEBIET! BETRETEN VERBOTEN!
BORDER AREA! NO TRESPASSING!

This is promising. Cycling round the sign, they come across a field that slopes down, then rises in the distance. In the furthest part of that field they see small dots moving. *Cows?* Manfred pulls out a pair of binoculars, looks through the glass and grins. 'Tractors!'

He inspects the wheels, the doors, the paint, and to Manfred, who's been trained in mechanical engineering while on military service, it is obvious. '*West German* tractors!'

If they can get to that field, they'll make it. Manfred scans the horizon with his binoculars. They need to know what else is there, what to watch out for. Further in from the tractors there's a line of trees. Then hay bales. Cows. A barn. Then suddenly – a mass of grey concrete. Manfred recoils, whizzing the wheel with his finger, trying to focus, and that's when he realises what he is looking at: a watch-tower.

Raising the binoculars slowly, scared of what he might find, Manfred squints through the glass lenses, edging up and up until he sees a window. Spinning the wheel, he refocuses, and that's when he sees them, a pair of eyes looking straight back at him through binoculars.

Border guards.

Jumping on their bikes, hearts banging against their chests, Manfred and Joachim cycle frantically round the sign, back to the road, waiting for the noise – a car sent to find them, or a warning shot – swivelling their heads to see if they're being followed, but they're not. They make it home a few hours later.

That night they decide that this field with its watch-tower is their best chance. It's too dangerous to keep doing recces and there'll never be a perfect escape route. They make plans to leave, work out who to tell, what to take. Then they wait. Their best change of escaping is on a dark night, that's the only way to get past that watch-tower.

And so, for the third time in his relatively short life, Joachim finds himself preparing to escape.

17

The Watch-tower

<hr/>

I T'S DUSK ON 28 September, two weeks after that recce. Joachim and Manfred are at the pub, drinking with friends, and when they leave, Joachim looks up and sees them. 'Oh man. The clouds are gathering.'

He knows it's time.

At home he changes, putting on two pairs of trousers, three jumpers and a winter coat – clothes for his first winter in West Berlin. Then he puts a few things in a plastic bag: his school certificates, birth certificate, ID card. He's doing all this in secret, doesn't tell his mother or sister: this way out of East Berlin is too dangerous for them, he doesn't want to say anything that could get them into trouble when the police come. If his mother is suspicious about all the activity over the past few weeks, she doesn't say anything. She's learnt there are things she'd rather not know.

A friend gives Joachim and Manfred a lift into the countryside, leaving them just behind that no trespassing sign. They creep towards the field, lie down on the grass, and wait for their eyes to adjust to the dark. They've chosen their night well; it's almost pitch-black, the moon and stars obscured by low clouds, scudding overhead. The VoPos won't spot them easily. The downside is that Joachim and Manfred can barely see where they're going.

Crawling down the hill, they are blind to everything except what's ten metres in front, and as they crawl, all they can think about is that watch-tower. Crouching down, they take it in turns to watch while the other person clambers forward, their East German military training finally proving useful, until eventually, they reach the bottom of the field, their clothes wet with dew.

Joachim checks his watch. It's three in the morning; they've been crawling for four hours.

The night is quiet. All Joachim can hear is the sound of his own breathing. Stretching his hands in front of him, he searches the undergrowth for something he's sure should be there, his skin prickling with fear when he can't find it. 'The barbed wire – where is it?'

He's expecting something to mark the border – a fence, barbed wire, anything that would indicate they're crossing into West Berlin – but there's nothing. Just brambles and bushes. And something else – water. Joachim lowers one foot gently. It's a river; perhaps the border is just beyond it. He puts his other foot into the water, then—

WHACK WHACK WHACK WHACK WHACK WHACK!

There's a deafening noise, it sounds like an explosion or machine-gun fire, but then he sees them – hundreds of wild geese taking off into the night, swirling and gliding through the sky, the flapping of their wings making a terrible noise, a noise so loud that Joachim and Manfred are sure the border guards in the watch-tower will hear.

Squinting into the dark, heart thumping, Joachim looks for any movement. All he can see are the silhouettes of trees; behind any of them could be a VoPo. It's too dark to know if they're alone, but they've come too far to go back and so he slips into the river, the shock of the cold water pulling his breath in. They wade through it, no idea how deep the river gets, so they hold their bags high as they push through the water, and to their relief, just as the water hits their thighs, the ground slopes up. Scrambling up the bank, they run in a crouched position, their thigh muscles trembling, their multiple pairs of wet trousers whipping and smacking around their legs. They don't know where they're running to, they can't see the tractors, can't really see anything, but they run and run and run until, finally, it begins to get light.

In the dawn glow a gravel track appears, trees either side. Instinctively, they join the path, trudging along until, out of the pink haze, a cluster of buildings emerges. As they reach the first, Joachim sees a blue light glowing in a window: *a fire station perhaps?*

But there's no time to keep guessing because, as Joachim looks through the open window, he realises he's looking at the outline of a man's head, a man who's sleeping, head perched on his hands. And it's only then that Joachim realises he has no idea where they are, whether they've made it to the West or whether they're still in the East, this man in front of them a VoPo.

Somewhere in the fog of his dreams the man must have heard something, for right now, he is opening his eyes. Startled, he is quick to compose himself, and as the hairs on Joachim's neck bristle, the man leans forward.

'Well, boys, where have you come from in the middle of the night?'

18

The Camp

———

THEY STUTTER, NOT knowing what to say.
The man looks back at them, a smile curling around his lips.
'Boys, stop looking for words. I know exactly where you've come from.
There were two young men just like you. Came through here a couple
of days ago, escaped like you. Congratulations, you've made it!'

Joachim falls into Manfred's arms and they collapse to the ground
with relief. Lying there, Joachim notices that his heart feels light, as
though a stone has fallen from it.

They look up and read the words on the banner, high above:

DIE FREIE WELT HEISST SIE WILLKOMMEN!
THE FREE WORLD WELCOMES YOU!

This is the entrance to Marienfelde Refugee Camp in the American
sector in West Berlin. It's where anyone who escapes into West Berlin
comes after they arrive, for though they have only crept a few miles to
the other side of their city, this is who they are now: refugees.

It's now around eight in the morning, and Joachim and Manfred are
tired, wet and cold. All they want are warm clothes, food and a bed, but
they must join the queue of refugees waiting to be processed by the staff
at the camp – mostly church workers and wives of Western soldiers. There
are twenty-five apartment blocks here, each three stories high, and most
are full, following the deluge of people in the months before the Wall was
built. Sometimes there were as many as two thousand a day: farmers,
teachers, doctors, factory workers, parents, crying babies, grandparents.

Then, hidden among them are the spies, sent by the party to find
out what is happening in the West. The camp is full of them – as well

as agents from the American CIA and the British MI6, poised to interrogate new arrivals at the refugee camp and mine them for information
about East Germany. For Berlin is now the spy capital of the world.
With the threat of nuclear war, the West and the Soviet Union are
desperate to understand more about each other – their armies, weapons,
any plans for attacks. But with the world carved in two, it's almost
impossible to sneak spies into each other's territory – except in one
place: Berlin. Seventy intelligence agencies operate in the city, all in the
business of recruiting and training informants, assigning listening posts
and drop zones, then sending their spies into the East or West. But since
the Wall appeared, the flow of information into West Berlin is drying
up: it's become harder for spies to wander in and out of East Berlin and
there are fewer people escaping to West Berlin. Anyone who makes it
is a precious resource.

Joachim is now at the front of the line. He gives his name and age
and a man takes him down a corridor to a small room. Inside, a man
in dark trousers and crisp white shirt sits at a desk.

'And how did you get here?' he asks, no introduction, as Joachim sits
opposite. Joachim is intrigued. The man's German is flawless, but the
accent isn't quite right. He tells the man his story, how he'd grown up
in the East and wanted to leave.

'And what were you doing before you left?'

There it is again. That accent, that hint of somewhere else. *American?*
CIA? It's a good guess. The CIA had just started a new initiative, putting
German-speaking officials into the camp to interview all new arrivals.
Joachim tells the CIA officer about his escape – the field, the river, the
watch-tower. The man looks bored; he's heard these escape stories a
hundred times. Then he asks Joachim what he'd been doing in the East,
and Joachim tells him about his university course. 'And then there was
my time in the army reserves.'

CIA guy looks up. 'Which unit?'

'Torgelow, in Mecklenburg.'

Now the intelligence officer looks interested; here's someone who's
recently been in the East German army. He might know things, however
small, which could be useful. He stands up, walks to the back of the
room. 'Which military company was this?'

'Telecommunications,' says Joachim. 'News division.'

The American walks to a large metal unit at the back of the room and opens the top drawer. Inside, a neat row of index cards. He pulls one out. 'Is the company chief in that unit still Senior Lieutenant Schmidt?'

Joachim is impressed; the CIA officer knows the names of all the senior army officials in the unit Joachim had been trained in, though their titles are out of date.

'He's now a major,' says Joachim, feeling useful.

The American looks back at him, smiles for the first time. 'There's a house, not far from here. We can put you up for a few days. The food's better there. You'll have your own room, somewhere to sleep. Just have a few more questions.'

Joachim says no, he wants to go and find his aunt and uncle in West Berlin, but the CIA officer is persuasive, putting Joachim in a car and driving him, his plastic bag and his drenched clothes to a small house in Grunewald, a forested area in the far west of Berlin.

Joachim doesn't know why he's here, what this place surrounded by pine trees is, but there's a bed to sleep in and right now that's enough. He drops into bed, and soon his eyes close, his breath deepens, and finally he sleeps, his first night in West Berlin.

The next morning he wakes to the smell of toast. Downstairs, breakfast is laid on a small table and there's a man and two children sitting in silence. Later Joachim will discover that the apartment is a CIA safe house, the man at the table a high-ranking official from East Berlin who'd defected to the West, but in this moment he doesn't care about any of that. Instead, he's distracted by what's on the table: a generous spread of cereals, toast and jam. Picking up a piece of toast, Joachim butters it, smears on a rancid-looking jam, takes a bite and . . .

Inside he melts.

It's marmalade but not like anything else he's ever tasted. He takes another bite. It's pineapple, the man tells him. Joachim has never eaten it – after all, citrus fruits were rare in the East – he'd only seen pineapple in photos. Now, here he is, eating a sugary, gooey version of this rare fruit and he's addicted. He eats pineapple marmalade for breakfast, lunch, then supper, answers a few more questions, then goes to bed, dreaming marmalade dreams.

19

The Spy

29 September 1961

A s Joachim sleeps, a few miles away a hairdresser called Siegfried is queueing at a checkpoint, waiting to cross the border into East Berlin. Siegfried clutches his bag, hoping he'll make it through without attracting attention. Around him, the trains whistle and screech, the sound bouncing off the iron roof of Friedrichstrasse station, swirling down through the maze of platforms.

Friedrichstrasse is the busiest border crossing between West and East Berlin. In a quirk of East German rules, the authorities only allow people with West *German* passports to cross into East Berlin to visit friends and family. At the end of their visit, they must return to West Berlin. VoPos patrol the platforms, machine-guns in their hands, watching as people make their way to the checkpoint next to the station, a huge hall nicknamed *Tränenpalast* – the 'Palace of Tears'. For this is where visiting relatives say goodbye to those stuck in the East – wives leave husbands, brothers leave sisters, mothers leave daughters. A trapezoid of glass, the ceiling reaches high into the sky, dwarfing the border-crossers, who are funnelled into narrow booths as they go through security.

Siegfried stands in line, his bag heavy with the weight of what he knows should not be in there. When he's called forward, he squeezes through the booth, a green-uniformed-TraPo (transport police officer) monitoring from behind the glass. Siegfried hands over his West German passport, then waits, as they all do, for the buzzer that means the door into the East is about to open, but the sound never comes, for the TraPo is motioning to Siegfried's bag.

Pulse racing, Siegfried obediently opens his bag, revealing hundreds of smuggled cigarettes and several bottles of alcohol.

In a side room, Siegfried answers the TraPo's questions about the smuggled cigarettes and alcohol, bluffing about going to a party, knowing his story sounds ridiculous. After an hour, the TraPo takes him into another room and there, sitting behind a desk, is a man. No uniform.

Siegfried's stomach bottoms out.

The man sitting in front of Siegfried is a Stasi officer, one of hundreds of thousands of employees spread between the Stasi's fourteen regional offices. Like most Stasi employees, he's been taught martial arts, how to use disguises to follow suspects (mostly wigs and fake moustaches) and how to conduct interrogations. It's not a bad life; his salary is generous, he shops in special supermarkets stuffed with Western food, and he knows that if he does well he can go on luxurious holidays, perhaps one day own a villa in a private compound with a swimming pool and cinema. But to keep these perks, and stand a chance of promotion, he must reach a target: recruit twenty-five new informants every year. If he fails, he could be demoted. For it is these informants that set the Stasi apart from every other secret police force in history.

The *Inoffizielle Mitarbeiter*, or IMs – 'unofficial employees' – are not Stasi employees working in Stasi offices, but they are ordinary people who spy on colleagues, friends, husbands and parents, even their own children. These informants are considered so important to the Stasi that they refer to them (rather poetically) as their 'breathing organs'. And these informants are everywhere: in hospitals, schools, universities, charities, businesses, environmental groups, hotels, bars, knitting clubs, even the Church (some estimate that as many as 65 *per cent* of church leaders were working for the Stasi).

Informants are separated into different categories depending on their importance: there are IMs, FIMs (unofficial collaborators running other unofficial collaborators), GMSes (low-level IMs), IMBs, IMEs, IMKs, all sending information into the ZAIG – the Stasi's central processing group in Berlin.

And what makes this network of informants so effective is the sheer number of them: 173,000. In Hitler's Germany, there was one Gestapo agent for every 2,000 people; in the Soviet Union, there was one KGB agent for every 5,830 people; in East Germany, there was one informant for every *sixty-three* people, and if you include part-time informers, some say there were as many as one informant per *six* people. Even the police, military and border guard units were stuffed with informants. They were there the night the barbed wire went up, spread among construction workers and soldiers, making sure they obeyed orders, and it was Stasi informants from the Twentieth Directorate who'd climbed onto the roofs of Dresden, looking for Western-pointing aerials, drawing up that list of names in Joachim's newspaper.

Helping Stasi officers achieve their target of finding twenty-five informants a year is their training in the science of recruitment. Directive 1/79 sets out different strategies they can use. First, the directive says, try political persuasion to win people through loyalty. If that doesn't work, bribe the potential informant with money or medicine. If that still doesn't work, there's the more forceful approach: blackmail.

The Stasi officer knows he has a good chance with Siegfried. He's been caught smuggling cigarettes; the threat of prison will probably be enough to turn him. But the officer is about to discover something even better: he asks Siegfried where he was taking these cigarettes.

'They are for a woman in the East,' Siegfried says.

'What for?' the Stasi officer asks.

And that's when Siegfried crumbles, admitting everything: how he brings this landlady a bottle of Vermouth and two packs of cigarettes every week so that he can spend evenings in a room that she rents to his lover.

Siegfried pauses. And then, in a moment of inexplicable honesty, he adds another detail: his *male* lover.

This changes everything. Not only is Siegfried guilty of smuggling, but he's guilty of a more serious offence: homosexuality. In 1960s East Germany – as in most of the world – homosexuality is illegal. Only a few decades before, Berlin had been the gay capital of Europe, the Ku'damm stuffed with bars and private clubs where it was the height of cool to turn up with someone of the same sex. Forty years on, in both East and West Germany, homosexuality is seen as deviant bourgeois behaviour, a threat to the state.

Siegfried knows he's in trouble. He waits for the Stasi officer to arrest him, take him to prison. But the Stasi officer doesn't arrest him. Instead, he tells Siegfried that there is a way out.

20

The File

———•———

WE KNOW ALL this from the files the Stasi wrote about Siegfried Uhse after his first interrogation. They're kept in a vault, alongside millions of other files, in the former Stasi headquarters.

It's a long, labyrinthine walk to get to that vault, through fluorescent-lit, stale-smelling corridors and down clunky lifts until, eventually, you come to a pair of locked double doors. Through those doors, at the top of a flight of steps, you look down onto a room containing row upon row of heavy white pull-out shelves, each containing thousands of files. The room feels like a morgue, white and clean with the whiff of bleach. The only sound is the hum of air-conditioning – the files must be kept at a constant eighteen degrees so the paper doesn't disintegrate.

Everything about the way those files are stored is as meticulous as that air temperature. They've been painstakingly catalogued so that any file can be found should someone ask to see it. And the files in that vault are only a fraction of what exists.

When the Wall fell, protesters broke into Stasi buildings across the country, and, like detectives in a crime scene, they searched every room, looking for evidence that revealed what the Stasi had been up to for forty years. They discovered videos of protests, rallies and church meetings. They found samples of people's handwriting, torn from letters and posters, along with graphological reports analysing their style. Then – the strangest discovery – thousands of jars, all numbered, each containing torn pieces of cloth. These pieces of cloth had been placed in suspect's armpits or crotches during long, sweaty interrogations, then put in sealed jars as smell samples, ready to give a sniffer dog should they need to find the suspect again.

As well as the jars, the handwriting samples and the videos, protesters found tens of thousands of sacks containing shreds of paper – the remains of the Stasi files. In the Stasi's final hours, when they knew the end was near and as protesters surrounded their offices, they started shredding. When the shredders broke, they ripped files with their bare hands. The protesters took those sacks to Berlin, where they sat, under the care of the new government, for five years while the country debated what to do. Should the files be read, or would that open old wounds and stop the country healing from the past?

Eventually, it was agreed that the past should be known, every inch of it, and so began the maddening task of putting the shredded files back together. In a building in a village near Nuremberg, a small group of men and women sat at tables reconnecting these dislocated pages, solving A4 puzzles of people's monitored lives.

It was then they realised just how many files there were, hundreds of thousands, the first dating from 17 June 1953 (the evening of the uprising that Joachim was part of), the final report dating from November 1989, weeks before it all ended. If you were to lie the pieces of paper on the ground, end to end, they'd stretch for over two hundred kilometres.

When I began my research, I asked the Stasi Archives for everything they had on Siegfried Uhse. Two months later, they'd gathered the files together. All 2,735 pages. I went through them with my German translator Sabine, trying to work out who and what each one was about, a task made harder by the black lines put through some names by officials at the archives. But we soon learnt the lengths of certain names, deducing from that and the occasional flick of a letter above or below a black line whose file we were holding.

The first report about Siegfried Uhse dates from 2 October 1961. It's the six-page account of his arrest and interrogation, carried out by Stasi officer Hans Joachim.

The first page notes the department that interrogated him – Department II: counter-intelligence. Then it sets out his personal details. His full name: Siegfried Alfred Helmut Uhse. His date of birth: 9 July 1940 – which makes him twenty-one years old. His profession: hairdresser.

Then his appearance: he's 1.67 metres tall with a narrow build, back-combed ash-blond hair, grey eyes, a 'pointed nose, a wide mouth', and they make a special note of his slightly 'inflamed eyes'. Then there are questions about his childhood, which, it turns out, is surprisingly similar to Joachim Rudolph's.

Siegfried Uhse grew up in a working-class family in East Germany and was thrown out of his house by soldiers, like Joachim, after the war. Aged four, he'd come to Berlin with his parents, though his father died when Siegfried was fourteen. (Cause of death redacted.) In 1958, three years before the Wall, Siegfried followed his mother in moving to West Germany, and that detail is important as it meant he had West German citizenship, which is why Siegfried could go in and out of East Berlin. Recently, he'd moved to West Berlin, where he now lived by himself, renting a small flat just off the Ku'damm.

The Stasi interrogator asks about his job.

Siegfried lists every hairdressing salon he's worked in, their addresses and his weekly salary.

His savings?

Siegfried says he has 60DM in his flat (worth £5 back in 1961). Then Siegfried turns out his pockets to show his interrogator a few coins he has on him right now.

In asking these questions, Hans is following the training he'd been given by the Stasi for recruiting informers. He would have been taught the Stasi's '101-point system', against which Stasi officers assessed potential recruits. They were taught to extract information about every area of a future informant's life: their friends and family, their job, social position, political views, hobbies, books, body language, dress sense, 'brain power', moods, skills, living conditions and, finally, their sexual behaviour. Nothing was off limits, everything was important. There it was again – that principle of *flächendeckend* ('covering all areas').

As you read the report, through Hans Joachim's forensic questioning, Siegfried Uhse comes to life: a man who waters his beloved plants every morning, reads widely and collects drawings that he carries around in a small notebook. Hans adds, 'there's a certain softness in him', before suggesting dismissively that it's probably because of his homosexuality. At night, Siegfried goes to bars and restaurants with friends, smokes cigarettes (Stuyvesants), eats meals he can't afford, all washed down with his favourite drink, cognac.

Siegfried says he's not into politics, but Hans Joachim would have been pleased when Siegfried tells him that he was part of the Free German Youth when he was a child and, more importantly, that he reads the party newspaper when in East Berlin. And it's now that you see Hans Joachim, the Stasi interrogator, beginning to warm to him.

'In a longer conversation with Uhse,' he writes, in typical Stasi-understated-language, 'it could be stated he's not unintelligent. In political matters, he is not ignorant.'

By now, it's the middle of the night; Siegfried's interrogation has gone on for two hours and this is when it turns.

From talking about politics, Hans introduces a more intimate subject, with no warning.

'When did you discover you were gay?'

Siegfried pauses. 'When I hit puberty.'

'Have you ever been with a woman?'

Another pause. 'No. I've always run away from them.'

'What kind of men do you like?'

'Pretty men,' says Siegfried, 'like actors and singers.'

'Do you have sex for money?'

'No.'

'Do you have anal sex?'

'No, I masturbate.'

'Do you have sex with children?'

'No.'

'Where do you meet men?'

'Through my hairdressing clients or out on the streets, but I want a steady boyfriend.'

'Do you think of your homosexuality as a criminal offence?'

'No.'

'Have you ever tried to cure your "illness?"' (By illness, Hans means his homosexuality.)

'Yes,' Siegfried says, 'I've been to the doctors several times to cure myself, but I always fall back into it. My mother doesn't know.'

Reading through this part of the report feels voyeuristic. The questions are intrusive and offensive, but in the file, there's only one moment where you get a sense of what Siegfried might have been feeling. Hans notes that: 'it takes a while for Siegfried to open up about "his problem"'.

It's hardly surprising. Siegfried is sitting in front of a Stasi officer in the middle of the night, answering questions about the most intimate parts of his life, talking about things he couldn't tell his mother. And the unspoken backdrop to these questions was the threat of prison: something Siegfried knew all about. The report notes that in West

Germany, where homosexuality was also illegal, someone had discovered Siegfried was gay, told the police and he'd been arrested, given a suspended sentence. Siegfried knows where he could end up today if he doesn't do what the Stasi officer wants.

It's now morning; Siegfried has been answering questions all through the night. No sleep. No rest. No food. No water. But now, finally, Hans offers Siegfried breakfast. After Siegfried finishes eating, Hans delivers the proposition he has been building up to all night: come and work for us.

Holding the report of that interrogation is like looking at a version of Siegfried caught in amber, an unfinished version of the man he might have been had he not been caught that night. I picture him: a softly spoken, plant-loving hairdresser, just twenty-one years old and exhausted, a terrible choice having been forced upon him.

Like thousands before him, and many tens of thousands after, Siegfried has to pick a side. This is something East Germany excelled at: it's what they'd done when they built the Wall, forcing people to choose between East or West, and it's what they did every time they asked someone to become an informant. The choice was simple: collaborator or dissident. Saying no meant risking prison, your career, your family. Saying yes meant you were now one of *them*.

There are no details in the file about Siegfried's reaction, his emotions. After all the questions about his sexuality, would he have felt shame? Was he thinking about the unspoken threat of a prison sentence, wondering what life would be like as a gay man in a Stasi jail? Or did Siegfried see this as his chance to take revenge on West Germany, the country that had arrested him for his homosexuality?

It's impossible to know. None of that is recorded in the file. Instead, in a neat black line, typewritten at the bottom of the page, the file records the end of his interrogation:

'It came to a fruitful conclusion,' it says. 'At 10 a.m. in the morning on 30 September, Siegfried Uhse declared by his free will that he would work for us.'

The next page in that file is handwritten. In an elegant hand, it's Siegfried Uhse's so-called letter of commitment; every new informant wrote one. It's a clever move; new recruits would have felt part of something, no going back. In another bit of astute psychology, the Stasi even allow Siegfried to choose his own codename; they want their informants to feel a sense of ownership in their new identity. Siegfried's chosen name is so incongruous it's almost comical.

> *I, Siegfried Uhse, voluntarily consent to actively support the security forces of the GDR in their righteous fight. Furthermore, I pledge to maintain absolute silence to everyone about my co-operation with the forces of the Ministry of State Security. If I break this commitment I can be punished according to the current laws of the GDR. For my co-operation with the forces of the Ministry of State Security, I choose the codename Fred.*

Then, finally, they let him go.

A few days later, the Stasi send an investigator to Siegfried's house to check his story. The investigator talks to a group of cigarette sellers on the street, friends of Siegfried's, as well as other tenants in the building. The investigator is happy with what he finds. He notes in his report that Siegfried lives a quiet life, he's clean, polite, his finances are in order and he doesn't make trouble. Siegfried's recruitment is approved and the Stasi schedule their first meeting with him: 8 p.m. on 4 October at Presse Café in East Berlin.

Siegfried Uhse had made his decision, picked a side. He belonged to the Stasi now.

21

Evi and Peter (and Walter and Wilhelm Too)

December 1961

EVI AND PETER Schmidt sit in their living room in Wilhelmshagen, a quiet, leafy suburb of East Berlin, a fire crackling in the corner. It's a few days after Christmas, they've just put their baby to bed, and sitting with them by the fire are two friends – Luigi (Gigi) Spina – a tall, handsome art student and his shorter, funnier sidekick, Domenico (Mimmo) Sesta. Mimmo and Gigi are Italian; they'd come to West Berlin to study before the Wall was built and they'd got to know Peter at art school. With the Wall up, they were now separated: the two Italians in West Berlin, Peter and his wife Evi in the East. As foreigners though, Mimmo and Gigi could cross the border into East Berlin when they liked and they went almost every week, trying to convince Peter to escape to West Berlin.

Peter always said no. The Wall won't last, he'd say, we just need to wait. Five months on, Mimmo and Gigi could see Peter was struggling. He was distracted and anxious – like a caged animal, they thought. Peter had once worked as a graphic artist for a newspaper in West Berlin; after the Wall, he'd lost his job and he and Evi were now struggling for money. Peter spent most days at home, playing with their eight-month-old baby Annet, strumming his guitar. One afternoon, Peter was told he would soon have to join the East German army and the thought terrified him – guarding the border, shooting at escapees. He wanted to escape before the military came for him.

Evi wanted to get out too. Apart from her grandparents, there wasn't much tying her to East Berlin. When she was six, Evi's mother had caught tuberculosis, and to prevent Evi from getting it, her mother took her to live with Evi's grandparents, her mother isolating in a summer-

80

house in their garden. A few months later, Evi's mother died and her father then came for her – he'd divorced Evi's mother a few years earlier. But when Evi's father revealed that he was planning on selling her to an American major who lived in Munich, Evi's grandparents threw him out and raised Evi as their own.

They were kind, loving, but worried about who would look after Evi when they were gone. When Evi turned fourteen, though she was bright and dreamt of going to university and becoming a teacher, her grandparents said she must leave school and begin an apprenticeship to support herself. Evi had become a librarian, learning to write in a child-like neat handwriting as she catalogued thousands of books in a university library. But as she walked to work, in fact wherever she went in East Berlin, Evi felt the Wall looming and she wanted to escape.

Now, as Mimmo and Gigi ask that same question, with the threat of Peter's conscription hanging over him, Evi and Peter give a different answer: they say yes. It is time.

But how? If escaping back in September when Joachim had crawled through a field had been dangerous, trying to escape from East Berlin just a few months later was almost impossible. The Wall was taller and more heavily guarded, with ditches running along the front filled with *hockersperren* (metal shards known as 'dragons' teeth'), and trip-wires that triggered alarms and floodlights. And there were now dozens of observation towers from which VoPos scoured the border, looking for escapees with orders to shoot. And so the escapes had become more inventive.

There was Harry Deterling, a train driver, who'd hijacked a steam train with his wife and four kids, along with twenty-five others, and driven it full speed into West Berlin. 'The last train to freedom', he'd called it, and he was right: soldiers closed the railway line the next day. Others crawled through sewers or scuba-dived through the river. By the end of 1961, over eight thousand had escaped (seventy-seven of them border guards), but the risks were increasing.

Tens of thousands of VoPos now patrolled the border, catching and arresting anyone they found, and thirteen would-be escapees were now dead: four had fallen off roofs or out of windows, six were killed trying to swim across the river (one, a champion scuba-driver who'd frozen in the water) and three people had been shot. The party was determined that fewer people would escape in 1962 and the number of successful attempts had plummeted.

Peter and Evi needed to come up with a new kind of escape route, something the VoPos wouldn't expect, that would be manageable with a baby. They throw ideas around: maybe they could hire a lorry and smash through the barrier? Or what about a helicopter? Then Mimmo suggests something more subtle: a tunnel. But instead of digging from East to West Berlin as border guards might predict – this tunnel could run from *West* Berlin into the East. From freedom into repression. It's the only option that sounds half sensible and they agree to talk again soon.

After Mimmo and Gigi leave, Evi walks to the window. Her stomach is alive with nervous excitement; it's a relief to make this decision, but it feels strange to be so powerless in your own extraction, waiting for an escape route to be dug out.

Standing at the window, Evi looks towards her neighbours' houses. They know each other well, they talk, share problems, help each other out. But she won't tell them about this.

What she doesn't know, as she stares out into the darkening night, is that two of her neighbours have been spying on her and her family for months. Codenamed Walter and Wilhelm, they're informants for the Stasi and they've been instructed to watch Evi and Peter. All the time.

Walter and Wilhelm have been diligent. They've told their Stasi handlers all about Peter's life in East Berlin, how he lives beyond his means, and they even told their handler the moment they knew Evi was pregnant. They watch the front door closely, note the times Evi and Peter leave the house and return each day. In more recent reports, they've made a special note of the 'friends visiting from West Berlin'. They will try to find out what they're up to.

It's now late, and Evi pulls the curtains, cocooning the three of them in a house she hopes she will soon leave and never see again.

22

The Girrmann Group

JOACHIM SHIVERS. IT'S his first winter in West Berlin and it's freezing, the streets covered in ice. He's glad of the coat he smuggled out of East Berlin three months ago; he's kept it with him all this time, from the CIA house to Marienfelde Refugee Camp, and now here, the student dorms at the Technical University in Berlin where he'd enrolled to study communications engineering.

It had been a hard few months. When Joachim arrived in West Berlin, he missed his mother and sister so much it hurt, particularly when he heard how brave they'd been when the Stasi turned up at their apartment after he'd escaped. His mother had calmy batted them away: 'Oh, he's in Dresden studying. Why would you even look for him here?' The Stasi had badgered and questioned and threatened, but his mother stood firm and eventually they left. He missed that. Her spirit. But he had no idea how to get her to West Berlin.

That's when he'd heard about them: the Girrmann Group. It was formed the night the barbed wire went up, when a law student called Detlef Girrmann and a couple of friends decided they wanted to help people escape the East. Within a few months, they'd helped hundreds leave: borrowing passports from West German friends, they matched them with people in East Berlin who looked similar, then couriers smuggled the passports over the border.

Someone at university put Joachim in touch with the Girrmann Group, and he'd asked if they could help his mother and sister escape. Yes, they said, but they'd have to try something new. Border police were now onto the passport scheme, its officers given manuals containing dozens of photos of different-shaped noses, eyes, lips and cheeks, so they could spot the difference between the passport photo and the person in front of them. They'd caught hundreds this way and sent them to prison.

Now, the Girrmann Group were trying something new. Instead of using borrowed passports, they were buying *blank* passports from embassy contacts in Vienna, Belgium and Switzerland. This meant they could add the escapee's own photograph – less chance of a VoPo noticing the passport was fake. A month later, the Girrmann Group had found two blank passports for Joachim's mother and sister and smuggled them into East Berlin. The passports were Viennese, so his mother and sister filled their bags with Austrian schillings and tram tickets, learnt a few Austrian phrases, then crossed the border into West Berlin.

They were all in West Berlin now, trying to build new lives, but it wasn't easy. Joachim had spent so long thinking about how to get over the Wall that he hadn't thought much about life beyond it. He'd gone from a world where he had almost no control over his life to one where he could do whatever he wanted, whenever he wanted, and it was dizzying. He'd understood how to behave when there was something to push against, but here in West Berlin, like a zoo animal released from a cage, he wasn't sure what to do. And now Joachim was living in West Berlin full-time, no longer just a weekend visitor, he could see the cracks beneath the surface.

For the Wall had changed West Berlin too: when Walter Ulbricht built his Wall to stop East Berliners leaving, he'd effectively encircled *West* Berlin. For Berlin was 100 miles inside the Soviet zone in East Germany, which is why many described West Berlin as an 'island of freedom in a Communist sea'. An island of freedom that was now surrounded by a wall.

Immediately after it was built, West Berliners showed what they thought of the Wall, covering it in graffiti: *Es gibt nur ein Berlin* – 'There is only one Berlin' – and the letters 'KZ', the initials for a concentration camp. Though, technically, West Berliners were free to drive or fly to West Germany, with the Wall looming over them, they felt trapped. Unless they had West German passports, they couldn't cross the border to visit friends or family in East Berlin, so many West Berliners felt there was no reason to stay. Every day, hundreds flew to other cities in Germany until West Berlin had one of the lowest birth rates in the world. The government was so scared by the exodus that it paid *Zittergeld* – 'trem-ble-money', to people who agreed to remain or move to West Berlin. As ambitious, conformist types moved to Frankfurt or Hamburg for mainstream careers, radicals, waifs and strays moved to West Berlin, including those who wanted to avoid conscription to the West German army, as living in West Berlin meant you were exempt. And it was here, in this schizophrenic, confused city, that Joachim had to make a new life.

His first few months at university had been a culture shock. Back in the East, student life was strictly controlled: he'd been told which lectures to go to, there was no personal choice. Here in West Berlin, Joachim had to make his own decisions and it was overwhelming. It was freedom, but too much freedom and he couldn't cope.

As an outsider, he'd found himself gravitating towards other East Berliners in the student dorms; they would eat together in communal kitchens, cut each other's hair and talk over beer in the evenings. Today, he was just about to head out to meet some of them when there was a knock on his door.

Joachim opens it to find three friends standing there. There's Wolfhardt (Wolf) Schroedter – tall, blond and charming, always laughing. Wolf had grown up in East Germany and, like Joachim, his father died after the war. As a teenager Wolf had been a model socialist citizen – he was part of the Free German Youth, sang all the right songs with the right kind of enthusiasm. But aged seventeen, after long nights listening to radio from West Berlin and questioning what he'd been taught, Wolf decided to escape. He boarded a train to East Berlin, then crossed the border into West Berlin (this was pre-Wall) and lived in a church boarding house for boys while he finished school. Now, he was studying engineering.

Next to Wolf were the two Italian students – Mimmo and Gigi. Sitting on Joachim's bed, the three of them tell him why they're here. They tell him all about Evi and Peter, how they need to escape East Berlin as soon as possible and how they have an idea for a new kind of escape route: a tunnel. And they want to use this tunnel to help others escape too. They are ambitious. They want this to be the biggest single escape since the Wall went up and they are telling Joachim all of this for one reason: they want his help. As an escapee from East Berlin, they feel they can trust him. Plus, his background in communications engineering will come in useful.

Joachim looks out of the window, the streets below full of students, people like him who are free to do whatever they want. He thinks about the risks. It's not just escapees who are being targeted by VoPos; escape-helpers from West Berlin have been killed too.

A few weeks ago, a member of the Girrmann Group had been involved in an escape that had gone horribly wrong. Dieter Wohlfahrt was a chemistry student at the same university as Joachim, just twenty years old, and since the Wall went up, he'd helped hundreds escape. One evening, Dieter had driven to the border to help the mother of a friend sneak into West Berlin. Using bolt clippers and pliers to cut through two layers of barbed wire, Dieter was about to pull the woman through when she called loudly to her daughter waiting for her in West Berlin. VoPos had heard, ran towards Dieter, shooting at him, their bullets piercing his chest. Dieter lay there bleeding as West Berlin and British police watched helplessly, too afraid to trespass into the East. Eventually, after an hour, East German border guards had carried his lifeless body away.

If Joachim was shot by VoPos, he knew that police in West Berlin wouldn't help him. Then there was the other risk, the one almost too horrible to think about: what if the tunnel collapsed and he was buried alive?

Joachim thinks about his mother and sister, both now here in West Berlin, yet here are these students, asking him to tunnel back into the country he's just escaped, to rescue people he doesn't even know. There are so many reasons to say no, all more logical than the reasons to say yes, but Joachim, who had seen, aged six, how escapes could go badly wrong, Joachim who hates cold water, Joachim who loves numbers and circuits and electricity and still sometimes dreams of being an astronaut, Joachim finds himself giving an answer.

He says yes.

23

The House of the Future

SIEGFRIED UHSE, THE hairdresser, stands in front of the house. It's grand, imposing. Not what he'd expected. He pushes the door to see if he can sneak in, have a look around. But no, it's locked. He pauses. This is his first mission and he doesn't want to mess up.

Shortly after he'd become a Stasi informant, Siegfried had been asked by his handler, Lehmann, to infiltrate the network of students in West Berlin who helped people escape from East Germany. *Fluchthelfer* they were called – 'escape-helpers'. The Stasi were obsessed with preventing escapes; Erich Mielke had told his employees they were *all* responsible for stopping people fleeing, and he'd even set up a new department to co-ordinate the work. At first, the Stasi focused on breaking up escape plans hatched in the *East*; now they wanted to infiltrate escape networks in *West* Berlin.

It's hard to know what Siegfried would have made of his assignment. After all, he'd chosen to live in West Germany, and now he was hunting down people like him who wanted a different life. But if he had conflicted feelings about his mission, there was no one he could talk to – spies who broke cover could be put on trial in military tribunals, and serious infractions resulted in beheadings or a shot in the neck. Two hundred Stasi officers had already been executed.

Four months into his assignment, Siegfried didn't have much to show for it. Then one night, at a favourite jazz club, he'd got a tip-off. A guy he'd got chatting to had told him to go to a student bar called Berliner Wingolf. A few days ago, Siegfried went there and spun a story about wanting to get his girlfriend and mother out of East Berlin. Did they know anyone who could help? Yes, they'd said, and they'd told him all about the headquarters of the largest escape network in West Berlin – *Haus der Zukunft* – the 'House of the Future'.

'You'll find the guy who runs it there in the afternoon,' a student had told him, and so now, on 18 March 1962, Siegfried had set off to find it. He'd discovered that the House of the Future was in Zehlendorf, one of the wealthiest areas in West Berlin. Alighting from the train at Krumme Lanke station, Siegfried clipped along the cobbled streets, gazing up at the grand houses set among parkland and trees until he'd arrived at the House of the Future, a house so large it looked like a small castle. Behind it, a lake surrounded by meadows, maple trees, weeping willows and rhododendrons. This was the heart of liberal West Berlin: musicians from the Berlin Philharmonic played concerts here, Shakespeare plays had been performed around the lake, and now, here he is, a Stasi spy, trying to infiltrate this world.

Siegfried rings the doorbell and a few moments later, a man wearing dark-rimmed glasses opens the door. 'The eternal student type,' Siegfried will later tell his handler. Siegfried doesn't yet know it, but he's struck gold. This is Bodo Köhler, one of the three founders of the Girrmann Group, the same group that helped Joachim's mother and sister escape. Bodo had escaped East Germany a few years earlier and was studying theology at the Free University. In his spare time, he helped run West Berlin's most prolific escape network.

Siegfried gives him his cover story and Bodo listens, opening the huge door, welcoming him in.

Walking through the corridor, Siegfried has never seen anything like it – dozens of students huddled in groups, talking different languages. As well as a student hangout, the House of the Future is a hostel, and people from all over the world stay here, stuffed into its rooms from the ground floor to the attic, some helping to orchestrate escapes from East Berlin.

One of the foreign volunteers is an American called Joan Glenn. Originally from Oregon, she'd been studying at a branch of Stanford University in Stuttgart. A few months ago, she'd come to West Berlin, and was so affected by the Wall that she abandoned her studies and decided to help East Berliners escape. With her flawless German, Joan was brilliant at it, and she'd pioneered an efficient system that was getting hundreds out of the East.

In the morning, volunteer students from West Berlin would cross the border into East Berlin. 'Test people', Joan called them. They wandered around the East for a while, then returned through the checkpoint at the border, making a mental note of the VoPos' procedures that day. Back in West Berlin, they passed this information on to a second group: the couriers. That same day, couriers smuggled blank passports (usually Swiss or Belgian) into East Berlin, hand-delivering them to escapees, telling them about any new VoPo procedures at the border they should be aware of. Then they'd rehearse the details of the escapees' new identities with them – which usually meant reciting names of towns in Switzerland or Belgium. For the final stage of this VIP escape-service, the volunteers would follow the escapee to the checkpoint, standing a few people behind them. 'This gave the refugee a feeling of reassurance,' Joan later explained.

But that level of support came at a cost. A few months ago, one of Joan's American friends from Stanford had been standing behind one of his escapees when the East German was arrested. The VoPo had discovered that the East German's passport was fake and somehow guessed that the man standing three spaces behind him was connected. The would-be escapee got off lightly with a suspended sentence. The American student was sentenced to fifteen months in prison. The message was clear: escape-helpers would be treated more harshly than escapees. Yet Joan kept going, ignored the risks. There were rumours that she and Bodo were in love. This was the world that Siegfried had just entered, Bodo his guide.

Bodo takes Siegfried into a small office where they can talk discreetly. There, Siegfried tells Bodo more about his fictitious mother and girl-friend, but, at first, Bodo isn't interested. They're not planning any more escapes, he says; their last operation just fell through.

But then Siegfried mentions that he has West German citizenship and Bodo starts paying attention: here is someone who can cross into East Berlin when he likes, and that makes Siegfried a precious commodity. Siegfried could be a courier, delivering messages and passports to escapees in East Berlin. Bodo hands Siegfried a pre-printed form (that's how well organised his network was) and asks Siegfried to write his details – name, address, telephone number. Then Bodo says goodbye and Siegfried leaves.

Siegfried has done well. Not only has he entered West Berlin's biggest escape network, but now *they* will call *him* when they begin plotting their next escape operation.

All these details come from the Stasi report, written the next day by Lehmann after his meeting with Siegfried at 10 a.m. at the Stasi safe house 'Marienquell'. And it's here, in this report, that you get the sense that Siegfried is getting a taste for his new life as a spy. Because this is not the only intelligence gathering Siegfried does that week. He also invites an acquaintance – a blond, muscular metal-worker – to the Dandy Club, a jazz bar in West Berlin. They get drunk, the metal-worker oblivious to Siegfried mining him for information, and eventually Siegfried finds some: it turns out the metal-worker has a friend who works in American counter-intelligence and he gives Siegfried a photograph.

Then, for his hat-trick, Siegfried tells Lehmann that he's spotted a job advert in the *Berliner Morgenpost* newspaper for a hairdressing position at the McNair American army base in West Berlin. Lehmann is delighted and tells him to apply.

The report ends with a brief to-do list for Siegfried:

1. Go back to the House of the Future in two weeks.
2. Maintain friendship with the metal-worker to find out more about the American spy.
3. Get the job at the hairdressers in the army barracks.

Proving the perfect spy, Siegfried does all three.

24

The Factory

QUESTION: HOW DO you dig a tunnel into the most heavily guarded country in the world? How do you find somewhere safe to dig from and somewhere safe to dig to? How do you dig your tunnel when you can't use machines in case you're heard by one of the most powerful secret police forces on earth? How do you buy tools when you have no money? How do you avoid hitting a pipe and drowning? How do you see in the tunnel when there's no light? How do you breathe when the air runs out?

And if, somehow, you do all this, and you get to the other end, what if the secret police are waiting for you?

It begins with maps.

Wolf gets hold of some from a friend in local government and he, Mimmo and Gigi spread them over their dorm-room desks, running their fingers up and down streets, along rivers, checking the locations of underground pipes and the height of water levels, trying to find the best place in West Berlin to start digging. Too far from the Wall and they could be digging for months. Too close, and they could be spotted by VoPos over the Wall in East Berlin. Then there's the soil to think about: Berlin's foundations are mostly crumbly and sandy, prone to collapse. They need to find somewhere with clay-like soil where a tunnel might hold firm. And finally – water. The groundwater in Berlin is high, sometimes just a metre below ground. If they don't find high ground to dig from, the tunnel could flood and they'll drown. With pencils they circle potential digging sites along the border, but there's only so much they can tell from the maps.

A few days later, Wolf drives the three of them through West Berlin in his cream and brown VW van and they scope out sites along the border with East Berlin. Nowhere is off limits: they scamper round the Reichstag (West Germany's parliament building, which backs onto the border) and even the Brandenburg Gate. But neither site works: the soil is too crumbly, or the water table too high. Then they come up with another idea. Something that on the face of it seems crazy.

Bernauer Strasse.

It's crazy because this street is not tucked into a quiet corner of Berlin, but back in 1962, it was the site of the city's most famous tourist attraction: the Wall. For Bernauer Strasse is the street that the Berlin Wall carved in two, where people threw themselves from windows the week after it was built. The eastern side is deserted, grass now covering the cobbles, border guards patrolling day and night. But in West Berlin, the road throngs with tourists from as far away as Asia and Africa. Open-top buses drive along the mile-long street so they can see the Wall up close. Now and then the bus stops and the tourists disembark, walking up special viewing platforms overlooking the Wall, where they pull out long-lens cameras and zoom in on blank faces that look back at them: inmates in the world's first human zoo.

As well as the tourists, Bernauer Strasse bustles with those who live on its western side. It's the hub of a district called Wedding (or as some call it, 'Red Wedding'), a working-class area, once the heart of the city's communist movement. It's always busy: families promenade with babies in prams, groups of women in flimsy dresses buy groceries, children in pinafores play in makeshift sandpits, swinging upside down from climbing frames, and factory workers in flat caps smoke cigarettes during their lunch-break and watch the world go by. Observing all of them from guard-towers over the Wall are the men in green and black – the VoPos, with their binoculars and Kalashnikovs.

And it is here, under this street swarming with tourists and monitored by VoPos, that Wolf, Mimmo and Gigi want to start digging. It's partly because of the soil under Bernauer Strasse: it's firm, less chance of being buried alive by a collapsing tunnel. And since Bernauer Strasse is higher than other parts of the city, the water table is lower – less chance of the tunnel flooding. Finally, they want to dig here precisely because it *is* so crazy: who would suspect them?

Now they've decided on the street, they need to find somewhere discreet to start digging. They need a cellar, somewhere on Bernauer

Strasse where the VoPos over the Wall won't see them wandering in and out in mud-spattered clothes. On a bright April morning, just as the horse-chestnut trees are beginning to bloom, Wolf, Mimmo and Gigi take a walk down Bernauer Strasse. Peering through doorways and windows, they look for an empty building or apartment, but it's hard to tell which buildings are occupied and which aren't. Halfway down the street, just a block away from Bernauer Strasse station, they come across a four-storey building set back from the street. The front is smashed in – bombed during the war – but a section at the back is still intact.

Creeping round, they come to a courtyard. It's quiet – no sound, no sign of movement – and in the corner, there's a door. Pushing it open, they tiptoe up the stairs, emerging into a large room. It's the sound they notice first – the efficient whirr of machinery at work – and following that sound with their eyes, they see hundreds of plastic cocktail straws flying out of an assembly line. Just as it sinks in that that they should not be here, they hear footsteps and a plump, blond man appears: 'What are you doing in my factory?'

Mimmo and Gigi step back, looking at Wolf, deferring to him and his German. Wolf's chest tightens. He knows the Stasi have spies in every part of West Berlin. If he tells this factory owner about their plan to dig a tunnel and he turns out to be informant, they could be kidnapped, driven over the border to East Berlin and thrown in a Stasi prison. He needs a cover story, and Wolf's brain – now racing – gives him one.

'Oh, we're a jazz band; we're looking for somewhere quiet to rehearse where we won't disturb—'

Plump blond man laughs. 'Don't tell me fairy stories!' he says. 'A group of young men wanting somewhere discreet on a street right next to the Wall? I know what you're up to!'

As Wolf prepares to run for it, the factory owner tells them his name – Müller – and starts sharing *his* story, describing escaping from East Germany after his porcelain business was confiscated by the government.

Wolf listens. There is no way of knowing if Müller is telling the truth; this could be a cover story, a way of reeling them in so they spill secrets. But, having guessed what they're really up to, Müller is now telling them they can dig from his cellar, and not only that, they can use his water and electricity, and Wolf, Mimmo and Gigi find themselves saying thank you as Müller gives them a key and tells them they must tidy up after themselves. Then they leave, laughing at their luck, still wondering if they've done the right thing to trust him.

Now they have a cellar to dig from in West Berlin, they need to find a breakthrough site in East Berlin, somewhere close to the Wall so they don't have to dig too far.

There's only one place they can think of: an apartment on Rheinsberger Strasse belonging to a Bulgarian engineer they know a little. It's perfect: just three streets away from the Wall. They hear that the engineer is having his birthday party the following week, so, after wangling an invite, one afternoon Mimmo and Gigi queue at the checkpoint, use their foreign passports to cross the border, then make their way to the engineer's apartment.

At the party, Mimmo and Gigi drink a little, chat and dance, and slowly edge to the hallway where they see a bunch of keys hanging on a hook among the coats and hats. Sneaking downstairs, they try each key until they find one that smooths into the lock and the door opens, revealing a small, dark cellar. It's perfect. All they need now is a copy of the key, so that when Evi, Peter and their baby – and the other escapees – come to the apartment on the day of the escape, they can get into the cellar. It is Mimmo who has the idea of running to a shop to buy plasticine and pressing the key into it, before returning the key to the peg. Back in West Berlin, Mimmo takes the makeshift mould to a locksmith, who makes a duplicate key.

The diggers are now all set: they have a digging site and a breakthrough point. They agree a date for the escape: 13 August – the first anniversary of the building of the Wall. It's four months away – should be enough time to dig the tunnel.

They aren't the first to dig an escape tunnel; others had tried, but most ended badly – either betrayed by Stasi agents or the ceiling had fallen in. From those attempts, they'd learnt a few lessons: don't get spotted before you reach the Wall, make sure the earth holds firm and most important of all: make sure the Stasi don't find you.

25

Concrete

I T IS JUST before midnight on 9 May 1962 and the night is warm and muggy. Mimmo, Gigi, Wolf, Joachim and Manfred (Joachim's friend from back home) squeeze into Wolf's windowless van and drive to the factory. They've got a small bag with them. Inside, some hammers and chisels.

Arriving at the factory, they walk down to the cellar where they pace the floor, muttering, looking for a good digging spot.

They've never seen a real tunnel before, never met anyone who's dug one, but they've seen footage of some on TV – those that failed – and that's sparked a few ideas. With a piece of chalk they draw the outline of a rectangle on the floor in the corner of the cellar. Like surgeons pencilling the site of an operation, they want absolute precision when they break into the floor, no unnecessary mess. The area marked out, they kneel down, pick up their chisels and begin.

No one can remember who made the first blow, because after a while, they're all at it, hacking into the concrete floor again and again, the sound ricocheting off the walls of the cellar and returning in a maddening way. Chips of concrete fly up and the smell of hot metal fills the room, their nostrils filling with dust. It's hot in the cellar and they're soon topless, sweat flicking off their shoulders as they smash through the top layer, the smaller pieces giving way to larger pieces, the sound of hacking deepening as they reach further under the floor. They hack, hack, hack and hack, until—

The floor breaks open.

Pulling back jagged shards of concrete, they throw them to the side with loud clangs, then use the chisel to extract more concrete until they come to a layer of screed. Now it's back to the hammers to pulverise the screed, smashing it again and again, until suddenly, the sound changes.

They've hit clay. This is good, they're getting somewhere. But as they start digging into the clay, they realise this is going to be much harder than they anticipated. They'd picked the site for the firmness of its clay, but now they discover the drawback: the mass of dense black earth is almost completely resistant to their attempts to loosen it. Using pickaxes, they chip away pieces so small they wonder how they'll ever dig a tunnel here, but after a few hours they learn how to work with the clay, now bludgeoning off big sections until, finally, they have something that looks like a hole. Surrounding it, they look down.

This is it. No going back now.

Abandoning their university classes, they dig all the way through that first night, sleep during the day, then dig again through a second night, then a third, and it's only at the end of that shift that the hole is finally deep enough. It's just over four metres – the length of a VW Beetle – the ideal depth to avoid digging into the city's water table or tram lines. They've worked it all out in forensic detail using the maps.

Now they're deep enough, it's time to start digging horizontally towards East Berlin. They bring a ladder to the cellar and prop it against the wall of the shaft, climbing down into the dark. With a spade, they sketch out a triangle on the clay wall – the safest structure, they think, for the tunnel. Then, taking it in turns to dig at the front, they use spades and an electric drill to bore into the clay. After a few days of drilling, they have it: the beginning of a tunnel.

It's small, just one metre by one metre, barely big enough to crawl in, and the only way they can dig inside it is to lie flat on their backs, feet pointing towards the East, holding on to a large spade, which they push down with their feet, scooping out the earth then tossing it behind them into a small wooden cart.

To get to the cellar in the East, they will have to dig like this, lying down, for 120 metres – the length of a football pitch. But there are only five of them to do it.

It is painfully obvious: they have underestimated the whole thing. If they are going to make it by August – just three months away – they need more diggers.

26

The Cemetery

JOACHIM PULLS HIMSELF to the top of the gate and looks down: hundreds of gravestones glinting in the moonlight. Cat-like, Joachim drops onto the grass and crouches behind a grave. Ahead of him, in their first tunnel mission, the two new recruits.

First, there's Hasso Herschel – charismatic, tall, with broad shoulders, thick beard and dark hair. Born in Dresden in East Germany, Hasso had led a quiet life until the day he was arrested, aged sixteen, for taking photographs of people queueing at a shop. He'd become angry, resentful, and in 1953 joined the uprising that Joachim was part of. The day after those protests, at five in the morning, the police came for him, throwing Hasso in a cell with twenty other prisoners, leaving him there for six weeks. After that, his life unravelled: Hasso was expelled from school, and though he was desperate to go to university, nowhere in the East would take him. When he was twenty, Hasso was arrested again, this time charged with illegally selling cameras in West Berlin, and he was sent to a labour camp. Four years. Four years in a communal cell, only one loo. Every day Hasso would look through the bars to the world outside; he loved it when he could see a streak of red in the sky and he'd say to himself: 'One of these days I'll be out there, standing at a tree, taking a piss.'

After the Wall was built, Hasso was desperate to escape East Germany. In October 1961, with the help of the Girrmann Group, he'd used a blank Swiss passport to cross the border at Checkpoint Charlie. As he'd walked past the VoPos, he was filled with an urge to give them the finger, but he'd controlled himself, made it into West Berlin. Since then, he'd been looking for a way to bring his sister, Anita, to West Berlin with her toddler and husband, and he'd vowed not to shave until they were here. He'd heard about the tunnel from Mimmo and Gigi, and agreed to help as long as Anita and her family could join the list of escapees.

The second recruit is a friend of Hasso's – Ulrich (Uli) Pfeifer. Uli was born in Berlin, but his family left when he was seven to avoid the bombs. In horrific timing, they arrived in Dresden a few days before the city was annihilated by firebombs from American and British planes. Uli still remembers his grandmother turning up at their house, covered in ash, having wandered through the night. After the war, as East Germany turned to socialism, so did Uli's family: his father became a party member, proud owner of a photograph of him with Walter Ulbricht, and Uli became a passionate communist, his friends calling him 'Communist Pfeifer'. Communist Pfeifer spent his days building toy bridges from modelling sets bought for him by his engineer father and dreamt of following in his footsteps.

But Uli lost his communist calling. It was partly the elections, seeing the way the party always won, despite the suspect vote counting. Then there was the time a group of children in his class were failed in their exams, simply because their parents weren't party faithfuls. Uli drifted, saved up for a motorbike, fell in love with a beautiful nurse called Christine, and they spent their time driving around East Germany, sunbathing on Baltic beaches. They'd swim in the sea and laze on the sand, imagining their lives together, their wedding, their children.

On 12 August 1961, Uli and Christine went to the cinema in West Berlin. At the end of the night, they crossed back over the border to their flat in East Berlin, went to bed and woke up to the barbed wire.

They made the decision to escape that morning. Uli and Christine hated being trapped in the East: they'd had dreams of travelling the world together, but now it was impossible. One day they'd walked to the Brandenburg Gate and stood looking at the border, trying to summon the courage to jump the barbed wire, but they couldn't, they were too scared. Then a friend of Uli's told him about a plan to escape through the sewers. There was space for one more person; did he want to join them? 'All right,' Uli said, 'I'll go ahead, test the route and get Christine out afterwards.'

On 7 September 1961, at 2 a.m., six of them (two girls, four boys, all students) met at Schönhauser Allee in East Berlin. Using a metal hook, they lifted a drain cover and climbed down the metal ladder. They went in silence, except for the moment Uli stepped on the fingers of the girl below and she let out a cry.

The sewer was large, tall enough to stand up in at a stoop, and the six of them fumbled along in the dark, feeling their way along the pipes. They were all wearing their smartest outfits, the only clothes they could bring to the West since there was no space for bags. In their high heels, stockings, dresses and suits, they sludged through the raw sewage, the smell wafting up as they dredged it with their feet.

Arriving at the other end of the sewer, under a street in West Berlin, they discovered a grate blocking the exit. For a moment they considered sloshing back again through the shit, but then they saw a torch flickering from the other side of the grate – it was the students who'd co-ordinated the escape. Spurred on, Uli felt around the grate with his hands and found a gap at the bottom. There was just enough space to wriggle under and slip through to the other side. There, they climbed a ladder, up into West Berlin and into a VW van. They'd made it.

A week later, Uli had wangled Christine onto another sewer-escape operation. But as Christine climbed down the ladder, she heard shouts and saw VoPos running towards her, loud in their heavy black boots. Leaping up from the ladder, Christine ran away, but the VoPos arrested two of her group, interrogated them, and a few days later the Stasi came for her.

Uli only discovered Christine had been arrested a few days later; heard she was to be put on trial. He was terrified for her, felt powerless to help. With no phone lines and all letters intercepted, Uli had to wait for coded messages from friends. Eventually, a friend in East Berlin sent a telegram:

ALL THE CELLS IN THE HUMAN BODY RENEW
THEMSELVES OVER THE COURSE OF SEVEN YEARS.

Uli knew what it meant: Christine had been sentenced to seven years in jail. In an instant, the life he'd imagined for them – marriage, children – vanished. His beautiful Christine was trapped behind the Wall and he knew he might never see her again. From that moment, Uli was full of hate: hate for East Germany, hate for the Wall, for Walter Ulbricht, the Stasi and a party that could throw a young woman in prison for seven years, just because she wanted to be with her boyfriend. The hate grew, ate at him from the inside, so when Hasso asked if he wanted to help dig the tunnel, Uli said yes. What better way to take revenge against the country that had ruined his life than by tunnelling back into it, being part of the most ambitious escape operation so far? And it felt particularly sweet to be using the engineering training he'd received in East Germany to do it. For Uli was now a qualified engineer working in a construction firm – which made him the perfect recruit.

With Hasso and Uli they had two more diggers, but, without tools, that wasn't much help. Which is why on this warm May evening they find themselves in the cemetery. It was Hasso's idea – he had a part-time job there, tending the garden, and he'd seen tools lying around. Creeping around in the dark, Joachim, Hasso and Uli grab whatever they can find: pickaxes, spades, shovels, even wheelbarrows, and they throw them over the gate to Wolf Schroedter, who puts the tools in his van and drives them all to the factory.

27

Shift-work

———————

JOACHIM IS AT the front of the tunnel. In jeans and bare-chested, he's digging out the earth as he lies on his back, droplets of sweat falling onto the mud floor. He's halfway through a shift, feeling calm as he works his arms and legs, his muscles now used to what's required of them, the pushing, pulling, digging and hauling.

He stops a moment and looks back at the cellar, now around ten metres away – the length of a large room. With the extra tools and diggers, they've been making good progress: as one digger hacks out clay, another shoves pieces of wood into the walls to hold the earth back, so the tunnel doesn't collapse. The wood came from the father of a university friend who owned a sawmill. He'd given them the wood free of charge as long as he could get friends out through the tunnel. One morning, his son came to the cellar, took off his jacket, revealing sticks of dynamite with trailing fuses, then pulled out a double-barrelled shotgun. 'Will these help for digging?' The diggers dragged him out of the cellar – *are you insane?* – thanked him for the wood, told him never to come back.

Now, sitting at the front of the tunnel, the cart full of earth, Joachim calls to the others in the cellar. He needs them to wind the winch and pull the cart of earth along the tunnel, back into the cellar. But there's no reply. The tunnel is now so long that when he's at the front, people in the cellar can't hear him. *Solve one problem*, he thinks, *and you create another.*

That day, after the end of his shift, Joachim walks to an American army shop in West Berlin. He's looking for a radio or telephone, something to help them communicate when they're in the tunnel. On a shelf along with walkie-talkies and old scraps of uniform, he sees them: two US army telephones, from the Second World War. Dark green with black handsets. They look perfect. Joachim buys the telephones and takes them to the cellar, where he inserts batteries and sets one telephone into the wall of the tunnel, covering it with cloth so no mud gets in. The other telephone he attaches to a wall up in the cellar, the two connected by a black cable that he fixes to the top of the tunnel with a hook. Then he crawls to the front of the tunnel, winds the telephone and – Brr Brr! He hears it ringing in the cellar. Smiling, Joachim shows the other diggers how it works and they all joke about how this is one of the only private telephones between East and West Berlin. Now, when Joachim is at the front of the tunnel with a cart full of earth, all he has to do is use the phone to alert the team in the cellar. They then turn a winch to pull the cart through the tunnel, up the shaft, where they take it off the winch, empty the earth into a wheelbarrow, dump it in a corner, then send the cart back down into the tunnel.

There are now eight of them: Mimmo, Gigi, Wolf, Joachim, Hasso, Uli, Joachim's friend Manfred (who they call the Tall One) and another digger called Orlando Casola, a friend of Mimmo and Gigi's who's so shy he never says a word, wearing sunglasses all the time, even in the cellar.

The eight men soon find a steady rhythm. Divided in groups, they work eight-hour shifts, their rota written on a piece of paper on the wall. Each shift, they come to the cellar with a packed lunch or tea, change into old clothes and begin. One digs, another fits the wooden supports and a third man dumps the earth in the cellar. After eight hours, they're exhausted, arms shaking, eyelashes clumped with mud.

At the end of his shifts, Joachim returns to his university dorm and collapses into bed, hands curled protectively around the ends of his blistered fingers. Within seconds, his eyes close as he drops into the darkness of a dreamless sleep.

28

A New Name

———◆———

SIEGFRIED UHSE, THE hairdresser-turned-spy, gulps a mouthful of beer and looks across the table at Lehmann. He can never work out what Lehmann, his handler, thinks of him, but he hopes that tonight he will prove what a good spy he is.

Since his visit to the House of the Future two months ago, Siegfried had met Lehmann regularly at a safe house called 'School', where they began every meeting with a coded exchange:

Lehmann: Excuse me, were you at Bela's party yesterday?
Siegfried: No, I was with Anni at Birgit's place.

Then, over dinner and cognac (always cognac) paid for by Lehmann, Siegfried would tell him what he'd been up to. And there was always lots to tell. First, there was his job at the army base, where Siegfried worked six days a week, attending to American soldiers, trying to coax information as he performed buzz cuts. He'd already found out about a three-day manoeuvre involving 3,000 American soldiers, then he'd flirted with a female guard at the gate to the barracks, somehow persuading her to give him an access pass. Walking around the barracks, Siegfried memorised the layout, later drawing a sketch and giving it to Lehmann. Then there were his regular visits to the House of the Future, where Siegfried had got to know Bodo Köhler and his team of escape-helpers.

You can tell Lehmann is impressed. Like a proud teacher, in his reports he writes extensively about Siegfried's character and the qualities he's discovering in his latest informant.

He is a very friendly and helpful person. He always appeared modest at the meetings but was pleased when he was offered a good meal at

the meeting . . . he seems . . . shy on the surface, however this is
deceptive as he is objective and determined in discussions . . . he
has good general knowledge, he is mentally fit and active and he
knows how to intensify this by refinement. He makes good
connections with people, especially men. He always follows the
instructions of the employee but also makes suggestions to carry out
various tasks. He has not yet refused any assignments.

These last two sentences are particularly interesting. Some Stasi spies
who felt pressured into informing found ways of resisting – agreeing to
carry out certain tasks, but making sure they never discovered anything
the Stasi could actually use. From Lehmann's reports it's clear that Siegfried
isn't one of those spies. He's proactive, goes beyond what he's asked to
do. But why?

Lehmann seems to have the same question, as every time they meet,
he asks Siegfried why he's doing the work. Siegfried says he finds it
'beneficial for his personal life'; his only regret is that he hasn't been
more successful. He says he's not doing it for 'material gain', though the
Stasi are now helping him with rent for a new flat and paying him a
regular salary – around 100DM (worth roughly £9) every week. Given
that Siegfried enjoyed an expensive lifestyle, one he could barely afford,
it's hard not to suspect that money was part of it.

Siegfried says the main reason is political. Lehmann isn't so sure. He
writes that Siegfried isn't clear about what his politics are, that 'he has
an open mind but has to be corrected in some respects'. In Lehmann's
accounts of their conversations, Siegfried's political ideas seem rehearsed,
as though he's parroting lines he's heard in the newspaper or on TV:
'East Germany is the real German state,' Siegfried says, 'and the objectives
of the GDR are the ones that appeal to me most.' Then Siegfried says
something revealing: 'It is always right to join forces with the strongest.'

Perhaps there was something in this. Perhaps, having been shamed in
his initial interrogation, made to feel like a pervert with those questions
about his sex life, finding self-worth through pleasing the most powerful
force in his life made sense. A kind of Stockholm-syndrome. Or perhaps
this is reading too much into one line. It's tempting to do that with
Stasi files.

Whatever his motivation, Siegfried's work for the Stasi goes so well that Lehmann promotes him. No longer is Siegfried just a Contact Person – an entry-level informant. Now he's a *Geheimer Mitarbeiter* – a 'Secret Informant'. To mark his promotion, the Stasi allow Siegfried to change his codename and this time he chooses one that suits him better, this spy who is determined to prove his worth.

Agent Fred becomes Agent Hardy.

And it was Agent Hardy who'd called this meeting on 22 May 1962, phoning Lehmann to say there was something important to tell him, something that couldn't wait till their next meeting. Siegfried wasn't sure that phoning Lehmann was the right thing to do; he was still working out the rules – there was no handbook to consult, no list of dos and don'ts. Lehmann hadn't said much on the phone, just gave Siegfried the address of a bar in East Berlin. Siegfried had jumped onto a train, crossed the border and taken the U-Bahn to Magdalenenstrasse. As he walked towards the bar, Siegfried realised he was just a few streets away from the Stasi headquarters. Lehmann must have been working there when he called him.

It was late by the time Siegfried arrived at the *Eckkneipe*, or 'corner bar'. Filled with regulars who drank there most nights, always in the same seat, Berlin's corner bars were a kind of shared living room for people who lived in nearby streets, who came there to drink and smoke into the morning, squished around vinyl-topped tables. Through the smoke, Siegfried sees Lehmann sitting in a corner. Pushing through the drinkers, he sits opposite. Lehmann is excited to know what Siegfried has for him.

Exhilarated, knowing this is the best piece of intelligence he's discovered so far, Siegfried tells Lehmann how a few days ago he'd gone to Joan Glenn's house – the American student who helped organise the Girrmann Group's escape operations. While he was there, Joan had told him something she shouldn't have: that a 'violent breach at the border' was about to happen. And the people involved were armed. Siegfried was desperate to know more – he wanted to know the time and place – but he didn't want to ask too many questions, was scared of losing Joan's trust.

Lehmann listens. The information is tantalising. Siegfried has told him enough to know that something bad is about to happen at the Wall, but not enough to do anything about it.

At the end of the meeting, feeling uncertain, Siegfried asks if he'd done the right thing in phoning Lehmann. Like a teacher encouraging a keen pupil, Lehmann reassures him: 'It was the right thing to do,' he says; 'with information like this you can always call me.'

Sitting in that cosy living-room corner bar, his belly full of beer, you can imagine the warm glow this must have given Siegfried the spy, who so desperately wanted to please his handler. The two of them then set a date and time for their next meeting, just over a week away at 5.30 p.m. on 30 May, at 'School'.

29

The Bomb

Four days later

MIDNIGHT ON 26 May. Two VoPos in khaki uniforms and black leather boots are patrolling the Wall along Bernauer Strasse, Kalashnikovs cradled to their chests. It's quiet and they hope it stays that way as they count down the minutes to the end of their shift.

Then they hear it: an explosion. Months of training kicking in, they run away from the Wall, towards the sound of the blast, but a few seconds later, they hear another, much louder explosion from behind. Then two more. They'd been duped. The first explosion was a decoy to distract them: when they sprint back to the Wall, they find a six-foot hole, shards of rock and concrete lying in the street. Nine months since the Wall was built, this is the first time anyone has blown a hole in it, and the story makes headlines all over the world, including in the *New York Times*:

FOUR BLASTS IN 15 MINUTES RIP REDS' WALL IN BERLIN

Underneath that *New York Times* headline there's a photograph of two West Berlin policemen looking through the hole. You can't see their faces, which is a shame. If you could, you might have seen the one on the right smiling, as it was him who'd set off the blast, working for the Girrmann Group.

The policeman – Hans Joachim Lazai – had come to them with the idea himself. He'd been on duty at the Wall nine months ago when Ida Siekmann had jumped out of her window to her death, and that moment had replayed itself again and again in his mind. As the months went on and Hans felt more powerless, he'd snapped. He wanted to do something, something dramatic at the Wall that would make a statement. He'd heard about the Girrmann Group and went to them with a proposition: were they up for blowing a hole in the Wall?

Of course they were. And Hans was the perfect man to do it. As a former riot officer, he'd been trained to work with explosives, and as a policeman, he could get close enough to the Wall to light the blast. That May night, Hans lugged six kilos of plastic explosives to the Wall, along with sandbags to ensure the blast pushed east towards the Wall, not west. After setting off the decoy, Hans lit the fuse for the blast with a cigar. As he later said: 'I intended this signal not just to cause a sensation in the West, but also to give the people in the East a sign of hope – you have not been forgotten!'

This was the 'violent breakthrough' that Siegfried had been warned about, but the warning he'd given Lehmann had achieved nothing. It taught Siegfried an important lesson: to be the perfect spy, you needed to get right into the heart of an operation and know every detail. He wouldn't make that mistake again.

30

Blisters

ULI, ONE OF the new diggers, holds his breath. He mustn't move. Down in the tunnel, eyeing the bubble of air on the theodolite, he moves the small tripod to steady it and locks the legs in place. Spirit level fixed.

He breathes.

Now for the vertical plummet on the bottom. Again, he holds his breath, adjusts the knobs, locking them in place, and moves his eye towards the lens. He looks for the crosshairs, that point in the middle that will tell them if they're tunnelling to the East or if they've been digging at an angle without realising. With articulate fingers, he twists the wheels on the sides of the theodolite, fixing it in place. He pencils down the angles, horizontal and vertical, then sits back. Breathes again. There are some perks that come with being engineering students: borrowing a theodolite and tripod from the university's engineering department while digging an illicit tunnel is one.

When the tunnellers cross-reference Uli's results with their map, they see to their relief that they're digging the right way. But they're not as far as they'd hoped. The digging has been hard, harder than they'd imagined. Some days, after an eight-hour shift, lying in that mud-tomb, arms enfeebled with exhaustion, they realise they've only dug ten centimetres.

But no one complains. They've got used to this strange new existence: spending whole days in the dark of the cellar (it's too risky to have breaks outside), napping on a mattress in the corner, relieving themselves in open sewer pipes and living off sandwiches and coffee.

At the end of each shift, as Joachim clambers out of the tunnel, back into the cellar, his whole body pulses. Muscles ache that he didn't even know existed. The worst pain is in his hands. Translucent domes have bubbled up on the end of each finger that make digging excruciating when they pop against the spade. Joachim finds himself seeking out cold surfaces, pressing his fingertips against them to soothe his skin.

Two weeks digging, and despite the long hours, the exhaustion, the blisters, they don't have much to show for it. The tunnel is still firmly in the West and at this rate, Joachim reckons, it will take them a year to get to the cellar in the East. They need better tools and more people. But there's only one way of getting that.

31

The TV Producer

—⋅—

August 1961 – nine months earlier

REUVEN FRANK TOOK his seat on the plane. It was half empty: not many people were flying from New York to West Berlin. The plane lumbered towards the runway, bumping across the tarmac before lurching forwards and lifting into the sky. As it gained altitude, Reuven looked at the flight time: twelve hours. Twelve hours to work out what he was going to film in Berlin.

Reuven Frank hadn't set out to work in TV. He'd started out in newspapers, the night city editor at the *Newark Evening News* in New Jersey, when one day he'd got a phone call from a friend at NBC (the National Broadcasting Company), a radio network in the US that was branching out into TV. Was he interested in coming to work for them?

No he wasn't. Back then, Reuven couldn't see the point in TV, nor could any of NBC's radio staff who, in 1950, were all suspicious of this strange new medium.

Would he at least come to NBC headquarters in New York and take a look?

Like most journalists, Reuven found it hard to say no to anything, and so in August 1950, he'd come to the corner of Park Avenue and East 106th Street, walked into the NBC building and sat down in the screening room, a lone bespectacled figure surrounded by hundreds of velvet seats.

Then—

A click. And the purr of a projector coming to life. On the screen in front of him, footage of Russian and American soldiers appeared. This was Berlin, a city he'd seen plenty of photographs of, but now he was looking at *moving* pictures. Behind him, at the back of the theatre, he heard whispering, two men conspiring in hushed tones.

'Open with a shot of the crowd for about seven seconds. Then a couple of scenes of the jeep driving up, then the general gets out for about five . . .'

It was the NBC news writer and his film editor, cutting a short news piece. Reuven Frank watched the screen as they played around with the footage, deciding where to start, how long to give each scene and where to end, turning incoherent fragments of film into a story. He'd never seen anything like it. In that moment, the power of TV hit him in the stomach. 'I thought: what a wonderful way to live!' Reuven Frank immediately gave his notice to the *Newark Evening News*, and two weeks later, he started at NBC as a TV news writer where he discovered that NBC management had as little faith in TV news as he'd once had.

Radio was the big thing, TV its little brother that NBC management ignored and no one thought would last. It was partly down to technology: to film anything you had to use hand-held cameras, powered by a large metal key on the side. You could only film for one minute and ten seconds before you had to turn the key again to power the motor. Compared to the ease of radio, TV was cumbersome and time-consuming, which meant camera-crews spent most of their time filming ice-cream-eating contests and beauty pageants. They left the serious news to the radio staff.

What TV really needed to prove itself was an epic story, a human drama, and in the early 1950s the perfect story appeared: the Cold War. Here was a *new* war, unlike any other, that was spreading to every corner of the world, involving the US and its greatest enemy: the Soviet Union. Like a Marvel film on steroids, the Cold War story promised action against the constant threat of total nuclear annihilation.

The only problem for the TV networks was that this new war was characterised by stalemate and inaction, or – even worse – drawn out UN General Assembly meetings, with incomprehensible votes won and lost. But there was one place where this story came to life, where the two superpowers, the US and the Soviet Union, faced each other with soldiers, tanks and machine-guns: Berlin.

Here, American camera-crews could peer behind the Iron Curtain and film their new arch-enemy, the Soviet Union. NBC started making

When Joachim Rudolph and his family walked to Berlin in 1945, they joined one of the largest forced migrations in human history.

After a barbaric fight for the city, the Soviets fly their flag over the Reichstag in Berlin. May, 1945.

Joachim Rudolph in his early twenties.

By the end of the Second World War, huge swathes of Berlin had been destroyed. Yet, for the city's children, the rubble and tanks turned Berlin into an adventure playground.

The uprising of 17 June, 1953. The first time unarmed East German protesters came up against the might of the Soviet military.

Before the Wall, it was easy to cross the border from the world of queues and empty shelves in East Berlin (above), to the glitzy lights of the Ku'damm in West Berlin (below).

Erich Mielke, Head of the Stasi, and the longest-serving secret police chief in Eastern Europe.

Walter Ulbricht, the leader of the German Democratic Republic (GDR).

The orderly enthusiasm of the Junge Pioniere (Young Pioneers) – the communist youth organisation.

Though the barbed wire went up in one night, the Wall itself took longer
to build. In the early days, many took their chances and escaped
through gaps in the barrier, including construction workers.

Divided families hold up newborn babies
at the Wall for relatives on the other side.

After the Wall was built, VoPos were instructed
not to lose a single escapee. They fought for
each one, including seventy-seven-year-old
Frieda Schulze, who leapt out of her window
on 24 September, 1961.

When Hans Conrad Schumann leapt over the barbed wire into West Berlin,
it created one of the most iconic images from the time of the Wall.

The Wall changed the geography of East Berlin, creating dead-ends
where children would play.

The Berlin Wall was 96 miles long: 27 miles separating East and West Berlin; and – less well-known to the outside world – 69 miles separating West Berlin from the East German countryside.

Evi Schmidt.

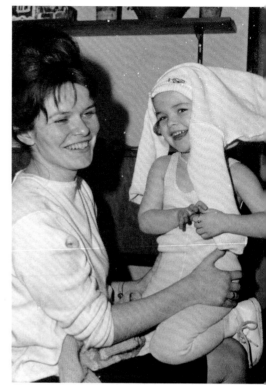

Evi Schmidt with her
daughter, Annet.

Wolfhardt (Wolf) Schroedter.

mutual exchange deals with European broadcasters such as the BBC, agreeing that each broadcaster could use each other's footage. Night after night, NBC would stream European pictures into American homes: Russian tanks rumbling down German streets, protesters throwing stones and bricks, American soldiers patrolling West Berlin, Chesterfields hanging out of their mouths. They'd never seen anything like it and American viewers drank it in.

Before the war, this story would have been a hard-sell. Back then, Europe felt a long way from the US, its politics of little relevance to an isolationist country. After the war, Europe felt closer. Americans knew that what happened in Europe could change things in the US, and, as millions of soldiers returned from fighting in European cities, they'd brought tales from the very places that were now appearing on TV.

By 1952, seventeen million American homes had televisions. The Cold War had given this novelty medium a sense of purpose, and it was clear: TV was here to stay. Reuven Frank had arrived in TV at the perfect time. With the medium new and unproven, there were no rules yet, no one to say, 'that's not how we do it', and so Reuven Frank, a born disrupter, helped invent them. It was Reuven Frank who first sent reporters onto the floor of American political conventions, telling them to talk live into the camera, and it was Reuven Frank who helped draft the blueprint for election-night coverage. He'd seen how powerful TV could be and spent hours in edit suites, weaving footage into stories that spoke to the gut as well as the brain. As he later wrote in a famous thirty-two-page memo: 'the highest power of television journalism is not in the transmission of information but in the transmission of experience'. And it was Reuven Frank who'd created *The Hunter–Brinkley Report*, a nightly news show presented by Chet Huntley and David Brinkley, with Reuven Frank behind the scenes, orchestrating quick cuts between reporters from different cities. Then, at the end, a sign-off that Reuven had invented, that felt revolutionary at the time in its friendliness: 'Good night, David, Good night, Chet. And good night from NBC news.' It was corny, but audiences loved it and the show was the most watched TV programme in the US for ten years.

Now, in the summer of 1961, as Reuven Frank sat in the plane, arcing down to West Berlin, his star-presenter David Brinkley beside him, he was one of the most powerful TV executives in the US, with TV the undisputed king of mediums. Once a niche product, with only 9 per cent of households owning TVs in the 1950s, TV-watching was the new normal, and by 1960 over 80 per cent of American homes had a set. Whenever anything happened, the first question was: how do we tell this story on TV?

And that was the question that Reuven Frank would be asking in a few hours, for the plane was due to land just before noon on Saturday 12 August 1961, and in an astonishing bit of good timing the biggest story of post-war Europe was about to unfold around him.

It wasn't until nine the following morning that Reuven Frank heard about the barbed wire. He'd spent the previous afternoon filming escapees in refugee camps with David Brinkley, then they'd collapsed in their hotel rooms, exhausted after their long flight. On Sunday 13 August, after a lie-in, Reuven Frank had come down for breakfast and was drinking coffee while reading a paperback when the buzz of conversation around him got so frenetic he realised something must have happened. He went to the hotel reception to find out.

'They've closed the border,' the man at reception said.

'Who?' Reuven asked.

'The East.'

Within minutes, Reuven Frank and David Brinkley were at the border between East and West Berlin, David Brinkley talking to camera, recording pieces that would tell the world what had happened, that showed the barbed-wire barrier still going up behind him. When they heard that Russian tanks had been seen in the district of Wedding, they drove there, filming hundreds of West Berliners shouting and screaming at the Russian soldiers protruding from the top.

For forty-eight glorious hours, the Berlin Wall story was theirs and theirs alone, their network rivals (ABC and CBS) racing to West Berlin from West Germany. The first footage that American audiences saw of the Berlin Wall was NBC's, and at a time of intense rivalry between networks, this was one of the sweetest feelings Reuven Frank had ever had.

On the Tuesday evening, exhausted after two days of filming at the border, Reuven Frank sat in the NBC bureau, talking to the man running it – Gary Stindt. Gary Stindt was one of the greatest cameramen of his day. He had an eye for pictures, the nose for a story and the stomach to see it through. Born in Berlin, the son of a cameraman, when the Second World War broke out he was sent to live in New Jersey. There, he'd joined the Air Corps, becoming a cameraman like his father, filming into plane cockpits while strapped to the wing. After the war he'd returned to West Berlin and become a cameraman for NBC, filming the American planes in 1948 as they came in to land, delivering food during the Soviet blockade. And it was Gary Stindt who'd had the ingenious idea of renting the attic of a bakery across the street from the prison where the seven last survivors of the Nazi leadership (including Rudolf Hess and Albert Speer) were serving out their sentences. Using a long lens, he filmed them in their army greatcoats and pillbox prisoners' hats as they shuffled out their final days in the prison exercise yard, the footage making an award-winning documentary.

Also with them in the bureau that night was Piers Anderton, NBC's correspondent in West Berlin – a tall, dashing Princeton graduate who served in the navy during the Second World War, then became a journalist. Charismatic, his dark hair streaked with a white quiff, Piers was admired by Reuven Frank for his rare combination of competence and brilliance. That night, they all got talking about the best way to tell the story of this new Wall between East and West Berlin.

Reuven Frank had long been looking for a more powerful way to explain the Cold War, one that went beyond a ten-minute snippet on the news. The era of TV documentaries was just beginning and Reuven Frank had seen how powerful they could be, but he wanted to push the format further, make the kind of story that no one had seen before. TV documentaries were now where the networks fought their ratings battles; they all wanted to be the ones to tell a story that would grip the country.

With this new barbed-wire barrier, an idea came to Reuven: what if Gary Stindt and Piers Anderton were to find an escape story? Not an escape that had already happened, but one that was just beginning? They could film it in real time, every twist and turn, not knowing how it would end. This idea was revolutionary. Ahead of his time, Reuven Frank had seen that if news journalists borrowed techniques from the world of drama and film, they'd have the power to *move* people, not just impart information. As Reuven put it: 'Every news story should, without any sacrifice of probity or responsibility, display attributes of fiction, of drama. It should have structure and conflict, problem and denouement, rising action and falling action, a beginning, a middle and an end. These are not only the essentials of drama, they are the essentials of narrative.'

Reuven knew that if they were to find and film an escape, it would give them the most gripping drama of the Cold War. Reuven Frank told Piers and Gary to start looking immediately. 'If you find something interesting', he said, 'start filming. I can pay for it. Whatever you need.' That's the kind of thing you could say if you were Reuven Frank.

Then the hotshot TV executive got a car back to the airport and took off into the night, the newly divided city disappearing beneath him.

32

The Deal

May 1962

NINE MONTHS AFTER Reuven's visit, Piers and Gary still haven't found an escape to film. It's not because they hadn't been looking. They'd put word out with their fixers that they were looking for an escape story, but every time they heard something promising, jumping in a car or driving to a field to film it in action, something always went wrong.

Once, Piers had climbed into the sewers, only to crawl into the torchlights of VoPos from the East. Another time, he'd lent walkie-talkies to a couple of West Berlin students who were orchestrating an escape, on the condition that he could come and film. Lying in a field, Piers had listened helplessly as one of the students crawled into the barbed wire and disappeared, never to return.

But Piers hadn't given up. If anything, he was more determined than ever to find an escape story – he wanted audiences in America to know what was going on, how desperate people were to leave East Berlin. He'd seen the aftermath of escape attempts: open manhole covers, bullets in the Wall, but that wasn't the same as filming one from the start. He was beginning to think it would be impossible to ever find one. Escape operations were shrouded in secrecy as they kept being infiltrated by Stasi informants, with disastrous consequences. A few months ago, a group of students had finished digging a tunnel from West to East Berlin. Crawling into the East to bring through the escapees, a student called Heinz had found the Stasi waiting for him. Flashing his torch into their eyes, Heinz scrambled as fast as he could back through the tunnel to West Berlin, Stasi soldiers shooting after him. By the time he arrived back in the West, blood was streaming from a bullet hole in his chest. Heinz looked up at his friends: 'Those swine shot me,' he panted. His last words.

By the end of May 1962, while Piers and Gary were still sniffing around for an escape to film, Joachim and the other diggers had just begun their hunt for money – for tools and to pay for more diggers. And they hadn't done badly: first, an aide to the mayor, Willy Brandt, had put them in touch with a political party which donated 2,000DM (around £170 – a substantial sum).

Then they discovered that Peter's mother (who also wanted to escape) had 3,000DM (£270) in a West Berlin bank account that she was happy to donate. The only problem was that Peter's mother was stuck in East Berlin and couldn't cross the border into West Berlin to withdraw the money. Mimmo and Gigi came up with an ingenious idea. They crossed the checkpoint into the East to see her, taking a pack of cigarettes. Peter's mother then wrote a note, giving Mimmo and Gigi power of attorney on a thin piece of cigarette paper. They rolled it with tobacco and placed it in the cigarette packet. If they were searched at the border, they could smoke away the evidence. Mimmo and Gigi got the note safely through the checkpoint and took it to a bank in West Berlin, where they withdrew her money. It was a lot, but they'd spent it quickly, on tools and a second VW van – this one with no windows, better for hiding diggers on their way to and from the cellar.

Now they needed more. And it was down to Wolf Schroedter, the blond fixer, to find it. If anyone could, he could. Charming, with twinkly blue eyes, Wolf started the hunt. His first idea was to go to *Der Spiegel*, West Germany's largest newspaper. It was an obvious thought: a few months earlier the newspaper had done a deal with the Girrmann Group, paying 6,000DM (around £500) in return for a front-page scoop about their escape operations (not giving away any names). With the Wall so recently built, escape operations were exciting and sold papers. Escapees became instant celebrities – two had even met Robert Kennedy (the president's brother and US attorney general) in his hotel room when he'd visited West Berlin that year.

But *Der Spiegel* said no, they'd already run one escape story, they weren't after another. But they had a suggestion: what about talking to MGM, an American film company in West Berlin? They were shooting a Hollywood blockbuster about an escape tunnel from January that year, but maybe they'd be interested in filming a different tunnel as it was dug? The diggers knew all about the film company, most people in West Berlin did, because the crew had built a 275-metre fake plaster wall near Tiergarten Park that was so convincing they had to stick a sign on it, explaining it was an imitation. On the first night filming, when shooting a scene by the canal, close to the real Wall, VoPos had spotted the film-crew, shining their searchlights into the cameras. The producer of the film was ecstatic, calling the *LA Times* to tell them all about it. 'Talk about realism!' he gushed.

Wolf made some calls, found the address of MGM's German publicist, and a few days later, he, Mimmo and Gigi turned up at his door. Did he want to come and see a real tunnel?

Of course he did, and so a few days later, they bundled him into Wolf's new windowless van and took him to the tunnel. He was impressed but scared: he knew what he was doing when it came to shooting in a fake tunnel, but didn't have the stomach to shoot in a real one where anything could happen.

MGM said no.

Just as Wolf was giving up hope, he had another idea: what about trying an American news broadcaster? If American audiences were so interested in escape stories, maybe they'd be interested in a film showing a real one while it unfolded? Wolf asked around and a friend put him in touch with a fixer at the NBC bureau in West Berlin. Finally, word reached Piers Anderton, who couldn't believe it: after months looking for a tunnel, a tunnel had found him.

Two days after the bomb blast, on 28 May 1962, Piers meets Wolf, Mimmo and Gigi at their university. Mimmo does most of the talking. Gigi doesn't say much. Wolf sits in silence, fiddling with the bolt on his newly acquired automatic – with all the stories flying around about Stasi spies infiltrating escape operations, he wanted protection. The diggers tell Piers all about the tunnel, how they can't finish it without more money.

Piers listens, nodding. 'How much do you need?'

'Fifty-thousand dollars,' Mimmo replies.

Piers gulps. 'Can I see it?'

The diggers agree. But only if Piers reassures them that he won't tell anyone about the tunnel – where it is, where it's going. Wolf, ever the businessman, draws up a contract:

> I hereby declare, on oath, that I will maintain absolute secrecy regarding the location of the operation of which I was informed on 28th May, 1962, by Mr Wolfhardt Schroedter. If I break this agreement, I agree to pay $50,000 to Mr Wolfhardt Schroedter.
>
> Piers Anderton.

A few days later, Wolf collects Piers Anderton in his windowless van and drives him to the tunnel. As soon as he sees it, Piers knows this is NBC's best chance of filming an escape. All he needs now is approval from Reuven Frank, and timing is on his side. For this week, Piers Anderton is due to fly back to New York to get married.

33

New York

——•+•——

June 1962

'I'VE GOT TO talk to you!' Piers Anderton pulls Reuven Frank aside,
looking serious.

Reuven laughs. 'Come on, not now!'

It's Piers Anderton's wedding day; he's just married his Swedish
air-hostess girlfriend, Birgitta, and they're all at the Four Seasons Hotel
in New York at the wedding breakfast.

But Piers is insistent.

Let's meet back at the office then, says Reuven, and so that evening,
after the party ends, they meet a few streets away at the NBC bureau.
As soon as they're in his office, Piers tells him: 'We have a tunnel!'

Reuven is confused. 'What do you mean, you have a tunnel?'

'Some students came to us and they're digging a tunnel under the
Wall and we want to make a deal with them.'

'What d'you mean, you want to make a deal with them?'

'They need money for equipment. They're engineering students and
they're going to build a proper tunnel.'

'How much?'

Piers tells Reuven about their request for $50,000.

'That's crazy! We can do $7,500. Max. Make a deal with them where
we will supply the material. They have to give us a bill and we will pay
it. And in return, we have the right to film. Period.'

And with that, Reuven Frank has just made one of the most controversial decisions in the history of TV news. A top American news
network has agreed to fund a group of German students digging an
escape tunnel in one of the most dangerous cities in the world.

34

Cameras

20 June 1962

I T'S EVENING IN Berlin, it's pouring with rain and a VW van is sloshing through the streets. Inside, two men wearing blindfolds. The van slows, turns and stops. A door opens, the men are pulled out and they fumble down a track, arms outstretched in front. At the end of the track, their blindfolds are removed and the two men blink their eyes open, through the rain that streaks down their faces, and straight ahead they see a door. Pushing it open, they creep inside, down to the cellar, and there it is.

The tunnel.

Looking at each other, the two men draw reassurance. They're brothers, Peter and Klaus Dehmel, and they work for NBC – Peter on camera, Klaus lighting. They don't mind the blindfolds; they know the diggers don't want to take risks. Peter takes a camera out of a small fibreboard case and climbs down the ladder. At the bottom of the shaft, he crouches and sizes up the tunnel. It is unthinkably small. Mimmo is inside, digging, and somehow Peter needs to get in behind him.

Folding his body into the tunnel, Peter turns onto his back, and scoots down the tunnel, cradling his camera. Once his feet are almost touching Mimmo, he stops, props his camera on his chest, points it down his body towards Mimmo and begins filming. Behind, his brother Klaus lies on his stomach, holding a battery-powered light, illuminating the scene.

Peter films for exactly 150 seconds before he stops. The tunnel is so small there's only space for the smallest and lightest of cameras, a 16mm Arriflex that holds just two and a half minutes of film. Peter peels off a plastic wrapping, the only thing protecting the camera from mud, reloads the film and begins shooting again. After a while, the brothers reverse through the tunnel, climb into the cellar and film the rest of the operation.

The first piece of footage from that day is a hand on a bright white rope. You see the hand pull down and a cart rises slowly from below. Full of earth, it sways with the weight, around ten kilograms. Then you see Mimmo. Bare-chested, the sweat on his back glistens in Klaus's hand-held light as Mimmo empties the earth from the cart in the corner.

Peter and Klaus film for a few hours that day, returning the next day and the day after that. As the diggers sweat, haul and heave the earth, winding the cart up on a pulley again and again, carting it off to a corner of the cellar in a wheelbarrow, the footage gives you nothing of the grunts and groans, the sound of metal against wood. There's no room for a sound recorder in the tunnel, so the footage shows everything in an eerie silence. There is one moment though, when the brothers take down a microphone. In the footage, you hear a click, then suddenly you feel as though you're down there with them. You hear the low rattle of a tram running along the ground just above their heads. Then a bus. Then footsteps – you can tell they're a woman's from the clip-clip-clip of her high heels. These are the sounds of Bernauer Strasse, the street above their head with all the tourists walking along it, looking at the Wall. Joachim finds the noises comforting. A reminder of the world of light and fresh air outside the tunnel.

The day after filming begins, American Secretary of State Dean Rusk arrives in West Berlin and tours the Wall. At Bernauer Strasse he makes a speech for the cameras, commanding that 'the Wall must go!' As Rusk stands there, under his feet, deep below the flashpoint of the world, the diggers burrow closer to that Wall under the lights of the NBC cameras, all of them now characters in a TV drama, the script unwritten.

35

Umbrellas

S IEGFRIED CLOSES THE door to the House of the Future, a grey umbrella in his hand. Heart thumping, he begins walking. This is it. Three months after joining West Berlin's largest escape network, finally, he's been asked to join an operation. The American, Joan Glenn, had told him about it a few weeks back. They were shaking things up, she said, changing the way they got people out of the East. Now, in a new VIP-service, groups of escapees would be assigned separate escape-helpers in the West. Was Siegfried up for taking a group on?

Of course he was.

Siegfried was assigned four people: two teachers and two students, all hoping to escape immediately. Then Joan had told him about the codes. Because so many escape operations had been busted by the Stasi, they would now communicate in a secret code, written on pieces of paper, hidden in umbrellas and smuggled over the border. She wanted Siegfried to deliver one of these umbrellas to the teachers tonight. And so Siegfried had come to the House of the Future and picked up that grey umbrella, a typewritten secret nestled within its spokes.

Now, after checking he's not being followed, Siegfried takes the umbrella to a Stasi safe house called Orient to meet his new handler, Puschmann. Siegfried arrives at eight. He's always on time, to the minute. He gives Puschmann the umbrella – a proud cat delivering a mouse to its owner.

Puschmann places the umbrella on a table, takes a photograph, then opens it, finding the container and the piece of paper inside. Written on the paper, a series of letters. Puschmann takes another photograph, refolds the paper and inserts it back into the secret compartment.

They talk. Siegfried is excited. He wants to take the umbrella to the teachers now, finish the job tonight. But he is nervous. He asks Puschmann to follow him, 'in case of an incident'. Puschmann agrees and off they go.

Siegfried makes for Malmöer Strasse, the address given to him by Joan. He walks down it until he finds the right number, walks up to the door and presses the buzzer.

Nothing.

He waits, then buzzes again. Nothing. He tries one last time. Nothing. All that tension, all that build-up, only to find no one in. It's the second time he's failed. First, not finding out about the bomb, and now this.

The next day Siegfried gets a phone call from Bodo Köhler and things get even worse: Bodo tells Siegfried not to come to the House of the Future again. Siegfried is worried. Are they on to him? Did they spot Puschmann behind him last night? In a panic, he calls Joan. 'What's going on?'

She's friendly as usual; nothing in her voice suggests a problem.

'So why weren't the teachers there when I went to see them? Did you give me the wrong address?'

Joan says the address was right, they just weren't at home. But he shouldn't worry, as the teachers have found someone else who can help. They don't need Siegfried's help any more with this escape.

None of this reassures him. Siegfried is suspicious, feels as though he's being edged out. 'So why can't I come to the House of the Future and see you all?'

'Haven't you read the paper?' Joan asks.

'Which one?'

'*Neues Deutschland*,' she says (the party's official newspaper in the East). 'Read it tomorrow,' Joan tells him. 'Then you'll understand.'

A few hours later, Siegfried meets Puschmann and tells him what's happened. Puschmann writes up the meeting in report 13337/64. He's worried, thinks Siegfried could be burnt. Puschmann writes: 'the Secret Collaborator should be extremely careful in his questioning so that he does not attract attention'.

The next day, Siegfried reads the newspaper and everything becomes clear. An escape tunnel was infiltrated by the Stasi just two days ago, a tunneller shot and killed. The Girrmann Group were rattled. Yet another death.

The party newspaper had left out the details: how the tunnel was dug by men in West Berlin who'd been separated from their wives in East Berlin, how one of them – a twenty-two-year-old who hadn't seen his baby since the Wall went up – had crawled through into the East only to find Stasi agents waiting. They shot him, interrogating him as he lay dying. Their wives were all arrested.

The Stasi informant who betrayed them was the brother of one of those women. His reward – a small bundle of cash.

36

The Death Strip

JOACHIM SITS BACK and inspects them: hundreds of stove pipes, bought by him over the past few weeks. It's the end of June, they've been digging for forty days and they're almost under the Wall. The tunnel is so long now, around thirty metres, that when they're digging at the front, the air runs out. Panting, heads pounding, they get dizzy, short of breath. They need fresh air, but how to get it down to the front of a thirty-metre-long tunnel?

That's when he'd had the idea of the pipes. Standing, he grips one pipe and sticks it to another using strips of white tape. Then he tapes that pipe to another, then another, until he's connected 160 pipes all the way from the tunnel to the factory door. There, he hooks the final pipe into a ventilator, and fresh air rushes in.

Lighting his way along the tunnel is a string of electric bulbs, installed a few weeks ago. Another Joachim invention. Then there's the cart that zooms along the rails after he'd attached a motor and electric winch. This tunnel is now the most high-tech escape tunnel under the Wall and you can tell Peter and Klaus are impressed as they lovingly film all of Joachim's electrical wizardry. The only problem Joachim hasn't yet solved is a small leak – water is coming into the tunnel but it's manageable for now.

NBC are now getting their side of the deal: footage. And the diggers are getting theirs: money, lots of it, brought to them by Piers Anderton, who'd stashed $7,500 down his trousers on his flight to Paris, driving it through East Germany all the way to West Berlin with his wife Birgitta on their honeymoon.

The diggers buy steel to make a rail for the cart. They buy pulleys. Ropes. Spades. Wheelbarrows. Pickaxes. And that means they can recruit more diggers. It's not easy, finding people willing to spend hours underground, but eventually they have twenty-one diggers, people they think they can trust. Most are students at the Technical University, refugees from East Berlin. Some have people they want to get out. Others want revenge.

When they recruit them, there's one thing that Mimmo, Gigi and Wolf don't tell them about: the NBC film deal. They're worried it will put people off, that they'll think it's too risky having an American TV network involved. They create a careful schedule, only allowing Peter and Klaus to come to the cellar when the core group are there: Mimmo, Gigi, Wolf, Joachim and Hasso. The others will find out in time, just not yet.

A few days later, the tunnel reaches the border between East and West Berlin. To mark the moment, they make a sign, a replica of the one you'd see above ground when you crossed the border:

YOU ARE NOW LEAVING THE
AMERICAN SECTOR OF BERLIN!

Every time they crawl under it they laugh. They were good at that kind of thing. Tunnel humour. And they need that humour, for now they are under the death strip.

It's a section of land next to the Wall patrolled by armed border guards and Alsatians. Watching. Listening. The strip is festooned with trip-wires, studded with spikes, and raked sand reveals the illicit footprints of intruders. At the end of the tunnel, as Joachim digs, it's now silent. The sounds from the street – the bicycles, horns, trams, buses – have disappeared and all he can hear is the sound of his own breathing, dank, fast and shallow. The scuffle of spade on clay. The metallic whirr of the cart as it zooms towards the cellar. In the tunnel, just one metre by one metre, those sounds disappear as fast as they arrive, absorbed by the clay. And in the silence, Joachim learns what it's like to feel entombed, the weight of the earth tightly packed in all around him. He looks up at the tunnel ceiling, a handspan above his head. If it were to collapse, as other tunnels have, he'd drown in the clay. Thinking about that sends a drowsy terror through his veins.

Then he thinks about what's above him: the VoPos. He knows they're on the lookout for tunnels and he knows about the listening devices that they place on the ground. If they detect movement they'll dig a hole and shoot into it or throw in dynamite. At any moment the earth above him could break open, a bright flash of sky before it all ends.

Some nights he hears them talking. And he knows that if he can hear them, they can hear him. So there's no talking in the tunnel. He switches off the ventilator. It's too loud.

Now he struggles to breathe. He gets headaches. His ears ring.

And then there are the times when he stops digging, just for a moment, and lies there, lost in time, the black hole against his feet seeming to lead down into forever. He can hear the wind, he can hear things falling on the ground above, he can hear vibrations that seem as though they're coming from inside the tunnel, then one of the lightbulbs flickers and winks out and panic flows through him like a drug.

Is there something in here? Is it the Stasi? Are they coming for me?

37

Wilhelm, Again

———

20 June 1962   BStU

Main division II/5

- Operative Group -

Report on the Schmidt family

Following a detailed discussion about his opportunities and his contact with Peter and Evi Schmidt, it was unanimously concluded that 'Wilhelm' will have good opportunities to further monitor these persons if things are done right.

Furthermore, 'Wilhelm' will spend his whole holiday at his weekend property in July and August this year, and thus he will be there every day, and he declared himself willing to do his utmost in this respect. In order to have more contact with Peter and Evi Schmidt it was agreed that he will carry out some work in their house and garden. After carrying out the work, Peter should be very hospitable and engage Wilhelm in conversations with Schnapps and beer.

Next meeting: 2 July, 1962 at 9.30 a.m.

Signed, _____

Second Lieutenant

[Enclosed: Floor plan of Peter and Eveline Schmidt's house]

38

Ground Rules

———

I's THE MIDDLE of the night and Piers Anderton is lying in bed, his wife Birgitta beside him. She's deep in sleep. His eyes are wide open. Slipping out of bed, Piers pulls on a sturdy pair of boots and drives to the factory, arriving just as Joachim, Wolf and Hasso are beginning their shifts. Inside, the Dehmel brothers are filming.

Piers likes to see the tunnel growing, getting steadily longer each week. When the diggers take breaks up in the cellar, he talks to them, his notebook out, writing by the light of a candle, inhaling deeply on his cigar. On one shift, over apples, beer and cigarettes, Mimmo tells him about his childhood. How his father died when he was six months old fighting Franco. His mother died soon after. He doesn't trust any government, he says, communist or capitalist; people have to do things for themselves. Then Mimmo describes seeing the Wall go up, women in East Berlin weeping because their husbands were in the West and they'd never see them again. 'The East Germans are swines,' he tells Piers, 'not because they are communists but because they keep people living lives full of fear. People should live happy lives with good food and love, not by an idiotic theory of a future one hundred years from now. We must do something to help friends whose freedom has been stolen. The East German government should know that there are simple people who want to do something against inhumanity.'

Piers never stays long, just an hour or two, then drives back to his flat, where Birgitta is stirring. She looks at him, his clothes spattered with mud, the earth caked on his boots. She knows not to ask questions, teasing him about his 'crazy American news business'.

Later that day Piers will phone Reuven to give him an update. He calls Reuven every couple of weeks, never saying much as he knows the phones are probably bugged – after all, West Berlin is 100 miles inside the communist zone and, as Reuven put it, 'only a fool would assume nobody is listening'.

Reuven and Piers had agreed the ground rules right from the start. First, they would only tell Reuven's boss at NBC about the tunnel, no one else – definitely no NBC lawyers. Reuven even hired a separate accountant outside of the usual NBC channels, against which he charged cameras, lights and any other tunnel costs. Second, they agreed that Reuven Frank would never come to West Berlin while they were filming – a hotshot TV executive from New York spending time there would raise questions. Third, the Dehmel brothers would never take the same route when they went to the tunnel and they would never meet any diggers in public. Finally, Piers agreed he would never tell anyone where the cellar was, not even Reuven.

The fewer people who knew, the better.

39

The Leak

———◆———

JOACHIM IS SOAKED.

Water runs down his face, his shoulders, into his ears and down his back. Crouched at the entrance to the tunnel, now around thirty metres long, he looks at the water that's filling it, the earth that's as soft as soap. The wooden boards that once held the earth back are floating on top of the water, almost touching the ceiling and every hour, chunks of the tunnel wall fall in.

Joachim looks down at his knees, wedged into the soft clay, pools of stagnant water swilling round them, the air filled with the musty smell of wet clothes. It's dark and airless in the tunnel now; one by one his lights have sparked out, and some of the pipes that funnelled fresh air have fallen in. Now he reaches forward to pull the Second World War telephone off the wall before it, too, is lost to the water. All of his beloved inventions are now redundant. Two months of digging; two months of blisters, exhaustion, and a life that Joachim had given over entirely to this tunnel, forgetting the above-ground life he was supposed to be living at university; and it had come to this: sludge.

Joachim trails his hand in the water that's still rising. The leak had begun three weeks ago. First, just a bit of moisture on the ceiling that they all thought was nothing to worry about. Then plump drips. Then a trickle of water that streamed in steadily hour after hour, day after day. Joachim thought it was just the rain – Berlin was in the middle of its wettest summer in years, the Wall-tourists above sploshing through giant puddles in the streets. But soon the water was gushing in and he knew there was more to it, probably a burst pipe somewhere nearby. It was then Joachim realised that, despite their calculations on the route and length of the tunnel, they had made one mistake: they'd dug the tunnel down at an angle, which meant the water was collecting at the front, almost impossible to remove. Standing in a line, their clothes sodden, the diggers had scooped out thousands of buckets of water. Still the water came. Using a hose borrowed from a local fire station they pumped out 8,000 gallons of water in one week by hand, dumping it into an overflow pipe that ran through the cellar.

Still, the water came.

Joachim climbs out of the tunnel up into the cellar, where the diggers are arguing about what to do next, pacing the room in their underwear – wet jeans and T-shirts drying over electric cables in the corner. One digger says it's time to give up, abandon the tunnel: look at it, it's half-wrecked already. The others nod, but then Uli jumps in; that knot of revenge in his stomach that has got him this far is now pulsing and he can't bear the thought of giving up now: 'No! Let's keep pumping, or . . . or there are other things we could try, like . . . why don't we go to the water authorities, ask for their help?'

There's a burst of laughter; the idea of wandering into a West Berlin local authority office and asking for help is so ridiculous that some of the diggers start gathering their clothes to leave. Others are terrified at the thought of doing something so reckless and they shout back at Uli: 'Are you crazy? Do you want to be kidnapped? Taken back to the East, thrown in prison?'

As they all know, Stasi informants aren't just operating in East Germany; West Germany is crawling with spies too. In the late 1950s, Markus Wolf (then deputy minister of the Stasi, supposedly the inspiration for John le Carré's fictional spymaster Karla), recruited hundreds of informants from East German universities, trained them in espionage, and sent them to West Germany. Like caterpillars, they wriggled into the fabric of West German society, into government, media, business, even its intelligence services, and now, ten years later, having reached the top, the brightest of these Stasi butterflies had been activated. The *Perspektivagenten* – 'sleeper agents' – are run from Markus Wolf's foreign wing of the Stasi, the Hauptverwaltung Aufklärung (HVA). As well as these spies, there are the former Nazis working in West German politics, blackmailed by the Stasi, who threatened to reveal their past if they don't spy for them. Then there are the low-level informants, the Siegfrieds of this world, who've been recruited to work for the Stasi in West Germany.

Joachim thinks of the stories he's heard, the Stasi agents who infiltrate student groups and escape networks in West Berlin, the cars that sidle up on the street – footsteps and a hood pulled over your head.

It was a well-known practice: Stasi agents would often kidnap (or, in their words, 'retract') people off the streets of West Berlin, smuggling them over the border to Stasi prisons. It's what happened to Karl Wilhelm Fricke, a well-known journalist, who on April Fools' Day in 1955 had his cognac spiked by Stasi agents, who then bundled him into a car, drove him to East Berlin and put him on trial. He was sentenced to four years of solitary confinement. Fricke was one of the lucky ones: many 'retracted' people were never seen again.

They all agree it's too dangerous to get the water authorities involved; they should just keep pumping the water out instead. But later that evening, as more of the tunnel collapses and they realise they only have a few days before they lose it completely, they decide that though the West Berlin water department is the riskiest solution, it's the only one they have.

Sitting in the water utility department, looking at the man in charge of water supply for Bernauer Strasse, Mimmo and Gigi come straight to the point: 'We've seen water, on the pavement on Bernauer Strasse, and we think it must be a burst pipe.'

The man looks back at them, says he's surprised. How would they know it's a burst pipe? It's very observant of them.

For a moment there's an awkward silence. Mimmo's mind races; he looks at the man, trying to work out from his face whether he could be a Stasi informant. But just as Mimmo is about to try out a story on him, the man asks them, straight out, whether they're digging a tunnel and Mimmo finds himself admitting it.

'Okay,' the man says, 'I'll help you. But you need permission.'

Mimmo looks blank. 'Permission? From whom?'

'The intelligence services.'

That night, there's a phone call for Mimmo at his university dorm. Running to the corridor phone, he picks it up and a man on the line introduces himself as Egon Bahr and says he wants to help.

Mimmo knows exactly who Egon Bahr is. He is one of the most trusted advisors to Willy Brandt, the mayor of West Berlin. Egon Bahr hates the Wall as much as Willy Brandt does (though while Willy Brandt calls it *die Schandmauer* – 'the Wall of Shame' – Egon Bahr calls it the *Scheissmauerr* – 'the Wall of Shit'). Egon Bahr is known for supporting any plans to attack the Wall – it was Egon who had given the Girrmann Group the go-ahead when they bombed the Wall, and right now he is very excited about this tunnel, the most ambitious escape attempt since the Wall was built. He says he wants to help, but first they need to meet someone in West German intelligence.

The following day, Mimmo and Gigi meet a man called Mertens. They know it's not his real name; they barely know anything about him except that he keeps an eye on all escape operations hatched from West Berlin, not just for West German intelligence, but also for the CIA. The Western intelligence agencies liked to know about escape operations for two reasons: first, so they could mine new arrivals in West Berlin for information from the East (as they'd done with Joachim after he escaped). More importantly, they didn't want any nasty surprises at the border if an escape went wrong – they all knew that a shoot-out could escalate into nuclear war.

Most of the time, the West German and American intelligence agencies didn't get involved in escape operations – they were in favour of them (they supported anything that undermined East Germany), but they'd watch things play out from the background. Occasionally though, like West Berlin police, who sometimes gave covering fire to help escapees over the border, they would find ways to work a little magic.

Mimmo and Gigi tell Mertens all about the tunnel, the people they want to rescue and about the leak. Mertens listens. He is inscrutable, they are uncomfortable talking to him, they have no idea whether they are right to trust him, but at the end of the meeting, he too sends them onto someone else: the Americans. And he gives them an address: 9 Podbielski Allee.

Mimmo and Gigi find it on a map. It's in south-west Berlin, which makes sense – that's where the Americans base most of their operations, including the offices of RIAS, the American radio station that Joachim listened to in East Berlin. Arriving at a large, nondescript house, Mimmo and Gigi walk into 'P9', and there they explain the situation. For a fourth time.

The Americans are interested. Very interested. They want names and addresses of everyone involved in the escape. Mimmo and Gigi write the names, hand them over to the Americans, then leave, the Americans thanking them – adding that help might come soon. Mimmo and Gigi have no idea if they'll hear from them again.

A few days later, a group of men in flat caps arrive at Bernauer Strasse, just outside the cocktail-straw factory. Joachim and Uli are on digging shift that day, and they pull aside a drape that covers the window to watch the men as they hack into the pavement. Also watching, from their guard-towers over the Wall, are VoPos. Straining their eyes through binoculars, the VoPos watch as the plumbers break into the concrete and remove pieces of pipe. The VoPos know that people are digging escape tunnels in the streets near the Wall, they're always hunting for evidence of one, and now Joachim and Uli are terrified that the VoPos will guess from the repair work that there is something that shouldn't be there underground.

It doesn't take the plumbers in flat caps long to fix the leak, but when they finish, Uli and Joachim watch as the men walk up to the next block and start hacking into the other parts of the pavement. They're confused – at first they think the leak must go further than they thought. It's only later they discover that this was a charade, performed entirely for the benefit of the VoPos. Just general repair works – that's the impression the plumbers are trying to give. Nothing to see here.

That night, down in the tunnel, Joachim checks the water level. It's stabilised, the water is no longer streaming in, but though the leak is fixed, the tunnel is still full of water. He calculates that it will take months to pump it out and for the earth to dry.

A week later, at the end of June, Mimmo and Gigi cross the border to East Berlin to see Evi and Peter, and they tell them about the leak, explain that the tunnel won't be ready by 13 August.

Evi and Peter are devastated; they know the army could come for Peter at any moment. Every time there's a knock at the door they think his time is up. But there is nothing they can do except wait.

40

The Second Tunnel

———◆———

IT's JULY 1962 and the Wall has been up for almost a year.

In East Berlin, the streets next to the Wall are quiet. The houses are empty, except for rats, and barbed wire hangs from chimney to chimney like Christmas decorations. Streets that once thrummed with cars are empty and the shops and bakeries that once stood here have closed. The Wall has changed the shape of East Berlin; bus routes have been re-drawn, walks to school diverted.

But every now and then, there are bursts of life. There are the children who play in the streets next to the Wall, taking advantage of these roads-to-nowhere, playing football or hide-and-seek. There are the protests, when people in West Berlin come to the Wall with banners and shout into the East. There are the songs, which separated lovers play to each other over the Wall. And then there are the vans that drive up to the Wall playing propaganda and music through loudspeakers: Soviet songs on one side, American on the other. A kind of musical warfare.

When the Wall was built, many in the East thought it wouldn't last. A year on, they realise it's here to stay – as are they. The idea of trying to escape now is terrifying, because the Wall has changed: there are now trip-wires, guard-towers, landmines, triangular tank traps, electric fences, metal spikes, spotlights, a second inner wall – and should someone somehow make it through all that, the VoPos are armed with pistols, machine-guns, mortars, anti-tank rifles and flame-throwers. Along Bernauer Strasse, there are makeshift memorials all along the street for those who've died here trying to escape, their names carved into wood: Olga Segler. Ida Siekmann. Rolf Urban. Bernd Lunser.

For Walter Ulbricht and his Socialist Unity Party, the Wall has been a great success. It's blocked the haemorrhage of people that would have destroyed the country and the party now has a second chance. And there are some who still believe that life in the East will improve, that things will get better if they wait long enough. But for many East Berliners, the Wall is a constant reminder of the life on the other side that they can't live. People who live closest to the Wall describe feeling constant anxiety and fear, and East German psychiatrists will soon invent a new word to describe this: *Mauerkrankheit*, which translates as 'Wall-sickness'. And statisticians who measure the country's death rate note that the suicide rate has shot up. All of which makes the next addition to the Wall feel even more insidious: the party instructs VoPos to attach a wooden screen to the top to make it taller. Not to stop people escaping, but to stop them waving to people in West Berlin. In a strange way, you can see their logic: if you're in prison, waving to a friend or your mother over a wall, you're still dreaming of a life on the other side, and the party doesn't want that. That's why they've blotted out West Berlin on all new maps. East Germany should be enough.

But it's not enough. And every month, some of those who dream of life beyond the Wall escape – eighty-six in June, stuffed into the boots of cars or smuggled over the border with fake passports. By now, the diggers hoped the tunnel would be almost ready, but it is sitting there, waterlogged, and every day they wait, there's a greater the risk the Stasi will find it. They're desperate to keep going, but how?

That's when they'd heard about it: the other tunnel. A tunnel that had been dug into East Berlin, but then abandoned: one of the diggers had got ill, the others had left Berlin. Bodo Köhler from the Girrmann Group put Joachim and the others onto it. There was a list of people waiting to crawl through this new tunnel; why not add Evi and Peter and get everyone out at the same time?

It made sense. In theory. But it was risky; it would mean working with a new network of students in a new tunnel they knew nothing about. Some of the diggers say no straight away – they're out. But Joachim wants to take a look – after all, here they were, a group of diggers without a tunnel, and now a tunnel had appeared, in need of diggers.

On a sticky day in late July, Wolf drives Joachim and Uli to Kiefholzstrasse in the south-east of Berlin. Climbing out of the car, Joachim walks towards a small clump of trees and bushes, and there it is: a hole in the ground leading to the tunnel.

Holding a small torch, Joachim crawls in. It's tiny, not even big enough for him to crawl on his hands and knees. He slides in on his belly, broken tree roots scratching his skin. The tunnel runs under Kiefholzstrasse, a busy road, and every time a truck drives over the tunnel, sand pours into his eyes, but Joachim keeps going, now wriggling along in pitch-black as there are no lights, his breath rasping as the air runs out.

He'd never expected another tunnel to be as high-tech as his, with lights, telephones, motorised pulley systems and air pipes, but he can't quite believe there are tunnels as basic as this: with nowhere to hide the earth, no water supply, no electricity. And all this with the VoPos just a few hundred metres away over the Wall. But as Joachim inches out of the tunnel, reversing feet first on his tummy, he finds himself thinking up ways to improve it.

A few hours later, Joachim and Uli return with spades and pickaxes. Squeezing into the tunnel, they hack away at the sides hour after hour until it is wide enough to crawl through.

Two days later, they are happy with the size. Now they need to check the tunnel is pointing in the right direction. All Joachim knows is that the tunnel is meant to come up under a house in a street over the Wall called Puderstrasse, but down in the tunnel it's hard to tell whether it's actually heading that way. So they come up with a plan: one of the diggers crawls to the front of the tunnel, sticks a rod through the ceiling, right up into the air, while another crouches above ground, looking through binoculars to see where the stick comes out, to check if the tunnel is pointing the right way.

It isn't.

Back into the tunnel they go for another day's digging, correcting the route, then they excavate the final few metres until the front of the tunnel is under the house.

Lying there, underneath that house, Joachim realises he knows almost nothing about what's meant to happen next. All he's been told by the Girrmann Group is that the house is owned by a couple who'd said a few months back that their home could be used to help with an escape. Since then, the couple had gone quiet and no one had heard from them for months. As for the rest of the plan, all Joachim knows is that there is a list of forty people who are meant to be escaping through the tunnel;

forty people – plus Peter, Evi and their baby Annet, who've been added to the list.

Now the tunnel is ready, there is one final job. They need a messenger, someone to tell everyone on that list in East Berlin the date and time of the escape. With no phone lines between East and West Berlin, the only way to do this is for someone to cross the border from West to East Berlin and tell everyone in person. That messenger needs a West German passport, since only West Germans can go in and out of East Berlin. It is dangerous: if anything goes wrong on escape day, the Stasi will send soldiers to the checkpoints to find that messenger before they go back into West Berlin. And they know that the Stasi punishes escape-helpers more severely than the people they're rescuing. Unsurprisingly, no one wants to do it.

But just as they are giving up hope, they find someone – someone who will do it for the most primal reason of all.

41

The Lovers

W OLFDIETER LIES ON her bed, looking at her, his Renate, drinking
in every minute before he has to leave. He thinks about what
he's agreed to do, hopes he's made the right decision. It is the biggest
gamble of his life.

He thinks back to the first letter he wrote to Renate, aged eighteen.
A family friend had put them in touch: 'You could be pen-pals,' she'd
said. And so, from his home in the Black Forest in West Germany,
Wolfdieter had told Renate all about his childhood after the war: the
French soldiers who liberated his city, the constant hunger, his father
who died as a soldier in an unknown field in Russia. And from East
Germany, Renate had replied, describing in long letters how her family
had escaped from Polish soldiers towards the end of the war, arriving in
Dresden just before the city was bombed, the fear that ran through her
bones – even now – every time she heard a siren. Soon they wrote
about other things, the music they listened to (this new band called The
Beatles), and they shared their love of Russian literature – Dostoyevsky,
Tolstoy. Renate once wrote a letter all about *The White Rose*, a book
about a group of German students who'd led an underground resistance
against Hitler. They were caught, put on trial and hanged. Something
in it had sparked something in her.

After two years of letters, Wolfdieter and Renate met in Berlin. They
only spent a few hours together, but enough to know they liked each
other as much in person as on the page. They'd made plans to move to
Berlin, but then 13 August happened and now there was a Wall between
them.

And so it had come to this: weekend love. During the week, Renate
worked in the audiology department of a hospital in East Berlin and
Wolfdieter studied at the Free University in West Berlin. As a West

German citizen, Wolfdieter was allowed into East Berlin, so on Saturday mornings he'd board the train to Friedrichstrasse, wait in line to cross the border, then take another train to Renate's apartment. He hated those train journeys. No one talked, everyone looked down, shoulders hunched. Three hours after leaving his flat in West Berlin, when he arrived at Renate's apartment, they would fold into each other's arms and wonder how they could ever build a future together. For Wolfdieter, it was like falling in love with a prisoner.

Since the Wall was built one year ago, Renate had become depressed. She'd always struggled with life in the East, hated having to wear two faces – saying one thing but believing another. At one point she'd had dreams of becoming a special needs teacher, but she couldn't see herself standing at the front of a class teaching her pupils things she didn't believe in. And now, with the Wall between them, Renate wanted only one thing: to escape.

Wolfdieter had asked around at his university in West Berlin: was there anyone who knew how to help people escape from the East? And that's when he'd heard about the Girrmann Group. A week ago, Detlef Girrmann had come to see Wolfdieter. 'I have an opportunity for you,' he'd said. 'There's a tunnel and we can bring Renate through it. But in return you have to do something.'

Detlef Girrmann told Wolfdieter he would have to be part of the escape operation, crossing the border into East Berlin, going door to door to tell the escapees when the tunnel was ready and the details of the plan.

Wolfdieter didn't need long to decide. He knew this was the only way to get Renate out.

A week later, Wolfdieter had crossed the border into East Berlin for his first job as messenger. It had been easy, walking round to various addresses, telling people the date and time of the planned escape. But then the date had changed and he'd had to return to East Berlin. Then it changed again. Each time, Wolfdieter had to cross the border to East Berlin and tell everyone. And each time, Wolfdieter became more nervous, worrying that the VoPos would get suspicious. Given how long it took to cross the border, people didn't usually go to East Berlin as often as this.

Then there was the problem of the escape list. At first there were just forty people on it, but the Girrmann Group kept adding more until there were over sixty. Sixty people who would have to travel to that house on a quiet street near the border in East Berlin, on the same afternoon, and sneak down into a cellar without arousing suspicion.

And so the plan had become more complicated: the Girrmann Group had split the list into groups, drawing up a schedule so that sixty people wouldn't all arrive at the house at the same time. Some would walk, others would use the S-Bahn, and some would arrive in trucks. They had two already; now they needed one more: would Wolfdieter help find it?

In most cities, getting hold of a truck would be simple; you'd just hire one. In East Germany, with every company owned by the state, Stasi spies in most, it was too risky to walk into a car hire company and ask for a truck. Instead, through friends of Renate's, they'd found a lorry driver who agreed to lend his truck – as long as he and his brother could escape through the tunnel too.

The escape plan was getting ever more complicated, spinning out of control, but Wolfdieter knew it was too late to back out. And now, tonight, Wolfdieter looks around Renate's bedroom, hoping it will be the last time he sees it. For in just three days, at 4 p.m. on Tuesday 7 August, if everything goes well, Renate will crawl into West Berlin.

42

The Day Before

—◆—

Monday 6 August – East Berlin

I T'S THE AFTERNOON. Renate leaves Ostkreuz station in East Berlin and walks towards number nine Puderstrasse, the house with an escape tunnel underneath. With her is the lorry driver. They're doing a final recce, making sure they know exactly where the house is, whether the gates are wide enough for his lorry to drive through.

Walking over the bridge, the River Spree stretched out beneath her, shimmering in the August sun, Renate looks across the city – her half of it. If all goes to plan, the next day she will be just a few streets away, looking back on her old life in the East from over the Wall.

Arriving at Puderstrasse, Renate's breath quickens. Coming here the day before the escape is risky: because it's so close to the Wall, there are border guards patrolling, and if any get suspicious and stop them, the operation will be blown. Walking down Puderstrasse, they count the numbers until they see it: number nine.

It's a small house, set back from the road. There's a lumberyard next to it, some railroad sidings, then the border and its death zone are just a few metres away. In front of the house, there is a large set of gates through which the lorry can easily pass.

Relief washes over her; now all Renate has to do is go home and wait for Wolfdieter. Tonight he is supposed to come to East Berlin so she can pass on this final information about the lorry and the gates.

West Berlin

A few streets away, over the Wall, Wolfdieter is in his flat, ready to go to East Berlin. Just those last details to get from Renate, to check everything is okay with the third lorry. He calls Detlef Girrmann on the phone, says he's ready to go, and that's when it happens: the first crack.

'You can't go,' Detlef says. 'You've been in the East too many times and it's too risky now. We need to save you for tomorrow. Don't worry, I'll find someone else.'

3 p.m., House of the Future

Siegfried walks into the House of the Future. Bodo Köhler has asked him here for an urgent meeting. Siegfried is surprised: he knows Bodo is suspicious of him; maybe Joan Glenn had talked Bodo round. Siegfried and Joan had been meeting up a lot recently; he'd been paying Joan special attention and she was warming to him, he could tell. 'It's hard to describe how I noticed it,' Siegfried told his handler; 'it's something you just notice when you have a feeling for it. Joan seemed emotionally cold to me before and now that's changed.'

For the last week, the House of the Future had been buzzing with talk about an escape operation. Siegfried had even been asked to go into East Berlin at one point and look for a parking space for a lorry. He didn't know what it was for, what the big plan was, but he would wait, be patient. Twice he'd tried to get inside an escape operation; twice he'd ended up empty-handed. He didn't want to mess up again this time.

Now, Siegfried heads straight to Bodo's office, that room he'd first met him in five months ago. It's small, the handful of people there filling it, Bodo standing in front of them. 'It's happening tomorrow,' he says. 'The operation with the lorry. The—'

There's a loud ringing from the phone on his desk. Picking it up, Bodo listens a moment, then turns to Siegfried: 'Can you go to East Berlin right now?'

Siegfried's heart jumps. 'Of course!'

'I have someone for you,' says Bodo to the person on the phone. 'I'm sending him now.'

Bodo puts the phone down and gives Siegfried an address, a house on Mörchinger Strasse, just ten minutes' drive away.

'There's someone in that house,' says Bodo. 'He'll tell you what you need to do when you get to East Berlin.'

Siegfried leaves, jumps in a taxi (taking a receipt so he can claim expenses from the Stasi later), and rings the buzzer on the door of the address he's been given. A man answers. In Siegfried's notes from the meeting he describes him as around twenty-three years old, 1.78 metres tall, slim sporty figure, narrow face, short blond hair – 'probably a student'.

It is a good description of Wolfdieter Sternheimer. Wolfdieter has been told to give Siegfried the address of a flat in East Berlin where Renate will be that evening until 9 p.m. Since Wolfdieter can't go to East Berlin, Siegfried must go instead.

'Give her my best regards, then ask her about the lorry driver: where will he pick people up? And find out if we can get any more people on the lorry.'

'I'll do it,' said Siegfried and he leaves.

6.15 p.m.

Siegfried is now right in the middle of the operation. He crosses the border into East Berlin, but before he goes to the house to meet Renate, there is something he must do. He takes a taxi to Wilhelm-Pieck Strasse and buzzes at a tall, brown door. Inside, he walks swiftly through a corridor, into a small courtyard, then into another building where he runs up the stairs into a flat. This is 'Orient', a Stasi safe house, and there, sitting at a small table, is his handler, Puschmann.

Siegfried tells Puschmann everything, says that something big is happening tomorrow, something with lorries, realising, as he talks, that there are a lot of details he still doesn't know. Still, it is enough for Puschmann to make a phone call, put the Stasi on alert.

Leaving the flat, Siegfried makes his way to the address Wolfdieter gave him. He rings the doorbell. No answer. Renate had left already and now he has no idea how to find her.

Crossing back over the border into West Berlin, Siegfried goes home to his flat and to bed. He is close, but still not quite close enough.

43

7 August

<hr/>

East Berlin, dawn

IN THE SHADOW of the Wall, East Berlin sleeps. VoPos awaiting the start of their shift sleep, mothers who will soon leave for factories sleep, fathers who will soon rise to tend their crops sleep. But in the leafy district of Wihelmshagen, Evi is awake, packing and repacking to make sure that the one bag she can take through the tunnel has what she needs: ID cards, nappies, photos, clothes. Hasso's sister, Anita, is doing the same, as are dozens of other people – students, vets, doctors, librarians, children, grandparents – over sixty of them, all hoping that tonight they will crawl through a tunnel and sleep in West Berlin.

As the sun rises, Renate sits in her bathroom, wrapping her hands in bandages, the white cloth covering angry red streaks of eczema. It's never been so bad. She knows it's stress; she's barely slept the last few nights, keeps thinking about the tunnel – imagining it collapsing while she crawls, or the Stasi finding her. And then there's the lorry she's organised. Will it find the right parking spot? Will the escapees remember the codewords?

So many questions, so many things that could go wrong. She must stay focused and think of tonight, what it will feel like to be on the other side of the Wall with Wolfdieter. No more weekend love.

Full-time love from now on.

West Berlin, 12 p.m.

At the House of the Future, Bodo Köhler sits in his office, briefing volunteers on the final details for today. The escape will begin at

4 p.m., he tells them. Only four hours to go. He looks around the room, sees Siegfried Uhse standing there. Bodo had had his suspicions about Siegfried, but now, finally, he's beginning to trust him. Joan has put in a good word for Siegfried and now Bodo needs him. With his West German passport, Siegfried is one of the few people who can go in and out of West Berlin. Bodo talks through the plan for the operation and Siegfried listens intently, committing everything to memory.

West Berlin, 1 p.m.

Siegfried's head is full, so full he's scared he might forget some of it, so he spills out the information to Puschmann as soon as he's through the door of the safe house.

The escape will begin in three hours, he says, at 4 p.m. Three lorries, all with white strips in their windscreen, will drive to three separate spots in East Berlin, where they'll wait for people to arrive. There'll be volunteers from West Berlin dotted around the streets, ready to give out coded signals in case of problems. Combing hair means all clear, blowing their nose means come back in ten minutes, tying shoelaces means leave now, there's danger. When the escapees get to the lorry, they'll ask for a street that doesn't exist. The driver will say, 'the street must be near here', and people will get on. The lorries are for the elderly and children, he says, and the children will be given sleeping pills.

The lorries will then drive to number nine Puderstrasse and park through the gates, where everyone will walk into the house and escape into West Berlin.

'How?' asks Puschmann.

'I don't know,' says Siegfried. He knows a lot about the operation. But not everything: he doesn't know about the tunnel. And there's something else he doesn't know – the pick-up point for the third lorry, the lorry that Renate has organised.

Puschmann asks Siegfried how many people are expected.

'Around a hundred,' he says.

Puschmann writes it down quickly. *One hundred people.* This is the most ambitious escape from East Berlin that they've ever heard about, and they know almost everything about it: start time, the lorries, the location. His protégé has done well. Puschmann finishes his report. He needs to get it to the Stasi headquarters as soon as he can.

Time to set the trap.

Schützenpanzerwagen SPW MfS HA 113256

BStU

[Federal Commissioner for the Records of the State Security Service of the former German Democratic Republic]

000105

Main division VII

MINISTRY OF THE INTERIOR

1st border brigade (B)

5th border section

Report on the situation in the section of the 5th border section on 07.08.62 15.20 hrs to 08.08.1962

On 07.08.1962 at 15.20 hrs, the following orders were issued by the commander of the 1st border brigade (B), Colonel Tschitschke for the 5th section based on information from comrade Captain Stuhr from the Ministry for State Security (MfS):

– Reserve company from the 5th border section, one water cannon and one armoured personnel carrier must immediately move from the property to base III and wait under cover for further commands.

– The commander of the 5th border section, Captain Gürnth, must take all measures to prevent border breaches in cooperation with comrade Captain Stuhr.

1.15 p.m., Schönhauser Allee

After crossing the border into East Berlin, Wolfdieter stands at the meeting point on Schönhauser Allee. He watches as Siegfried hurries towards him, the man who came to his flat last night. Wolfdieter has been told to meet him here so that Siegfried can pass on everything from the meeting at the House of the Future that morning.

Siegfried arrives and tells Wolfdieter the plan – the timings, the coded signals. Wolfdieter is just about to race off to pass these details on to the escapees on his list, when Siegfried calls him back.

'There's just one thing I need to know,' he says: 'the address for your third lorry. Where will it pick people up?' Siegfried says he wants to get his mother and girlfriend onto it.

Wolfdieter pauses, unsure whether he should pass this information on, but he has no reason to be suspicious of Siegfried Uhse; after all, here's Siegfried telling *him* the details about the operation, so he gives Siegfried the address and the codeword. Then the two men say goodbye, Wolfdieter hurrying to the first house on his list, Siegfried rushing to give Puschmann this final piece of information.

3 p.m.

Joachim looks into the black hole in front of him. The tunnel stretches so far, all he can see is darkness. Hasso and Uli crouch beside him, the three of them having volunteered to carry out the most dangerous part of the operation: crawling to the front of the tunnel and smashing through the ceiling into a house they know nothing about, owned by people they know nothing about.

Rifling through a bag, Joachim checks they have everything: an axe, a saw, some hammers, a drill and a couple of walkie-talkies to keep them in contact with the rest of the team. There's quite a gathering of people, assembled just a few streets behind the tunnel: Wolf, Gigi, some of the other diggers, a few students from West Berlin's escape network and a couple of West Berlin policemen with machine-guns. Then, in an abandoned building a few streets away, there's Piers Anderton and the two NBC cameramen, filming from the top-floor-window. Finally, there's an ambulance. Just in case.

Next, Joachim goes through his second bag. It's heavy and there's a clank of metal and brass as he checks what's inside: two pistols, an old Second World War machine-gun and a sawn-off shotgun. Since they heard about the digger shot by the Stasi a few weeks ago, they'd decided they'd arm themselves. They've heard what Stasi interrogations and prisons are like. If they're caught, they're not going alive.

The weapons change the possibilities of the operation. This is the first escape operation to involve so many different people: the Stasi, West German police, tunnellers, messengers, escapees and American journalists. Even the US military in Berlin know about the operation, after the diggers went to the CIA safe house a few weeks earlier. If anything goes wrong and shots are fired, things could spiral out of control.

Joachim tries to steady his hands. After months of digging, the moment is here. It doesn't feel right: a shoddy tunnel, no idea about the house they're digging up into, and a huge list of escapees to bring through. But somehow, the series of decisions he's made, from his own escape to this one, has brought him here, to this moment, and like a Greek hero following his destiny, he follows the path. No looking back.

Looking at each other, Joachim, Hasso and Uli nod. Time to go. They begin crawling. Eighty metres to the other end.

As he crawls, Joachim can hear his breathing, the sound of his shoes hitting the clay. The sides of the tunnel are only inches away from his shoulders and when he brushes against them a dusting of clay falls down, coating his shoulders in soil. Getting into a rhythm, the three of them pick up speed, each crawl taking them closer and closer to the house.

Just before the other end, there's a bend in the tunnel. They crawl round it, then stop. They've made it. Nowhere to go now except up.

Picking up their saws and hammers, they begin.

4 p.m.

It's just a few minutes before the escapees are due to arrive and the house is surrounded by Stasi agents. Spiders waiting for flies. Spread along the streets, the Stasi agents hold newspapers and talk in small groups, trying to look inconspicuous.

Then they see it: a truck. Mimmo is on board and he's just about to tell the driver to park and unload the escapees when he sees the men in long coats and hats on the street. 'Keep going, keep going, don't stop!' he shouts and the truck screeches off. Shaking, Mimmo is relieved, but has no way of letting the others know the operation has been infiltrated. And right now, the first escapees, those coming on foot, are arriving.

They collect on the street, waiting for something, none of them sure what. Some try to hide, one Stasi files notes: 'it appeared that they were waiting for something specific. One of the wives waited in a bush by the cemetery wall for an extended period of time.' Eventually, one man approaches a Stasi agent, assuming he must be a volunteer from West Berlin, here to help with the escape. 'Is the operation still on?' he asks. 'Can we get any more people into the lorries?'

The Stasi agents can't believe their luck and they bundle the man into a car, where they pump him for information. One of the escape-helpers on the street realises what's going on; he tries to signal to those arriving that the operation is blown, but it's too late, and he's arrested. Soon there's a steady stream of arrivals – elderly people, couples, some with children in pushchairs – all oblivious to the men in long coats, and by the time they notice that something isn't right, it's too late, for the Stasi agents are swooping in, shoving everyone into cars and taking them away until there's no one left – just a single pushchair lying on the street.

A few roads away, Evi, Peter and their toddler Annet are racing towards the house. They're late because Evi was out when the messenger turned up at their house to tell them the escape was on. Evi was collecting a green dress she'd had made specially for this escape, the only item of clothing she would bring with her to West Berlin. When Evi arrived home, Peter was furious: 'Where have you been? We have to leave right now! The tunnel is ready!'

Grabbing their ID cards, nappies and money, they'd raced to the station, onto the S-Bahn. Now, as they approach the street, Evi's stomach churns because, apart from them, there's no one else there and she can't understand why it's so quiet. But they keep going, determined to stick to the plan, for they know the house is just around the next corner, and that's when they see them – a handful of men skulking on the street, and they turn on their heels, walking away as fast as they can, hoping that no one follows.

At the same corner, Renate is arriving with two friends – Peter and Britta – and they walk right into a Stasi agent, who stops them. 'What are you doing here? Papers. Now.'

Renate's stomach plunges as she pulls out her papers, and she watches as Peter and Britta hand theirs over too, the Stasi officer making a note of their names and addresses.

Renate's mind races; what excuse can she give for them being here? But then Peter starts talking about how it's his birthday today; how they've come to meet his sister who works in a factory nearby so they can celebrate. It's a good story because when the Stasi officer checks Peter's papers, he sees that, yes, today is indeed Peter's birthday: 7 August. He radios his commander, who radios someone else until they reach the factory to check that Peter's sister really does work there, and when the confirmation comes through, the officer returns their papers. All right then, he says, off you go, and Renate and her friends leave, trying to smile and laugh as though they're celebrating a special day out, while on the inside, they're falling apart as they realise the operation is unravelling and there's nothing they can do.

At the parking spot in Grünau, the lorry organised by Wolfdieter and Renate has just arrived. People emerge from the bushes where they'd been hiding, waiting for the lorry. One by one they board the truck, giving the codeword to the driver, who pulls out, oblivious to the Stasi truck behind. The Stasi follow them almost all the way to the tunnel, then drives them off the road, arresting everyone.

At the house on Puderstrasse, another lorry arrives, full of escapees. They get out, straight into the hands of the Stasi. And so the operation falls apart, the Stasi taking away family after family until, eventually, the streets are quiet.

It's now 5 p.m. The Stasi agents walk towards the house. They've arrested over forty people from East Berlin, but now they want the bigger prize – the people behind the operation, the tunnellers from West Berlin.

A few metres under their feet, Joachim, Hasso and Uli are hacking into the ceiling of the tunnel, pulling out chunks of clay. Finally, the ceiling breaks open and the first thing that hits Joachim is the smell. Coal-dust. Then he feels it. It pours out, onto his head, his shoulders and into his eyes until he's blind with it. They've hacked into the layer of coal-slag insulation under the house and there's nothing they can do except wait until the coal-dust stops flowing. Face blackened, nostrils clogged, Joachim looks up and sees floorboards: time for the drill. He makes four holes in the shape of a square, then picks up the saw, rasps it through the floorboards above. It's not easy. The saw keeps snagging on something, a carpet Joachim guesses.

Then – screaming. A woman's voice. 'Get away, get out of here! Get out! Now!'

They have no idea what's going on, why she's screaming, and they're terrified that someone will hear. Hasso tries to reassures her – 'Don't worry, you won't get in trouble; we'll give you money if you stop shouting' – but there's no reply. Just silence.

In the tunnel, there's a sudden burst of static as the walkie-talkie crackles into action, then there are muffled shouts from down the tunnel, though they can't hear what they're saying. In the distance, a car horn beeps, long and loud.

Something is wrong, they know it. Joachim looks at Hasso and Uli. An unspoken message runs between them and Joachim picks up the saw again and pulls and pushes it back and forth along the wood and the carpet, willing it to carve through. As his arm pumps above his head, shaking with the effort, a small voice inside tells him that this is the moment to leave, that there's still time to crawl back into West Berlin, but then images flash up in his head of families above him, just waiting for the tunnel to be finished. Mothers. Fathers. Children the same age he was when he first escaped, when it all went so horribly wrong. And now all he can think about is getting to them before the Stasi find them. He just needs to work faster.

Outside the house, Stasi Comrade Teichert and two officers are talking to the owner, a small man called Friedrich Sendler. They tell him to open the gate, they're here to inspect his house.

Mr Sendler falters, tries to put them off, but then his front door opens and his wife runs out, the woman who was screaming at the diggers.

The Stasi agents stop her, ask her what's going on.

'I feel sick,' she says, perhaps trying to distract them from entering the house.

'Why?' they ask. 'What's happening inside?'

She crumples: 'I was in the living room,' she says, 'and I saw holes in the floor.'

From over the Wall, standing in an abandoned elevated railway switch tower, Piers Anderton and the Dehmel brothers are watching everything. They know that Joachim, Hasso and Uli are still in the tunnel and all they can do is hope that Mr Sendler can hold the Stasi back. Filming everything, they see the Stasi agents talking to the couple and watch, with dread, as they all suddenly rush towards the house.

Powerless to help, they film the soldiers as they put down their weapons and take off their boots before walking inside the house, the door closing behind them.

Inside the living room, creeping around silently in their socks, the Stasi agents scan the floor and they see them: four small holes in the centre of the room, each surrounded by a sprinkling of wood chips. Then a noise from under the floorboards: it's the diggers discussing how they'll break through. The Stasi comrades tiptoe out of the room. They'll wait for the diggers to break into the living room and that's when they'll take them.

Underground, Joachim has given up with the saw. It's not strong enough to slice through the floorboards, and he's desperate to climb up into the living room and start helping people through the tunnel, the people he's sure are there, waiting for him. Picking up an axe, he starts hacking into the floorboards, the ceiling shaking, everything shaking, the noise so deafening he can feel it in his bones. The whole floor vibrates – whack, whack, whack, whack, whack – until eventually two floorboards crack open and a rush of cold air funnels down into the tunnel.

Silence.

Another buzz of the walkie-talkie. More shouts down the tunnel.

Joachim ignores them; he's so close, he just needs to keep going, stick to the plan. Rummaging in his bag, he pulls out a mirror, sticking it up into the room like a submarine periscope. He turns it in all directions to see what's there, hoping to find a sea of faces.

But there's nothing.

From the bag, he pulls out a small pistol. Holding it in one hand, he hoists himself through the hole with the other and clambers to his feet. In front of him, there's a small sofa, a side-table and a couple of chairs. It's dark, the only light coming from a window obscured by a net curtain. And right now, he has an urge to see what's behind it. He takes a step towards the window, the hairs on his skin prickling as he sees a shadow fall across the curtain. He flinches, but keeps going, taking another step, then another, compelled to see what's there, ignoring the voice in his head that tells him to leave right now and not look back. Hand trembling, he pulls the curtain to one side, his eyes confirming what he already knows.

Stasi.

Blood pumping loudly in his ears, he ducks down, mind racing, trying to work out what to do. He saw just one man, a Stasi soldier creeping under the window, but where there's one, there'll be more. He reckons he has a few seconds' head start, just enough time to jump back into the tunnel before they make it into the living room. What he doesn't know is that the Stasi soldiers aren't just outside that window, they're outside the living-room door, Kalashnikovs in their hands, watching him through a crack in the door.

6.45 p.m.

At precisely this moment, Wolfdieter is racing back to the border, skin tingling with excitement at the thought of being with Renate tonight, her first night in West Berlin. He'd taken the S-Bahn with Renate a few hours ago, accompanying her for the first part of the journey to the house, then he'd split off, boarding a train to the checkpoint at Heinrich-Heine-Strasse, one of the largest crossing points into West Berlin. He calculates that Renate should have crawled through the tunnel by now; once he's crossed the border, he'll take a train to meet her.

Walking into the checkpoint, a long table in front of him, Wolfdieter sees two men in uniform. They look at him strangely and something in his stomach stirs. It's as though they've been waiting for him. They motion to his pocket. 'Passport and visa.'

Wolfdieter gives them his papers.

They leaf through them and look up at him. 'Come with us.'

As Wolfdieter follows, he tries to reassure himself. This kind of thing often happens, jumpy VoPos going overboard with extra checks, but when they put him in a car, his knees start to shake. They don't tell Wolfdieter where they're going, but fifteen minutes later he arrives at a building near Alexanderplatz that he knows is the East Berlin police headquarters. *Still*, he hopes, *maybe it's a misunderstanding; they don't have anything on me, nothing to tie me to the tunnel.*

Inside the police station, two officers take his belongings – his ID card, watch, money – then give him prison clothes and put him in a cell. Wolfdieter sits there. Taking deep breaths, he calms himself, tries to use this time wisely. *Think up a story, think up a story.*

After a while, he's taken into a room and sat down at a table in front of four policemen. They ask what he's been doing in East Berlin and Wolfdieter tries out his story. 'Oh, I'm just a student at the West Berlin Free university and it was my day off today, no lessons! So I thought I'd go to the East and see the city . . .' He gabbles on, getting into the groove of his lie.

The policemen make notes. Ask questions. Send him back to his cell. Wolfdieter sits there again. Someone brings coffee, he drinks it and he dares to hope. *Maybe my story has worked,* he thinks. *Maybe everything is okay. Just stick to the story.*

Back at the house, the Stasi are still watching Joachim through the crack in the door. Hasso and Uli have now climbed up into the room, all of them trying to figure out what to do. The soldiers watch, and they are just about to burst in when they hear one of the diggers say, 'My pistol isn't working; pass me the machine-gun.' They hear the sound of a machine-gun being loaded and the soldiers recoil – they know their old Soviet Kalashnikovs are no match for Western machine-guns. The soldiers assess their next move: if they burst in now, they could be mown down by machine-gun bullets. If they wait for backup, the diggers might get away.

Inside, Joachim paces the room, not ready to give up. Then the walkie-talkie bursts into life and this time they hear the message clearly: 'Come back now! It's over!'

Through the door, the soldiers have made their decision. They radio for backup – more soldiers and weapons. They don't want to die over a tunnel.

Inside the living room, Joachim looks at Hasso and Uli; they know it's over, and the three of them jump into the hole, crawling frantically through the tunnel with their bags of weapons and tools swinging. Jeans snagging on tree roots, hands sliced open on pieces of rock and grit, they push themselves forwards, dreading the moment they fear will come when the Stasi burst into the room, jump into the tunnel and shoot, so they crawl as fast as they can in the tiny, dark space: crawling, crawling until eventually they see it – a small circle of daylight.

Minutes later, those extra soldiers arrive. Rushing into the living room, they run towards the hole. They're too late. But they're not empty-handed: they've got forty-three failed escapees and, best of all, they've heard that a messenger from West Berlin is sitting in the police station at Alexanderplatz.

3 a.m.

In his brightly lit cell, Wolfdieter has no idea of the time. He guesses it's the middle of the night, that midpoint between dusk and dawn when time seems to stretch out. Then footsteps, a key in a lock, and the cell-door swings open and a guard appears, marches Wolfdieter back to the room with the policemen.

Wolfdieter sits there, eyelids drooping, craving sleep, when a tall man with grey hair walks in, towering over Wolfdieter as he opens his mouth and screams: 'You are a liar! Tell the truth!'

But it's not what this man says that scares Wolfdieter. It's his clothes. He's not in uniform. And that means one thing: Stasi. He throws Wolfdieter out of the room, tells him to face the wall.

As Wolfdieter stands there, eyes fixed on the beige wallpaper in front of him, the air filled with the smell of stale coffee and sweat, finally, he accepts his fate. They have him. But out of the depths of a despair that is beginning to swamp him, Wolfdieter pulls a thread of light: at least everyone escaped through the tunnel before they caught him, at least his Renate is safe.

Then, from behind, he hears footsteps. They are light, a woman's he guesses. Risking a glance, his stomach lurches as he sees her: Britta, Renate's best friend; they were meant to escape through the tunnel together. Turning back to the wall, his body floods with panic, his mind racing with images of Renate – Renate caught in the tunnel, Renate arrested at home, Renate in a prison cell, Renate shot trying to run away – and he thinks back to the gamble they'd made, this decision to escape, to risk everything so they could be together, and now it's clear: they gambled everything and they lost.

44

Hohenschönhausen

———

W OLFDIETER SITS IN the van, handcuffed, no idea where he's
going. Sitting in the darkness, no windows, he listens to the
thrum of the engine as the van skulks through the streets, hour after
hour, lulling him in and out of sleep. For the first hour or so the van
had stopped and started constantly, the sea-sick rhythm of city driving.
He'd heard trams, people talking. Then the van picked up speed, driving
for long stretches, and he knew he must be a long way from Berlin.
From the outside, the van looked ordinary: just an old white fruit-and-vegetable truck. The Stasi had bought hundreds and butchered their insides,
creating five separate cells in each. Wolfdieter's cell is so small he sits
with his knees crunched against the wall.

Ferrying prisoners around in these vans was all part of the secrecy of
Hohenschönhausen Prison, a prison whose very existence was denied. When
you go there now, the first thing you notice is that it's a long way from the
centre of Berlin and it's hard to find. Right out in the far east of the city,
it's nestled in a warren of side streets. The Stasi didn't want people knowing
it existed: when you look at maps from the time, there's just a big black
smudge where the prison was. There were rumours about the so-called
'forbidden area', but no one could get close: surrounding it were checkpoints
manned by armed guards and tall steel barriers blocking the view.

The history of Hohenschönhausen Prison is the story of post-war
Berlin writ small: once a Jewish-owned industrial area, it was taken over
by the Nazis, who filled it with businesses and a small prison-camp.
During the war it was damaged by bombs; then, when Russian soldiers
turned up in 1945, they shot the factory owners, shipped the equipment
back to Moscow and turned the complex into the headquarters of the
Russian secret police in Berlin, filling it with tens of thousands of
ex-Nazis and anyone critical of the Soviets.

Prisoners called the prison the 'U-Boat' – the submarine – and once inside, you can see why. You can still walk through the tiny underground cells, cold and windowless, filled with the fusty smell of damp. Prisoners were stuffed in there, ten to a cell, taking turns to sleep on a thin wooden plank. They lived off cabbage soup, and to relieve themselves there was a bucket in the corner, no soap or running water. At the end of the corridor, you come to the cells where prisoners were tortured. In one, prisoners stood in a room of icy water up to their neck; another was lined with spikes, a medieval-looking yoke at the centre; then, at the end of a corridor, there's a sound-proof padded cell where prisoners lost their minds. After confessing, prisoners were marched up to the railway station behind the prison and shipped off to Moscow or Siberia, where many were executed. Then there were those who died in prison from cold or disease, their bodies chucked into bomb craters nearby.

Six years after the end of the war, in 1951, the Soviets gave the prison to the Stasi. At first, the Stasi ran it along similar lines to the Soviets, torturing prisoners to extract confessions. But by the end of the 1950s, the Stasi decided they wanted a new look, and they put their inmates to work, building 200 cells and interrogation rooms on top of the old Soviet submarine-cells. By the early sixties, Hohenschönhausen had become the Stasi's main remand prison, its cells filled with political prisoners awaiting trial, many of them failed escapees. And it was here that Wolfdieter was now arriving, inside that white fruit-and-vegetable van.

It shudders to a stop. The door is pulled open and Wolfdieter dragged from the pitch-black of the van into a huge white room the size of an airport hangar, festooned with bright lights. Many prisoners say this was the most terrifying part, the sudden noise and lights after hours of darkness – hibernating animals wrenched into a sudden summer. At the end of the white room, a door leads into the prison. There is no final snatch of fresh air, no glimpse of the walls of the prison; instead, Wolfdieter stumbles forwards, following the other prisoners as the guards yell at them.

'*Kleider aus!*'

Wolfdieter takes off his trousers and shirt.

'*Alles!*'

Then his underwear.

'*Bücken!*'

Now the humiliating strip-search.

Finally, they give Wolfdieter his prison clothes and take him to his cell: number 34. This is now his name.

In the other cells are most of the people arrested that night. A Stasi file lists all forty-three: a photo-lab assistant, a vet, students, mechanics, several 'housewives', a librarian, hairdressers, a lighting technician, an optician, an accountant, a carpenter, an architect, a fireman and a nurse. The oldest is sixty, the youngest fourteen.

A few hours after arriving, as Wolfdieter sits in his cell in the dark, the door to his cell opens and a guard walks in.

'*Nummer 34! Kommen Sie!*'

Wolfdieter follows the guard along the corridor to a small room, which, after the sterile anonymity of the cells, feels almost homely. There's a desk, a telephone, a set of cupboards, even wallpaper. Behind the desk sits a man with neat hair and a clean-shaven face. There's a typewriter in front of him. It is now six in the morning and Wolfdieter's interrogation is about to begin.

The Stasi were good at a lot of things – recruiting people, cataloguing their files – but there's one thing, perhaps above any other, they wanted to become masters of: interrogations.

In the fifties they'd got a bad name for themselves. People had come out of prison with terrifying stories about the Stasi: beatings, torture. And believe it or not, the Stasi cared; they didn't like the bad press so they wrote manuals forbidding beatings and physical torture. While some renegade officers still did it, most didn't have to resort to physical torture. Instead, they became masters of *psychological* torture, creating a special academy in Potsdam, a town not far from Berlin, where senior Stasi officers learnt 'operative psychology'.

Sitting in that interrogation room, Wolfdieter was about to be questioned by an officer who'd spent months learning how to break people down, an officer with a degree in the subject, and what Wolfdieter didn't know was that the process of interrogation had begun long before he entered the room. It had begun the moment he was put in that van, the journey and everything after it carefully designed to begin the process of breaking someone down until they gave up their secrets willingly. It was all part of the Stasi's strategy of *zersetzung* – 'decomposition'.

The journey to the prison should have taken half an hour. Instead, the Stasi guard drove the van for hours, taking a route that went right outside of Berlin and back again. It was all about disorientating prisoners, so they'd think they were a long way from home, their friends, their family.

Once in the prison, that burst of light, the shouting guards, the strip-search, all of that was to break prisoners down further. Apart from the instructions barked at them, none of the guards talked to the prisoners to explain where they were or what would happen next. The Stasi had learnt that ignorance was the best short-cut to fear. Then there were his prison clothes – they were far too big for him. That was deliberate. It's a minor detail, but imagine wearing clothes that don't fit you, all the time. You don't feel yourself.

Then his cell. And it is here you see *zersetzung* at its most insidious. Though the cells could pass for a modern prison in many Western cities from the time – clean, white, functional – there were small but important differences: the light switches were on the *outside* of the cell, as well as the button to flush the loo. It was all about control – or rather, lack of it. Prisoners had to plead with guards to turn the lights off at night, to turn them on in the day, to flush the loo when it stank out their cell. Political prisoners who arrived with confidence and self-worth soon felt insignificant. Inhuman. Worthless. Finally, in each cell there was a small window at the top, no bigger than your hand. Prisoners would peer through, hungry for a glimpse of the world outside, but the glass was designed so that they couldn't see anything. Like looking through spectacles with the wrong lenses, everything was a blur. The world was just outside Wolfdieter's window, but he could never see it.

And so by the time a prisoner arrived for his first interrogation, as Wolfdieter had now, they were a shadow of themselves. Sitting upright on a small four-legged milk stool, stripped of his name, hungry, tired, no idea where he is, an anonymous prisoner in ill-fitting clothes, number 34 waits for the first question.

It starts with the obvious ones.

Why did you go into 'democratic Berlin' (that's what the party calls East Berlin) on 7 August 1962? Where did you go? Who did you see?

Wolfdieter answers, giving as little information as possible, telling his interrogator what he guesses he already knows. Wolfdieter tells him about the Girrmann Group, the House of the Future, then about Renate and his plans to get her out of the East. He talks about the day of the operation, his trips around East Berlin, passing messages on, but gives no names.

His interrogator types it all up. 'Phone numbers?'

'They've slipped my mind,' he says.

At no point does Wolfdieter's interrogator beat him. Instead, he waits for Wolfdieter to disintegrate. Four hours in, sitting on the stool, hands on his knees, Wolfdieter's back begins to ache, pain streaking through his legs. Eight hours in, his voice rasps, there's no water and he can't remember when he last ate. Ten hours in and the room is now swaying, his ears ring, the edges of his vision darken and all he can think about is sleep.

Sleep.

Sometimes Wolfdieter drifts off mid-answer, crashing off the stool onto the cement floor, the bump wrenching him from his half-dreams. Each time, the interrogator strolls around from behind his desk, calmly places Wolfdieter back on the stool and the questions begin again.

The Stasi want to know everything about the operation, despite knowing a huge amount from their informant and from the tunnel itself. That night, like detectives at a crime scene, they'd spent hours measuring, documenting and drawing the tunnel, noting its height (1 m), width (0.8 m), depth (2.3 m), the lack of wooden supports and lighting system. The only measurement they didn't get was the length: they sent a dog into the tunnel, but it only went ten metres in, and none of the Stasi were brave enough to go further. They noted the tools left behind: an axe, 'two wood drills and a chisel', then turned to the rest of the house, listing everything inside, the 'upholstered chairs' and 'bookcases'.

Still, they want to know more.

'How did you keep in contact with Detlef Girrmann?'

'What was agreed with the West Berlin police?'

Question after question after question.

Now and then Wolfdieter's interrogator slips through a side door into another room and there's a rumble of conversation. Later, Wolfdieter discovers that the interrogators are monitored by other Stasi officers, people who listen in, check they're asking the right questions. Back in the room, his interrogator begins again. More questions. More falling on the floor. Dry mouth. Half-dreams. Finally, late in the afternoon, twelve hours after his interrogation begins, Wolfdieter is taken back to his cell.

Shuffling along the linoleum corridor, Wolfdieter is instructed not to talk to other prisoners, not even to look at them. He is told to look down at the floor, following markings that show him where to walk. At one point he hears footsteps approaching, another prisoner perhaps, but before he can snatch a glimpse of them, his guard pushes him into an empty holding cell. These cells are stationed at intervals along the corridor so that if two prisoners are walking along it, one can be taken aside. No chance of interaction, or a sympathetic gesture. No solidarity here.

If Wolfdieter were allowed to look up, he would see a thin piece of rope running along the corridor at head height – the prison's silent alarm system. Not that it was used much as no one ever tried to escape. Even if someone made it out of the prison, they would find themselves in a huge military complex, surrounded by factories that churned out Stasi paraphernalia: spy cameras, fake number plates, microphones. If someone made a run for it, the guards would tug the piece of string, triggering a red light down in the control room. There was no loud ringing. The silence was as much a part of this prison as anything else; there was no noise to find comfort in. To that end the prisoners were all given slippers, the guards too.

Eventually Wolfdieter arrives back in his cell and there, a surprise: another prisoner. At first Wolfdieter is grateful, he has someone to talk to. His cell-mate is pale, thin and inquisitive, and Wolfdieter answers his many questions. Only later does he guess that he must be a *zelleninform-ator* – a 'cell informant' – put there by the Stasi to find out what secrets Wolfdieter hasn't already given up. This was a common Stasi tactic; they knew prisoners were desperate to talk to people apart from their inter-rogators and they spread *zelleninformatoren* through Stasi prisons, instructing them to wheedle out other crimes from their cell-mates. The Stasi don't mind prisoners knowing these cell-informants exist. Sometimes they even spread false rumours that a prisoner is an informant, just to create distrust.

No solidarity here.

That night, Wolfdieter tries to sleep, tries to ignore his *zelleninforma-tor's* questions but it's difficult. Like all inmates, Wolfdieter is instructed to sleep flat on his back, hands over his blankets. If he rolls over, moves his hands, the door opens, a slippered-guard whispers in, wakes him, orders him back into position.

At midnight, Wolfdieter wakes to see a guard standing over him; he's pulled out of his bed and taken back into the interrogation room, the same man sitting behind a desk.

Round two.

As Wolfdieter's interrogator begins again, down the corridor other prisoners from the botched escape are answering questions. There's a vet who wanted to rescue his wife and one-year-old baby through the tunnel, but they were arrested at the house, his wife taken to a woman's prison along with their baby. During her interrogation, the Stasi took her baby away. She had no idea if she would ever see him again.

Then there's the couple who owned the house, Edith and Friedrich Sendler. Both say they had nothing to do with the tunnel, but their interrogators don't believe them: 'How do you explain the fact that your living room was hacked open from below? Why is it that tunnellers from West Berlin drilled through your living room floor in a perfect spot with no furniture on it? Your statements are completely illogical and unbe-lievable . . .'

In each room, behind the interrogator is a window. As the prisoners sit on stools, answering questions, the deal on offer doesn't need to be spelt out: confess and after prison you'll be *out there* again one day, in the world through the looking glass. If you don't, you'll stay here; who knows if you'll ever leave. Some prisoners spent years in remand prisons, refusing to confess to crimes they didn't commit. By the time they were released, there wasn't much of them left.

Across East Berlin, in various Stasi prisons, the students, vets, teachers and doctors answer questions about that night. Their interrogators fax the information around so that it can be cross-referenced and checked. Night after night it goes on: the official interrogations, the unofficial ones in their cells.

Wolfdieter loses track of what he's said. Loses track of time. Himself. What he's now experiencing is the Stasi's most effective interrogation method: sleep deprivation. The Stasi are proud that they've moved on from the barbaric torture methods carried out by the Soviets: Stasi prisoners don't usually leave their prisons with broken teeth and arms, yet the Stasi's brand of torture is still physical, only the damage is invisible. It happens deep within the body. As the CIA would later discover when using sleep deprivation as an 'enhanced interrogation technique' following 9/11, it is an incredibly powerful tool, one that strikes at the core of you, at the biological functions that determine your mental and physical health.

Fatigue comes first, then irritability, problems concentrating, reading and speaking. Your body temperature drops. You find it hard to make decisions. You lose your appetite, become disorientated and you hallucinate. As your body weakens, so does your mind and you begin to withdraw from everything around you. That information comes from research carried out by scientists who have only monitored what sleep deprivation does to the human body up to this point. For obvious reasons, they can't go further, though they know from research on animals that sleep deprivation eventually kills you. It seems that it's not because of a particular problem with any single organ: instead, your whole body, deprived of the regenerative function of sleep, collapses.

Wolfdieter is now in the early stages of this process. Tired. Cold. Confused. Withdrawn. You can see the effects of this in his forty-page interrogation, typed up neatly in his Stasi file. Wolfdieter begins to crumble, giving more names, places, dates. At the end of the third night, his interrogator gives him a confession to sign. Wolfdieter reads it. It's seventeen pages long and it contains everything he told his interrogator. Then, at the end of his statement, he reads something that even in the depths of exhaustion Wolfdieter knows he never told him: how the tunnel operation was all part of a plot involving West German and American governments. He's confused: *they have enough to send me to prison, why do they need to add these lies?*

'That's not what I told you,' says Wolfdieter, somehow finding the strength for a final moment of defiance.

His interrogator looks back at him blankly. 'You will sign it.'

Wolfdieter is shaking; he can barely read it, understand it, but something within him has stirred at this final insult, the lie in this typed-up confession, and though his body is broken, he wants to hold on to something: the simple truth of that day.

Looking at his interrogator, he tries again. 'No sir, I won't sign it.'

His interrogator smiles. 'Yes you will,' he says, the bored confidence of someone who's been through this many times. 'You will sign everything.'

And he is right. At five in the morning, Wolfdieter Sternheimer signs the confession.

When I ask Wolfdieter why, why he'd signed a statement that wasn't true, knowing this could lead to a tougher punishment, his answer is simple.

'I was so, so tired.'

45

Mole-hunt

S IEGFRIED IS NERVOUS. He's been summoned to the House of the Future and he knows why: they are trying to work out what happened, how the Stasi knew so much, who betrayed them.

It's two days after the operation and everyone is in shock, trying to piece it all together. Joachim, Hasso and Uli are lying low at university, wondering why it went wrong, and Bodo Köhler is on the hunt for the mole.

As Siegfried walks into Bodo Köhler's office, his mind races. Bodo had always been suspicious of him and now he's looking for someone to blame. How to keep cover? He needs to find someone else to cast a shadow on. Not too obviously; just enough to raise questions.

Siegfried looks around the room. There are only a few people there, several other escape-helpers from that afternoon, all waiting for Bodo to come in and begin.

Footsteps. Then Bodo's voice: 'Well, here's another corpse.'

Siegfried looks up to see Bodo looking straight at him and in a flash of panic he thinks Bodo knows everything, but then—

'Obviously you can't go to East Berlin any more,' Bodo continues, and Siegfried realises what he means: Siegfried is burnt. It makes sense: having been part of an operation busted by the Stasi, Siegfried can't be a messenger again. Too risky.

Bodo looks around the room, says they need to talk through the operation, go through every detail to find the cracks. Turning to each person, he asks them to account for their day, every minute of it, all the places they went to, and to tell him if they noticed anything suspicious.

When it's Siegfried's turn, he tells Bodo about the meeting with Wolfdieter. There was another man with them too at that meeting, he says, a vet who wanted to get his wife and baby through the tunnel. Like Wolfdieter, the vet had volunteered to pass messages on to people in East Berlin. Siegfried tells Bodo about that meeting, saying he noticed something odd: the vet was agitated, he says, and when he left, instead of walking to the train station, the vet took a taxi, which Siegfried thought was strange . . .

He tails off. *Is that enough? Be subtle. Not too heavy-handed.*

Bodo listens, pauses, then moves on.

At the end of the meeting, Bodo leaves the room and the others talk for a while and gossip. One of them has heard a rumour that the Girrmann Group is about to oust Bodo, blaming him for the mistakes in the last few operations. Siegfried listens, keeps quiet, drinks it all in. Then someone else mentions another escape tunnel; one that's being dug right now in West Berlin.

Leaving the meeting, Siegfried can't believe his luck. Not only does no one suspect him, but now, Bodo Köhler, the only person who'd been suspicious of him, was about to be kicked out. Then, best of all, this new intelligence about another escape tunnel. Siegfried knows he won't be asked to take part in this one, after all he's burnt, but maybe if he hangs around the House of the Future, he'll hear more about this new tunnel, find out where it is. Where it is going.

A few days later, Siegfried meets Puschmann, his handler, and tells him what he's discovered. Puschmann is impressed. 'The secret collaborator is of the opinion that he has undoubtedly gained and solidified the trust of these persons,' he writes, adding: 'work is already underway on a tunnel supposedly located in North Berlin. The Secret Collaborator assumes that he will receive precise knowledge of the exact location of this tunnel. He will inform us immediately.'

A few days later, a letter arrives on the desk of the head of the Stasi, Erich Mielke.

AIM 13337/64 part I/1

BStU

[Federal Commissioner for the Records of the State Security Service of the former German Democratic Republic]

000139

Ministry for State Security
Administration Greater Berlin
- Director -
Berlin, 15.08.1962

Proposal

Subject: Award and distinction of Secret Collaborator (GM) 'Hardy'.
It is proposed to award Secret Collaborator 'Hardy' the Silver Medal
of Merit of the National People's Army and 1000 DM West (one
thousand).

Reason:

Thanks to information from the Secret Collaborator, it was possible
to prevent a large-scale, violent border breach organised by a West
Berlin terrorist organisation and arrest the persons involved. Armed
bandits planned to enter the state territory of the GDR by means of a
tunnel from West Berlin to democratic Berlin and secure the border
breach with armed force.

The Secret Collaborator showed great dedication, reliability,
initiative and personal courage in performing his duties for the Ministry
for State Security (MfS). As a result of the Secret Collaborator's
cautious behaviour, it was possible to arrest a total of 43 persons,
including 4 West German members of the West Berlin terrorist
organisation who played major roles in the organisation and
implementation of border provocations in democratic Berlin.

Signed,
Colonel Wichert

Erich Mielke agrees to the award immediately. Siegfried Uhse will be
one of the first recipients of this new medal, a fitting prize for the spy
who prevented an embarrassing mass escape. But Mielke doesn't plan
on keeping this escape plot a secret. For the master of theatrics has a
grand plan for a great spectacle, Wolfdieter in the starring role.

46

Silence

———◆———

13 August 1962

J OACHIM LOOKS AT his watch: five minutes to twelve. Not much
time. Looking around the train, he sees it, a piece of string running
along the top of the carriage.

NOTFALL! EMERGENCY!

Reaching up, he places his fingers around the cord, ready to yank.

It's 13 August, six days after the escape that went wrong and the first
anniversary of the building of the Wall. In East Germany, the VoPos are
out in their thousands, expecting trouble. In the West, Mayor Willy
Brandt has announced a minute's silence at noon. Neither the governments of East or West Germany, nor the Americans, want any protests
or violence.

When the Girrmann Group heard about the West German government's anaemic plan for the anniversary, they were outraged – just one
minute's silence to mark a concrete Wall that had separated children
from parents, sisters from brothers, a Wall at which twenty people had
died trying to cross. The Girrmann Group wanted outrage, defiance,
noise, anger; they wanted to remind the world that their city had been
cut in half, their lives cut in half, and that this was not normal. If the
government wouldn't organise something more spectacular, they would.

At twelve noon, the minute's silence begins.

In West Berlin, all down the Ku'damm, along Bernauer Strasse, across
the whole city, people stop walking, stop talking and they are still. Traffic
stops. VW Beetles and lorries sit awkwardly in the middle of the road.

As people stand there, statues dotted around the city, the sudden departure from normal life kick-starts their emotions: grown men cry, elderly couples cling to each other, children curl into their parent's arms. But as the seconds tick on, despair turns into something else. Anger. Anger that their collective response to one year of the Wall is simply this.

Silence.

At 12.01, someone somewhere beeps their horn. A long, loud, angry beep. Another joins in, then another, until all over West Berlin car horns are blaring, and it's at this very moment, during this gesture of defiance, that on the S-Bahn, Joachim and dozens of other Girrmann Group volunteers pull the emergency cords, train wheels suddenly fix in their tracks, sending up sparks and the smell of burnt metal as the carriages screech to a halt in the no man's land between stations. It is a perfectly aimed piece of civil disobedience, for in a strange quirk of municipal politics, the whole of the city's train network is owned by East Berlin. Stopping these trains is a finger-up to Walter Ulbricht and his party and everything he stands for. Now, Joachim watches as a couple of angry East Berlin policemen (who are allowed to patrol the trains even in West Berlin) stride through the carriage towards him.

'*Dokumente*,' they order.

'*Nein*,' Joachim replies, with the sweet satisfaction of knowing that here in West Berlin, they are on *his* turf. They can't make him do anything. Instead, they hand Joachim to the West Berlin police, who give him a fine. A small price to pay.

Those broken-down trains, the blaring horns, seem to spark something, because later that day thousands of people walk to Bernauer Strasse, the street with the tunnel underneath, the street cut in half by the Wall, and when they arrive, in a rush of madness, they try to smash through the Wall, hurling stones and bricks at the concrete before being pushed back by West Berlin police with sticks.

Eventually, just after midnight, the protesters realise they'll never smash through the Wall and people peel off, beginning the walk home. A few metres under their feet, still intact, lies the tunnel, the first that Joachim and the others dug, the one that became so waterlogged it was unusable. Now, after the hot August weather, it's finally dry, just waiting to be rediscovered.

47

The Show Trial

I T IS THE night before his trial and Wolfdieter lies in bed, counting down the minutes before the guard returns. That night the guard had been in every ten minutes, turning the light on, padding over to Wolfdieter's bed, waking him. Wolfdieter was breaking the rules, he said, not sleeping flat on his back. But Wolfdieter soon realised it was just a ruse. Even when in the state-sanctioned sleeping position, the guard still came in. Just another Stasi game.

Wolfdieter thought back to that morning, the moment he'd been pulled out of his cell and he'd let himself hope that something had happened, someone had intervened – that he was being released early for some unfathomable reason. Pushed into a fruit-and-vegetable prison van, Wolfdieter was driven to another building and taken into a room where a man sat, neatly dressed.

'I'm your lawyer,' he'd said; 'your trial begins tomorrow.'

Sinking into himself, Wolfdieter tried to get a grip, a list of questions forming in his head, things to go over with his lawyer. But he needn't have bothered.

'We have thirty minutes to discuss your crimes,' his lawyer continued, 'terrible crimes that deserve proper punishment . . .'

As he went on, Wolfdieter wondered what kind of lawyer spoke to his client like this, but this was East Germany and everything went differently here. Wolfdieter knew what crimes he was being accused of; his interrogator had told him the day before: paragraphs 17 and 21 of East German Criminal Law. He was being charged with 'threatening acts of violence' and 'misleading people into leaving East Germany'. It was that first charge of violence that had stuck in Wolfdieter's throat.

'What violence?' he'd asked.

'If your escape plan had worked,' his interrogator answered, 'it would have spread fear and horror through our country. There's your violence.'

Instead of explaining these charges or his likely sentence, the lawyer asked Wolfdieter a few questions about his childhood, his time at university, then left.

Now, lying here in the darkness, thinking about his trial, Wolfdieter realises he has no idea about any of it: who will be in the court-room, how long it will go on for, what his sentence will be or where he'll be taken. The questions rattle around his brain, each spawning new ones, his stomach gnarling with adrenaline. And it no longer matters that the guard appears every ten minutes, for Wolfdieter knows that sleep will not come tonight.

Dawn. A guard brings Wolfdieter his old clothes, the clothes he'd been wearing when he arrived in prison. They are baggy – two weeks in prison have taken the fat off him – but their musty smell feels like home.

He washes, combs his hair, then follows the guard outside, climbing into the van. At the court building, he's taken into a side room with four other prisoners: two accused of spying, and two other escape-helpers, one of whom is the vet – the other messenger from the escape, the man whose baby was taken by the Stasi. A Stasi officer is in the room with them. He turns to each prisoner in turn, giving instructions.

To the vet: 'You must say you hate this country.'

To Wolfdieter: 'You must talk about six men coming into the tunnel with machine-guns. If you don't,' he says, 'we'll take you back for another interrogation, we'll find those secrets you never revealed and things will be much worse for you.'

It is only when Wolfdieter enters the court-room that he understands why he's been given this script. He'd imagined a small court-room, just a handful of people, but sitting on all sides of the court, eyes boring into him, are hundreds of people, all smartly dressed. He realises then that he is no ordinary prisoner.

Stasi jails were stuffed full of East Germans, but Wolfdieter was a *West German* student, involved in the most ambitious escape operation from East Germany so far. It was a huge political opportunity for the Stasi, and only a few days after they'd arrested Wolfdieter, they'd begun to organise one of the first great show trials. The Department of Agitation and Propaganda had written a letter to the head of the Stasi, Erich Mielke, asking for his approval, which he gave, and then, as if throwing a party, the department had sent hundreds of invitations to the great and good: police officers, soldiers, journalists, businessmen and party members. Two hundred and fifty people had accepted, now sitting there, sweating in the heat and the glare of the lights and cameras – for the trial was to be filmed and broadcast on TV.

The trial begins with a statement from the General Prosecutor, a man in his fifties in a smart suit and cravat. Streitt is his name. It means fight. He starts by talking about the escape, then, puffing out his chest, he broadens the narrative into a bigger story: a parable about the dangers of trying to escape East Berlin; the corrupting influence of West Berlin; the West German terrorists sponsored by the Americans who are trying to destroy East Germany. To add to the drama, he brings a witness on stage, a politics professor from Humboldt University who talks at length about the corrupting influence of the Americans and demands that they leave West Germany or they will spark a third world war.

Late in the afternoon, the first day over, as Wolfdieter leaves the courthouse, he realises that he is merely a puppet in a political drama, staged in this court-room theatre. He knows now that neither his testimony, nor his lawyer, will make a difference. As in most Stasi trials, the script has already been written. Yes, there are lawyers representing clients, judges to hand down sentences, it all looks and feels like a proper trial, but the real work happens off-stage, with judges given instructions by the party.

On day two, Wolfdieter's lawyer stands up to speak.

'The accused has carried out terrible crimes and must be punished,' he says, adding cursorily: 'but please take into consideration that Wolfdieter Sternheimer grew up in West Germany and was influenced and brainwashed by a capitalist system and a capitalist press.' And that is it. His lawyer sits down. Now for the sentence.

Wolfdieter has no idea what to expect. When you look at the kinds of sentences allotted to different political crimes, it's hard to predict what anyone would get in a Stasi court. There are cases of teenagers being given eighteen months for watching Western TV, people given two years for sticking political posters on their apartment windows – someone was even given two years for failing to report a friend who was planning an escape to the West. People caught escaping could get anything from six years to life imprisonment, or in some cases, the death penalty, which was carried out initially by guillotine, then by a single shot to the neck.

Wolfdieter looks at the judge, a nondescript man in his fifties who is enjoying his starring role. The judge reads out the sentences for the five prisoners: life imprisonment for the two accused of spying, twelve years for the vet, six for the other escape-helper. Seven years for Wolfdieter.

Wolfdieter looks down at his hands. Steadies them. Seven years is manageable. He'll be twenty-nine when he's out. Still time to build some kind of life. Then he catches himself: what about Renate?

From the court-room, Wolfdieter is taken to Brandenburg Prison, called 'the crystal coffin' because of its enormous glass roof. He spends his first week in solitary confinement, then he's taken to a cell, nine other men inside: murderers, thieves, rapists. In East German prisons, political prisoners are mixed with criminals; it's part of the punishment, being roughed up by thugs and murderers, and the criminals often work as informants.

At Brandenburg Prison, every day is the same. At four in the morning, Wolfdieter is woken with a piece of bread and coffee. He washes, makes his bed, then at six his shift begins. Like most prisoners, Wolfdieter is expected to work in prison. It boosts the East German economy, for the party sells products made in its prisons to West Germany.

Wolfdieter is in House Five, shift B: kitchen furniture production. Every morning he's taken down to a room in the basement, thick with dust and heat, where he uses outdated machines to build wooden carcasses for East German kitchens. He works in a 40-degree heat for eight hours straight, and there are times when he faints, when he sees men lose fingers and other horrific accidents that he puts to the back of his mind. At two in the afternoon, there's lunch, then it's back to his cell where he sits and looks at the wall, or reads the party newspaper that's delivered to prisoners as part of their re-education programme. Occasionally, there are lectures too. 'Red light radiation', the prisoners call it.

After four weeks, Wolfdieter thinks nothing can be worse than this, but then one day, without warning, he's taken to Pankow Prison, one of the oldest Stasi prisons in the centre of Berlin. And there, he's put in a cell on his own. Solitary again.

The first week is okay; he's done this before. Wolfdieter moves around, tries to keep his mind active. But it's hard to keep a routine – the guards bring food at different times and he struggles to frame each day. He craves his murderer cell-mates, the kitchen work, even the conversations with his cell-informant back in Hohenschönhausen. He replays lessons from school and university, and for a week his brain is blissfully busy, but soon his mind is exhausted and empty. He loses sense of time, of day and night. It is then that his memory hunts begin: scrolling back through his life, Wolfdieter searches for memories, stretching them as far as he can, hungry for every detail. First he goes for the recent stuff: the escape. Renate. University. Easy pickings. Soon he's craving the deeper stuff. Like an oyster diver, he swims down, finding fragments from school, his childhood, those memories that barely make sense, images and smells as incomprehensible as dreams. Then one night, around six weeks into solitary, he dives down and discovers that most precious of pearls: a memory he thinks he's never had before. He sees himself in his parent's bedroom, standing in front of their bed. It's empty. His mother sits on the floor, crying. It's the day his father left to fight the Russians. In the corner of the room he sees a chess set – the set he inherited once it became clear his father wasn't coming back.

Wolfdieter is intoxicated by the fresh memory, spends days with it, rolling it around in his head, until he no longer knows what's memory and what's a dream. He forgets the cell, forgets he's a prisoner, but then at some point, days later, he finds himself surfacing, coming back to the room, to the prison, to the other end of his life, back to his interrogation, and without warning, it hits him.

My interrogator asked me about everyone involved in the escape. Asked about them ten times – what they did that day. Their address. Their family. But there's one person they never asked about. Not one question. Siegfried Uhse.

Why? Why? Why?

As Wolfdieter sits there, going back over those nights in Hohenschönhausen, he can't believe he didn't see it before: Siegfried Uhse. He must be the spy, the man who betrayed them to the Stasi, the reason so many are now sitting in prison, separated from everyone they love. And now, his despair turns into an overwhelming sense of help-lessness for he knows Siegfried Uhse is the spy and he knows Siegfried is still in the network of escape-helpers, but Wolfdieter is stuck here, unable to warn anyone.

Two weeks later, a guard comes to Wolfdieter's cell, takes him out of the building and into a car, and drives him to a building he doesn't recognise. There, a guard takes Wolfdieter up the stairs into a room. A court-room. He's confused: he's had his trial; why would he need another?

Then he sees her: Renate.

The last time he'd seen her was on the S-Bahn, the day of the escape. They'd said goodbye at the train station, Wolfdieter leaving to cross the border back into West Berlin. He'd had no idea Renate had been caught by border guards on the street corner, or that they'd made up that story about her friend's birthday and got away.

The night of the escape Renate went home, relief flowing through her as she went to bed, assuming that Wolfdieter had made it back over the border. Then, at three in the morning, the doorbell rang, long and urgent, and opening the door, bleary-eyed, Renate found two men standing there.

'Get dressed,' they'd said, and they'd driven her away in a black car, one man either side of her in the back. Later she'd discover that her name and address had been given to the Stasi by someone in Hohenschönhausen Prison. Renate never found out who, but she didn't blame them. In the end, most people talked.

The men took Renate to Keibelstrasse, the police headquarters, and interrogated her all through the first night and the next. Since then, she'd been kept on her own – in solitary confinement. Now, back in the clothes she'd thrown on that night, she stands in the court-room, and sees Wolfdieter at the back.

Their eyes lock and her hands begin to shake, as do her legs, so much so that the judge – a woman – motions for someone to bring Renate a chair. Renate has never forgotten that: that small gesture of kindness. But she doesn't let herself hope that the judge might be lenient. She knows by now how it all works.

The judge looks at Renate. 'You are charged with committing a violent act, which endangered the state and created fear and terror.' She is being charged with the same crime as Wolfdieter.

Renate is given a chance to speak and, somehow, she finds some words. 'I didn't want to create fear,' she says. 'I just wanted to go to my Wolfdieter.' After the trial, many years later, she'll hear that the other prisoners in the court-room were moved by her words. Few dared say anything.

Meanwhile, standing at the back of the court-room, watching all of this, Wolfdieter realises that, in an act of chilling vindictiveness, the Stasi have brought him here simply to watch Renate be sentenced. The judge calls the court to order, then hands down her sentence.

Three years.

As the guards take Renate out of the court-room, she passes Wolfdieter and she puts out her still-shaking hand, he puts out his, and for a few seconds their fingers curl together, gripping tightly before their hands are ripped apart and Renate disappears out of the court-room, the door closing behind her with a bang.

48

The Butcher

―――・―・―――

COVERED IN SWEAT and mud, Joachim lies back in the tunnel. It's quiet. He looks at his stove pipes, the electric lights, the Second World War telephone, all his inventions that make this tunnel feel like home. Yes, it's hot and damp and dark and claustrophobic, but it feels good to be back.

The NBC camera-crew are here again too, Peter and Klaus lying in the tunnel with their tiny camera and light, filming the digging. And Piers Anderton had been dropping in now and then to see how they were all doing. Over the months Piers had become a father-figure to the diggers, though he would always remember what Reuven Frank had told him when he started filming: don't get *involved* – that would cross the red line of universal journalist principles. Piers was simply there to film and report the digging. Not be part of it. If the diggers ever asked his advice about the escape operation, Piers would redirect the conversation and they would talk politics, fantasise about a future where one day the world wouldn't be carved in two.

It is now late August, a few weeks after that failed escape attempt, and Joachim and the others are back in the tunnel. They'd gone to the cellar to check on it, the tunnel that had been waterlogged by the leak, and discovered it was dry, the clay no longer mush, but holding firm. That day, they'd started digging again. Peter and Evi were desperate to escape East Berlin as soon as possible, and now there were over twenty others on the list, including Hasso's sister Anita, all desperate to get out. And so the diggers had returned to the rhythm of their shifts in the tunnel: the eight-hour digging stints, the backaches, the blisters and the fear of being discovered.

Up in the cellar, Joachim's gaze falls on a newspaper photo of a teenager in a white shirt, with neat features and combed hair. Whenever he felt exhausted, like giving up, Joachim would look at the photo and he'd dig from somewhere deep within, anger fuelling each thrust.

The boy's name was Peter Fechter and he was famous all over the world for something horrific that happened on 17 August. It began when Peter and his friend Helmut crept into an abandoned factory in East Berlin near the Wall at Zimmerstrasse, not far from the American border post at Checkpoint Charlie. Peter and Helmut were eighteen years old, bricklayers working on a building site nearby, and they'd wandered to the factory during their lunch-break. They'd been talking about how they both wanted to escape, and in a heady moment of teenage-spontaneity, they decided to see how close they could get to the Wall without being seen.

Inside the factory, Peter and Helmut took off their shoes, padding up to a storeroom where they found the only window in the building that wasn't bricked up. It looked directly out onto the Wall.

Then suddenly: voices. Without thinking, they jumped out of the window and ran towards the Wall, scrambling over the first barbed-wire barrier. From behind, they heard the crack of automatic Kalashnikovs as VoPos caught sight of them, spraying bullets at the boys as they sprinted across the death strip in their socks. No one knows how they'll react to the sound of gunfire until they hear it: for Helmut, it made him run faster and he vaulted to the top of the eight-foot Wall. Looking down, he saw Peter, who'd had a different reaction.

He'd frozen.

With the Wall right in front of him, Peter no longer had the momentum to scale it, but he tried anyway, throwing his body at the Wall while the VoPos let off their weapons, thirty-five bullets streaming towards him, one hitting Peter in the hip.

Peter fell.

Slumped at the bottom of the Wall, Peter curled his body into a foetal position, cradling himself as the ground around him turned red.

'Help me! Help me!' he screamed.

The VoPos watched. Police in West Berlin watched. American soldiers from the nearby garrison watched. And they kept watching minute after minute as Peter cried for help, gasping for breath, his voice getting weaker. Later, the VoPos would say they didn't run in to the death strip to retrieve Peter because they were scared they could be shot by Western police. West Berlin and American police said they held back as they were following orders not to help escapees unless they'd already made it into the West. One American officer at the scene was said to have looked away, saying: 'It's not my problem.' They all knew that if shots broke out, it could spark World War Three. This was the Cold War in action. Or rather, inaction.

At Checkpoint Charlie, the American lieutenant on duty called the commander of West Berlin's American garrison, who managed to get a message to President Kennedy: 'Mr President, an escapee is bleeding to death at the Berlin Wall.' They wanted instructions.

None came.

Soon, word spread through West Berlin that something awful was happening at the Wall: reporters climbed ladders, taking photographs of Peter as he lay there, his life bleeding out of him. Hundreds of people climbed on cars, screaming at the VoPos, the West German policemen, the American soldiers: 'Do something! You cowards! You murderers! DO SOMETHING, DO SOMETHING, DO SOMETHING!'

Eventually, a couple of West Berlin police climbed onto the Wall and threw down some bandages, but by then, Peter had stopped crying and his face was pale. An hour after Peter had been shot, his body crumpled and went limp. Only then did the VoPos move in to collect his body, exploding smoke bombs around them to give cover. As the VoPos took his body away, to the chant of 'Murderers! Murderers!', the smoke cleared and a reporter took a photograph that would be printed in newspapers all over the world. It would become one of the most iconic images of the Cold War: Peter Fechter's body being carried away by three VoPos, his head flopping back, one bare foot.

Three hours later, a handwritten sign appeared in an East Berlin apartment window:

'He is dead.'

The American garrison sent a message to the White House: 'The matter has taken care of itself'.

The next day, and for three days after that, West Berlin exploded with rage. Tens of thousands of people filled the streets, setting cars on fire, barricading streets, swarming to the Wall, where they threw rocks and bricks, West Berlin police pushing them back with water cannons and tear gas. But the protesters kept going, because something about watching

Peter's slow and lonely death had made West Berliners feel powerless and ashamed as never before. Right now, they wanted to feel as though they could do something to change the monstrous thing that had happened in their city that made soldiers and policemen stand by and do nothing as a human being died in front of them. Thousands marched to Checkpoint Charlie to demonstrate against the American soldiers for abandoning Peter, holding banners reading:

PROTECTING POWER = ACCOMPLICE TO MURDER

As they raged, the reactions came in: the US commander in West Berlin called the event 'an act of barbaric inhumanity'. President Kennedy discussed Peter's death with his advisors, trying to work out a plan should this kind of thing happen again. *Time* magazine ran the story as their headline, describing the Wall as a 'Wall of Shame', a phrase that would stick.

But somehow, words didn't feel enough, and a few days later, the mayor of West Berlin, Willy Brandt, invited the Yale Russian Chorus to sing a German translation of Mozart's *Ave Verum Corpus* at the Wall. The men gathered at the Wall, the understated opening notes giving way to a soaring melody, the music lifting high above the concrete, high above East Berliners, who felt forgotten. From now on, they knew that whatever horrors happened at the Wall, the US wouldn't step in: the risk of nuclear war wasn't worth the life of a bricklayer, however long and painful his death.

While West Berliners could express their anger, East Berliners had to suppress theirs: Peter's horrific death was yet another indignity to rage about in private. They'd learnt from that uprising in 1953 what the costs of marching on the streets were. Peter's parents only found out what had happened when police burst into their home, searched it, interrogated them, then told them their eighteen-year-old son was dead. At the funeral a few days later, 300 people turned up, and as usual, the Stasi took the opportunity to monitor everyone who attended, arresting an American photojournalist and sentencing him to two years in prison for espionage. That evening, on his nightly TV show, East Germany's chief propagandist, Karl-Eduard von Schnitzler, got to work, turning Peter's death into a moral lesson for anyone in the East thinking of escaping:

'The life of each one of our brave young men in uniform is more important to us than the life of a lawbreaker. By staying away from our state border – blood, tears and screams can be avoided.'

East German newspapers buried the story, filling its front pages instead with stories about the latest Soviet space missions and the heroism of the volunteers who'd helped with that year's harvest. In the back pages, where they mentioned Peter's death, they blamed the West for inciting him to suicidal actions. By the end of August, after the rioters in West Berlin had exhausted themselves, all that remained to mark Peter's death was a white wooden cross near the spot where he'd died.

Looking back down from that photo on the wall to the tunnel, Joachim thinks about the weeks ahead. This final stretch of digging will be more dangerous than all the digging they've done so far, for now they are firmly under the East, VoPos patrolling above their heads all the time with their listening devices. And yes, the digging is hard, but after what happened at the other tunnel, all the people arrested, what Joachim finds harder is the fear, never knowing who to trust. Ever since the escape that went wrong, the mood among the diggers had changed; they still don't know who betrayed them to the Stasi, so they watch each other. All the time.

Towards the end of his shift, around six in the evening, as he lies in the tunnel, Joachim hears a strange noise.

Hmm. Hmm.

It's a humming, electrical sound. It starts, then stops. Starts and stops again. Putting down his spade, Joachim lies in the dark, listening to the sound of his breathing. *Is it a VoPo patrolling the death strip above? Have they heard me?* He begins to wriggle through the tunnel on his back, barely breathing.

Hmm. Hmm.

The hairs on his neck prickle as he hears the noise again, now louder, his eyes boring into the ceiling as he scoots back towards the cellar, imagining the tunnel ripped open, a VoPo smiling triumphantly as he throws in dynamite.

Hmm. Hmm. Hmm.

At the end of the tunnel, Joachim pulls himself out, scrambles up the ladder into the cellar and catches his breath.

Hmm. Hmm. Hmm.

The noise is louder here and he scans the room, looking for anything that explains it, and sees the fuse box – perhaps that's it. Walking towards it, Joachim freezes, for the cellar door is slowly opening, and an arm is sliding through the gap. Joachim is rooted to the spot; all he can do is watch as the door opens to reveal a man standing there. He is hefty, plump, with brown hair, an open face and – to confuse things – a big smile.

'I'm Claus,' he says.

49

Claus's Story

———•——•———

H E'S A BUTCHER, Claus says. Married, but he hasn't seen his wife,
Inge, since the night they tried to escape in November last year.
They'd taken their toddler, Kirsten, to the border with nappies and milk,
and were about to dash across when a VoPo appeared, pointed his gun
at them and told them to go home.

The border guard was short, much shorter than Claus, and it had
been too tempting not to take advantage of his height, so Claus punched
him and ran, thinking Inge and their daughter were following as he
squeezed through the barbed wire. Then he'd heard them, five shots,
and he dropped to the ground. As Claus stood up, astonished he wasn't
dead, he realised Inge and Kirsten weren't following, but were stuck
behind the barbed wire, trapped in the arms of the VoPo. In an instant,
Claus had lost his wife, his daughter and his unborn child – for Inge
was pregnant.

Since then, Claus had been living in West Berlin, feeling powerless
as he heard snippets of news from back home: he'd heard all about Inge's
show trial, how she'd been sent to prison, their daughter placed in a
children's home. He'd imagined Inge giving birth in a Stasi jail, but she
was released early and gave birth in hospital to their son, Uwe. A few
weeks later, through smuggled messages, Claus and Inge had agreed a
date and time to stand either side of the Wall in the hope they could
catch a glimpse of each other. On the appointed day, Claus went to the
border and held up a pair of binoculars through which he could just
make out the shape of his daughter (now reunited with her mother),
and Inge, holding Uwe high above the Wall, wrapped in a blanket. Since
then, Claus had spent every day trying to find a way to get Inge and
their two children into West Berlin. He'd helped dig two other tunnels,
but both collapsed. Then, walking down Bernauer Strasse today, he'd

seen clumps of clay in the courtyard, which is why he was standing here right now. Could he help dig the tunnel and use it to rescue Inge and his two children?

It's quite a story. Almost too much, and Joachim doesn't know whether to believe it. He wonders how a husband and father could escape like that, abandoning his family, not checking they were with him. It just doesn't sound right. Then this tale about finding clay in the courtyard.

Joachim thinks about the people arrested a few weeks ago, sitting in Stasi prisons all because of a spy, and now, here's someone they've never met with a strange story who just happens to have found their tunnel. If they let Claus join the group, and it turns out he's working for the Stasi . . . it's unthinkable.

The easiest solution would be to throw Claus out of the cellar, but now he knows where the tunnel is. And then, what if Claus is telling the truth? What if his wife and children really are stuck on the other side? If Joachim doesn't let Claus join them, the children will grow up without their father, just like he did. He must think carefully. Find a solution.

'Okay,' says Joachim, 'I need to discuss this with the others. Come back at ten tonight.'

At ten exactly, Claus returns and sees five of them standing there: Joachim, the two Italians, Wolf and Hasso. Joachim had told them all what was happening, said he needed their help.

'So,' says Joachim, 'tell them what you told me.'

'Well, I'm a butcher . . .'

Claus repeats his story and the diggers form a circle around him, listening to every word, scrutinising his body language, looking for any sign that he's lying. Then slowly, they close in on him, Claus inching back towards the tunnel until his heels are teetering over the edge of the shaft. As he stands there, Joachim catches Mimmo's eye and Mimmo gestures to the hole, and for a moment the thought hovers in the air between them, horrifying and unspoken. Joachim pictures it: if Claus were to fall in, they could bury him in the tunnel and no one would ever know. It would be a neat solution. But as suddenly as the thought appears, he pushes it away. He knows neither of them could do it. Even if Claus is a spy, they're not murderers.

Claus finishes his story. There's a short pause, then the diggers start firing questions: 'Who are you really? How did you find the tunnel? Where do you live? Who are you working for?'

Claus is scared. He stutters, repeating the same answers over and again, but after the horror of the betrayed tunnel, nothing he says can persuade the diggers he's not working for the Stasi. With each answer, the diggers get more worked up, and suddenly they rush towards him and there's a moment where it seems as though he might fall back into the hole, but instead they push him sideways onto a plank and Claus screams as a nail pierces his backside.

'What are you doing? I just want to help, please let me help!'

One of the diggers grabs a piece of rope, ties Claus's hands together. 'Are you armed? Where's your gun, where are you hiding it?'

Claus stutters, 'I don't have one. All right, yes I do. It's in my apartment.'

'Where is it? Keys! Give them to us!'

Claus pulls out his keys, gives them to Gigi and Hasso, who drive to his flat and search it. No gun.

Back at the cellar, they hover over Claus, shouting at him, 'Why are you lying? Where is it?'

'It's hanging behind a cupboard on the wall in my flat,' says Claus; 'it's on a piece of string.'

They drive back to his flat, find the gun, bring it to the cellar. More questions.

By midnight, they're all exhausted. They have no idea what to do: they can't kill Claus, but they don't trust him. As night falls, the city quietening, Wolf thinks of something. He leaves the cellar, drives home, picks up his phone and makes a call.

An hour later, Wolf is on the road, Claus in the back of his windowless VW van, hands tied. Wolf drives past Brandenburg Gate, around Checkpoint Charlie, then takes the road south through the city towards Tempelhof airport. Just before the airport, he turns off down a gravel lane towards a large building. Inside, a group of men who are expecting him. Wolf pushes Claus towards them, thanks them for their help, then leaves. He'll have his answer in the morning.

It's early when Wolf's phone rings. It's the men from last night – the *Verfassungsschutz*, West Berlin's intelligence agency. Since the tunnellers knew nothing about interrogating people, how to work out if someone was working for the Stasi or not, he'd taken Claus to people who could. The intelligence agents had grilled Claus all through the night.

'And?' asks Wolf, 'what do you think?'

Their answer isn't very helpful. There's no proof that Claus is a Stasi informant, they say, but no proof that he isn't. So be careful.

That morning, Joachim meets the others at the cellar. They agree that it's unlikely after everything that happened that Claus will return; he'll have been scared off by the whole experience. But a few hours later, there's a knock on the door and Claus appears, smiling.

'Wow, that was quite a night,' Claus says. 'You guys have the most amazing connections! It was pretty tough, but I don't blame you; it's better to be careful isn't it. I'm back now though, and I've got nothing to do with the Stasi – so please let me work with you?'

The diggers look at each other, shocked at Claus's cheerful persistence. Here's a man who's been tied to a chair, had a nail stuck in his bottom, been interrogated – twice – yet now he's back for more.

Claus looks back at the diggers, sensing their uncertainty. 'I'll do two shifts in a row, even three. I won't leave the cellar if you like; you can watch me all the time!'

Joachim says they need a moment to think. Walking to the corner of the basement, they weigh it up. So far there's nothing to suggest that Claus is a Stasi spy, and even if he is, there's not much they can do about it if they're not prepared to kill him.

'What if we let him dig,' says Joachim, 'but we don't tell him where we're digging to. Or the date of the escape?'

It's a clever idea. Even if he was a spy, without those details, the Stasi wouldn't know when or where the escape was happening. Plus, just looking at Claus's huge frame, it's hard to say no. They don't have long left to dig the tunnel and here's a man, built like an ox, who wants to help.

'Okay,' says Joachim to Claus, 'you're in.'

50

Paris

August 1962

CLIMBING OUT OF a taxi, dressed in an expensive suit, Reuven Frank walks towards the Parisienne restaurant, shiny shoes clicking on the pavement, the door opened effortlessly by a bellboy in red. In front of him, one of the most gorgeous rooms he's ever seen – red velvet seats, small intimate tables topped with art-deco lamps, a piano in the corner, and beautiful people everywhere. It's everything he'd hoped he would find at Maxim's, the most famous restaurant in the world.

Walking through the room, he sees the two of them, his Berlin correspondent, Piers Anderton, and NBC bureau chief, Gary Stindt. A few days ago, Gary had called Reuven, said he needed to talk. Since they'd agreed never to discuss the tunnel on the phone, whenever Piers and Gary wanted to talk to him, Reuven had to fly to Europe. It had happened once before, after the tunnel sprang the leak. Reuven had come to London, dined with Piers and Gary at the Savoy Grill, flown home the next day. It felt extravagant but Reuven Frank loved the romance of it, talking in hushed tones in luxurious European restaurants about the most daring escape operation under the Berlin Wall.

Sitting down at Maxim's, cocktail-eyes flicking round to see if there are any famous diners here tonight, Piers and Gary tell Reuven what's happened: water is coming into the tunnel. Again.

Reuven's heart sinks. The first leak had almost destroyed the tunnel; it was only down to the West Berlin water authorities that they'd been able to continue. With the tunnel so far under East Berlin, West Berlin's water department can't help now.

Piers looks down. He's devastated. He'd been going to the cellar for months, knew the diggers intimately, had seen them shake with exhaustion with each dig, felt their fear of the VoPos, of being buried alive; and now, it could all come to nothing. Then there was the other problem: if the tunnel was destroyed, what would happen to their documentary? They had 12,000 feet of footage boxed up in the bureau storeroom. It was worth nothing if the tunnel collapsed and no one escaped.

Reuven sits back. There's a long silence. He is desperate for an ending; most of his documentaries end in complexity and injustice, and he wants this story to do something different, give people the kind of ending that rarely happens in real life. Perhaps he'd been hoping for too much.

'Remember,' says Reuven, 'we didn't set out to make a programme about a tunnel. We set out to make a documentary about people who wanted to escape. And if this tunnel fails, well, we can still tell that story.'

Reuven talks about the tourists who swarm along Bernauer Strasse, taking photos of the Wall. 'Let's show these people who buy their Wall souvenirs what the Wall *really* means. We can tell them about other escapes as well as this failed tunnel: people who've jumped to their deaths, the forged passports, the idealistic student escape-helpers.'

His voice trails off. It's a valiant attempt at a pep talk, but they all know it: if the tunnel fails, their documentary will fail too.

Though they have footage of other escapes, all they'd been able to film was the aftermath: open manhole covers, policemen talking, a blank wall. Like every news crew, they were always too late to film an escape in progress.

Eventually they change the subject, sit back and enjoy the expensive taste of the wine, the smell of perfume and the sound of the room filling around them. Reuven asks for the bill, but before he pays, there's one final problem to discuss. The one back home.

A few weeks ago, a State Department official had come to see Reuven's boss, the head of NBC. He'd heard rumours, he said, that American TV networks were trying to film escapes in Berlin. CBS had been trying to film an escape tunnel – a different one – and he'd been to their office to tell them to stop. Was NBC filming one too? If so, they, too, needed to stop.

The White House was still terrified about Berlin, President Kennedy still obsessed by the city that he thought was the most likely place to spark nuclear war. After all, ten months ago, back in October 1961,

Siegfried Uhse was just twenty-one years old when he was recruited by the Stasi.

The Stasi's report about Siegfried Uhse following his recruitment. The report notes his ash-blond hair, 'pointed nose' and 'inflamed eyes'.

Siegfried Uhse's letter of commitment. Every new recruit wrote one.

Reuven Frank, later referred to as one of the founding fathers of broadcast journalism.

NBC News correspondent Piers Anderton (far left) talking to NBC News cameraman Peter Dehmel and Domenico (Mimmo) Sesta.

The tunnel, with its stove pipes, electric lights and the diggers' beloved border sign, replicating the one above ground: 'You are now leaving the American sector of Berlin!'

When the leak began, the diggers pumped 8,000 gallons of water out in one week, but still the water came.

Renate Reichelt.

Wolfdieter Sternheimer speaks for a few moments during his show-trial.

Hohenschönhausen Prison, one of the Stasi's largest remand prisons, where guards perfected the art of 'zersetzung' – decomposition. Many inmates spent years there. By the time they were released, most were a shadow of their former selves.

Dotted along the Wall between East and West Berlin were border crossings, like the famous Checkpoint Charlie.

Though Walter Ulbricht described the Berlin Wall as an 'anti-fascist protection barrier', designed to protect East Germans from spies and saboteurs in the West, the binoculars of the VoPos were always trained on their own people in the East.

The lifeless body of Peter Fechter, killed on 17 August, 1962.

VoPos searching an escape tunnel near the Wall.

In 1963, President Kennedy feared he might be heckled in West Berlin for his inaction over the building of the Wall, but he was welcomed as a hero.

During the summer of 1989, protests grew each week until tens of thousands took to the streets in Leipzig in November. It was the beginning of the end for East Germany.

And so the Wall came down. November, 1989.

they'd seen how a spat in Berlin could bring the world to the brink of war.

It had begun with a petty argument about American access to East Berlin. Walter Ulbricht was harassing American diplomats, hoping that if he made their life difficult when they drove into East Berlin, he could push the US out of Berlin entirely. He was banking on President Kennedy not retaliating. But he bet wrong. Kennedy had a new advisor in West Berlin: General Lucius Clay, the man who organised the American airlift in 1948 that kept West Berlin going during the Soviet blockade. The city had never forgotten him: West Berliners wrote letters to General Clay, and when they saw him in the street, they'd race over to say hello and shake his hand. General Clay thought Kennedy should have intervened when the barbed wire went up, but now he saw this spat as Kennedy's chance to show West Berliners that he still cared, by fighting for the city and standing up to Walter Ulbricht.

And so the next time East German soldiers made life difficult for American diplomats entering East Berlin, General Clay's response was tanks: four of them, bulldozer blades mounted on the front, driven right up to the border of East Berlin, guns pointing towards the VoPos. And over one week in October 1961, Clay sent those tanks to the border every time an American official was harassed by East German soldiers. At the end of that week, on Friday 27 October, the Soviets retaliated, sending ten T-54 tanks to the border, where they sat, engines running, guns pointing towards the American tanks on the other side.

This was a historic moment: never before in the Cold War had American and Soviet soldiers faced each other at point-blank range. American helicopters and Soviet MiG fighter planes buzzed overhead. Journalists from West Berlin, who'd heard that something dangerous was happening, scampered round the edges, taking photos. Further back from Checkpoint Charlie, hundreds of West Berliners stood huddled in the cold, desperate to know what was happening, aware it was dangerous to be there, but too afraid to sit at home, waiting passively for what might come. Rumours flew through the crowds: maybe the Soviet army was marching towards West Berlin right now to take their half of the city.

Behind the scenes, President Kennedy and Soviet leader Nikita Khrushchev telephoned their representatives in West and East Berlin, asking questions, trying to work out their next move. Only a few months ago, Khrushchev had begun new nuclear tests, and that week he was secretly preparing to test the most powerful nuclear weapon ever built – a thirty-megaton nuclear bomb that had a thousand times the explosives used in Hiroshima and Nagasaki combined. The fear of nuclear war had reached fever pitch; only a few days earlier, *Time* magazine had run a story with the headline:

[NUCLEAR] SHELTERS: HOW SOON – HOW BIG – HOW SAFE?

In Berlin, as the afternoon darkened, an East German commander switched on six searchlights, blinding the American soldiers. Tank warfare was now light warfare. Retaliating, the Americans switched on their own much brighter searchlights, dazzling the Soviet soldiers in their mud-covered tanks, the border now brightly lit as if for a play.

Night set in. It was cold. Hour after hour, the soldiers in tanks either side of the border looked at each other down their barrels, feeling the responsibility of the live ammunition in their tank racks, trying not to think about what could happen if a shaking finger accidentally pulled a trigger. Every so often a soldier would climb out of their tank and wander around to warm up, then clamber back in.

Back in their capitals, each president was making bigger moves. Khrushchev put his nuclear strike forces on special alert status, the first time he'd done so over a dispute with the US. Kennedy put American aircraft and warships on full alert throughout the world, ordering four submarines with sixteen warheads to be submerged in the North Sea.

Back in Berlin, the tanks sat there. The Soviet soldiers sat there. The American soldiers sat there. All of them straining to keep their eyes open, their bodies shutting down in the cold.

Just before dawn, Berlin time, Kennedy sent his brother, Bobby, to negotiate with a secret intermediary, a Soviet spy who passed messages to and from Khrushchev. No one knows exactly what was agreed in that meeting, as the material is still classified, but at 10.30 a.m., after a sixteen-hour stand-off, Khrushchev pulled back his Soviet tanks. Thirty minutes later, American tanks withdrew. And so ended what many describe as the most dangerous moment of the Cold War.

The US had stood firm, atoned for its anaemic response to the Wall, made it clear it would not be pushed around by Nikita Khrushchev or Walter Ulbricht. But there was a more sobering lesson: in the tinderbox of Berlin, a petty disagreement about American access to East Berlin could bring the world to the edge of nuclear war.

Since that week in October 1961, there'd been an unspoken agreement between the Soviet Union and the US. Neither wanted the situation in Berlin to spin out of control, leading to an accidental nuclear war. Instead, there was now stalemate.

It's why American soldiers had stood by as Peter Fechter lay dying. And it's why the White House wanted to stop TV crews meddling in escape operations. American soldiers could stand by and watch as an East Berlin bricklayer died a slow death in front of the cameras, but it would be harder to sit back if an American reporter got caught in the crossfire of an escape operation gone wrong.

Back in that meeting at NBC headquarters, Reuven Frank's boss had bluffed, not said anything to the State Department official about the film or the tunnel. He wanted to keep going, as did Reuven Frank, as did Joachim Rudolph, all of them determined to see the escape through, whatever the cost.

At the end of the night at Maxim's, Reuven Frank pays the bill, walks back to his hotel, and as he drops off to sleep in his Parisienne sheets, he knows that the next time he's back in Europe, the escape will either be on, or the tunnel destroyed.

51

Numbers

UNFURLING THE MAP, the diggers spread it out on the cellar floor. On a piece of paper are the latest numbers from the theodolite – the surveying instrument borrowed from the university's engineering department. The numbers will tell them where they are, what's above them. From the tunnel they can hear water trickling in. It's coming in more slowly than the first leak, but this time, with no way of fixing it, they guess they only have a week before the tunnel collapses. The only solution is to dig up from where they are right now. But where is that?

Joachim reads out the numbers. Scanning the map, the diggers cross-reference those numbers with buildings, street names, muttering quietly, calculating on the hoof, trying to work out where they are. Their fingers eventually close in on a street and an apartment: number seven Schönholzer Strasse.

They're just one street away from their target basement, the one Mimmo and Gigi checked out in the East, the one they have a key for. It doesn't look far on the map, but in tunnel time it would mean weeks digging. No chance of making a mad dash for it. Instead, tunnelling straight up is their only option. Sitting back, they discuss what that means.

First: they must smash into the cellar of a building they know nothing about. Once in the cellar, the diggers will have to force their way into the apartment. Finally – the most dangerous part – since they don't have a key to the apartment, they'll have to open it from the inside to let the escapees in. And the reason this is so dangerous is that Schönholzer Strasse is just one street away from the Wall, which means it's patrolled by VoPos, all the time, looking for people trying to sneak across the border. The escapees will have to walk past those VoPos, trying not to look conspicuous as dozens of them approach the same apartment and disappear inside.

The diggers fall silent. The odds are terrible. Every week there are reminders of what can happen when escapes go wrong. In the past month, three people had been killed trying to escape, the last one a forty-year-old carpenter called Ernst. He'd climbed to the top of a cemetery wall that led to the border. It was studded with broken glass to stop escapees. Cat-like, Ernst had weaved through the glass, ignored the border guards shouting at him to come down, and he'd almost made it, preparing to leap over the Wall, when a VoPo fired a shot from 100 metres away. Ernst fell, his body landing between two graves, his eyes open to the sky. After what happened with Peter Fechter, the VoPos were quick to move in, dragging his lifeless body away before journalists could film him lying there. But the VoPos couldn't remove all the evidence, for the bullet that killed Ernst had entered his head through his cap, and as Ernst fell off the Wall, his hat had floated over the top into West Berlin, where it fell to the ground. It was punctured by a single hole. 'The man with the cap' – that's how people who saw it described him. A few days later, a cross adorned with flowers and wreaths appeared on Bernauer Strasse near where Ernst was killed, just a short walk away from the diggers' cellar where they sit now, preparing to make the most difficult decision of the escape operation so far.

Digging up into a cellar on Schönholzer Strasse is crazy, they know it is. But somehow, they've ended up here, with this final choice: digging straight up or abandoning the tunnel forever. The diggers sit in silence, lost in memories of the months underground, the VoPos patrolling above their heads, risking everything to get this far. Friends of theirs are sitting in Stasi prisons, just as *they* could be if they carry on. Perhaps this moment, right now, is the time to back out.

But Joachim barely registers this moment as a choice, for what was the point in any of this if they give up; they just need to think, work out how to protect themselves.

And so the diggers agree to give it one last shot. But this time they will keep the final details of the escape plan secret – only the core group of diggers will be told the address of the cellar in the East. The only thing left is to set a date: Friday 14 September.

52

The Last Visit

—◆—

9 September

'IT'S TIME,' THEY say. Mimmo and Gigi have crossed the border and are now sitting in Evi and Peter's house. 'We have a date for the escape; get ready to leave in five days.' Not that there's much for Evi and Peter to plan. They can't tell anyone, not even Evi's grandparents, in case someone talks. And they can't bring much – just nappies, money and ID cards. Sitting there, Evi decides she'll wear her deep-green skirt suit again, the one she had made for the first escape that went wrong.

Mimmo and Gigi don't stay long, just a few hours. After they leave, 'Wilhelm', the Stasi informant who lives a few doors away, picks up a pen and makes a note of the visit.

Something to tell his handler when he next sees him.

53

The Messenger

10 September

ELLEN SCHAU SASHAYS down the terminal hall at Berlin-Tempelhof airport, enjoying the movement of heads swivelling her way, the eyes that admire her chestnut-red hair, her delicate figure and her elegant Düsseldorf dress. Scanning the crowds, she looks for him, her fiancé, her Mimmo. Ellen hasn't seen him for a year – they barely talk on the phone and she's convinced something is wrong – but then she sees Mimmo, his dark eyes, his caterpillar eyebrows, his arms outstretched, and the hurt is forgotten as she burrows into his chest. All this year, Ellen has felt lost without him, stuck at home with her strict father and sick mother – she has TB and doesn't have long left. But now, here with Mimmo, the man Ellen describes as her first close friend, she feels safe.

That night, they eat at a restaurant. It's small, intimate. Their knees touch under the table. Ellen is expecting a long, romantic meal, but instead Mimmo looks serious and says he has something to tell her. And so it begins. Mimmo tells Ellen about the tunnel. The escape that went wrong. The arrests. Then he tells her that they're going to try again in four days. Ellen laughs at the coincidence: 14 September is her birthday.

Then Mimmo picks up Ellen's hand, so tiny in his. He tells her how none of it will work unless they can find someone to be their messenger, only no one wants to do it. Everyone has heard about Wolfdieter's arrest and imprisonment. A girlfriend of one of the diggers said she'd do it, but she'd pulled out – said she felt ill, but everyone knew it was just an excuse. Ellen stops eating because she knows what's coming before Mimmo asks.

★

Lying in bed, in a friend's apartment a few hours later, Ellen thinks about Mimmo's proposition. She hasn't given him an answer yet; she's still shaking off the version of her trip to Berlin she'd been dreaming about, replacing it with this new uncertain one. She thinks back to her conversation with Mimmo; how he'd called her the perfect messenger: with her West German passport she can go in and out of the East and, being a woman, he says, she'd arouse less suspicion.

'But what if it goes wrong,' she'd asked, 'like that other tunnel?'

Mimmo says she'd have to get a train to Warsaw, then to Yugoslavia and ask the embassy for help.

Ellen can't begin to imagine doing all that and so she lies there, playing out different versions of the escape in her head. In each scenario, she gets caught. At some point in the middle of the night, Ellen falls asleep, and when she wakes, she finds a single thought running through her head: *If I don't do it, no one will, and I don't want to be the person who lets them down.*

54

Investigations

—◆—

EVERY DAY, THEY'RE learning more about it, this mystery tunnel in North Berlin.

Siegfried has been lurking around at the House of the Future, asking questions, and sometimes he gets answers. He hears about weapons requested. Plans to rip up floorboards. He passes every detail on to his handler, and the Stasi cross-reference these titbits with their other intelligence, the information they're getting from their prisoners in Hohenschönhausen Prison, and gradually, they are piecing together the details. Like the blind men and the elephant, they hope that with enough numbers and measurements they'll find the tunnel. They hear the tunnel is over 100 metres long. Then, their best intelligence yet: it begins in a cellar on Bernauer Strasse.

55

Maps

———◆———

TUCKED INTO A quiet corner of Café Bristol, just off the Ku'damm, Ellen and Mimmo hunch over a table, half-empty cups pushed aside, pencils and notebooks in their hands, the comforting smell of bread rolls and coffee washing over them. One by one, Mimmo recites the street names that she must walk to in East Berlin: Schönholzer Strasse, Bernauer Strasse, Wolgaster Strasse, Brunnenstrasse, Ruppiner Strasse . . .

Ellen listens and scribbles the names in her notebook, the notebook she will take into the East. She has to be clever about how she puts it all down: the numbers she disguises as birthdays, the street names she weaves into diary entries. Studying the map Mimmo has given her, Ellen tries to burn the layout into her mind. She's never been to East Berlin before, has no frame of reference, so she must remember it all. Over the Wall it will be too dangerous to ask for directions.

Yesterday, Ellen had met the other diggers – Joachim, Hasso, Uli and a few others in their university dorm. They couldn't believe she'd agreed to be their messenger, showering her with so much attention that she'd flushed pink with embarrassment. Gabbling at her through cigarette smoke, they'd all wanted to help Mimmo's glamorous girlfriend with directions. Ellen had got confused, bamboozled, which is why she and Mimmo were here alone. Somewhere calm to work it all out.

On the map, Mimmo identifies three pubs. In each, he tells her, there will be a handful of escapees, waiting. Mostly families with young children. When Ellen walks in, she must give a coded signal that the tunnel is ready, a different one in each pub. Once she's delivered all three, she must get out of the East. As fast as she can.

56

Reuven

———•———

13 September

H E COULDN'T RESIST asking. For months, Reuven Frank knew
almost nothing about this mysterious cellar in West Berlin from
which twenty men had been digging for four months, but now, the day
before the escape, it is time.

Two days ago, back in New York, Reuven Frank had received a coded
message from Piers Anderton: he needed to come to West Berlin now.
Reuven had flown to Tegel airport in West Berlin, along with one of
his top film editors, only the fifth person in NBC to find out about the
tunnel. At the airport they were met by Piers Anderton and Gary Stindt.

'How long do we have to wait?' Reuven had asked, guessing it would
be at least a week.

'They go through tomorrow night,' said Piers; 'the tunnel's finished.'
Reuven Frank grinned. 'Can I see it?'

Now, sitting in Gary's car, weaving through West Berlin, the long,
grey cement-curtain looming over them, Reuven is shocked by how
much the Wall has grown since he was here a year ago. Gary parks the
car outside the factory, tells Reuven that the tunnel is just underneath.

It's too risky for Reuven to go inside, so he sits in the car, looking
at the factory, imagining the tunnel below, this tunnel that NBC money
has helped fund, a tunnel 4 metres deep, 120 metres long, pointing into
the heart of East Berlin. Four months of digging and it doesn't feel right
that everything now depends on the next twenty-four hours.

Looking at the factory and the buildings around it, Reuven gets a
strange feeling – this part of West Berlin feels familiar. This was the
place, it dawns on him, where he'd set up the NBC camera a year ago

when the Wall appeared and NBC was the first to tell the world. Now, a year later, he's back at that same spot to tell another story – the story of what people will do to escape.

That afternoon at the bureau, Reuven watches the footage that Peter and Klaus gathered over the past four months, developed in secret by a film processor in West Berlin. There's twenty hours of it. Some is footage from the early days, when they were filming the aftermath of other escapes. It's boring; little to see – just open manhole covers and sewers.

Then Gary shows him the scenes from the tunnel. Holding his breath, Reuven leans forward as he watches every frame, as he watches the tunnellers digging, cart-hauling, dirt-emptying, sweating, shaking, exhausted, and he knows this is unlike anything he's ever seen.

He watches it for a long time, into the early hours of Friday morning – the escape day – and as he sits there in the darkness, taking it all in, just a few streets away, Ellen lies in bed, eyes fixed on the wall, lips moving as she whispers the names of those streets she must remember, '*Schonholzer Strasse, Bernauer Strasse, Wolgaster Strasse, Brunnenstrasse, Ruppiner Strasse*', the sound of those street names disappearing into the night.

57

14 September

—◆—

Ellen

S HE WAKES WITH her ears ringing, pain throbbing. An ear infection from the flight, she guesses. Sun pours in from the window onto her bed and Ellen lies there, trying to work out what to wear, suddenly realising that the only clothes she's brought with her are glamorous dresses that would draw too much attention in East Berlin.

She looks through her friend's wardrobe for something plainer, finding a skirt and sleeveless tunic. They're too big for her, baggy on her delicate frame, but they'll do. Then she covers her flaming red hair in a cream headscarf. At the kitchen table she tries to eat breakfast, but can't get much down, just a few sips of tea. She barely slept last night, her stomach is churning, but she stills herself, goes over Mimmo's instructions once more.

On her bed, Ellen lays everything out. Passport. Notebook with street names and numbers. Tissues. Make-up. Sunglasses. Cigarettes. Lighter. Then money: both Deutsche Mark (West German currency) and Ostmark (East German.) The Ostmark is her Plan B; she'll need it if the escape goes wrong, so she can buy a train ticket to Warsaw.

Mid-morning she leaves her apartment and walks to Bahnhof Zoo train station, where she meets Peter and Klaus Dehmel. They're here to film Ellen's trip into East Berlin; they want to capture as much of the day as they can. In the footage you see Ellen standing below the train station in her headscarf and sunglasses, handbag draped off her arm. The streets around the station are busy: smartly dressed men and women rush past; groups of children play on the ground. Among them, Ellen stands out – despite her efforts to dress down, she still looks like a glamorous sixties movie star. You see her check her watch: it's midday. Then she turns and strides into the station, heads turning as she clicks past in her white high heels. Peter and Klaus follow with the camera.

The next shot is Ellen, sitting in an empty carriage, looking out of the window as the train zooms along the elevated railway to East Berlin, slicing between trees and buildings high above the city. At the last stop before the border, Peter and Klaus leave the train and take a final shot as it crosses the canal and disappears into the East.

Evi, Peter and Annet

Evi comes running into her grandfather's house, not far from her own home, Annet, her toddler, perched on her hip. Peter is working there; he's been doing odd-jobs for Evi's grandfather through the summer to make some money.

'You need to come home right now!' Evi commands. 'People from the newspaper are here.'

Peter turns around, confused, then catches her eye and understands. 'Won't be back today,' he tells Evi's grandfather as they leave the house. 'See you tomorrow.'

As they race home, Evi explains, telling Peter all about a person who came to their house that morning to tell them that the escape would happen today. They should leave now and go to a pub near Schönholzer Strasse and wait for Ellen's signal.

Evi's hands are shaking; she'd been nervous all week, ever since Mimmo and Gigi visited and said the escape would happen soon. Evi knew what had happened to the people arrested at the other tunnel, the one the Stasi busted. She'd heard how they were all now in Stasi prisons, babies snatched from mothers and dumped in children's homes. Evi still remembers the moment when she noticed the men on the streets in the long coats and hats; how they'd only just got away in time. If it all goes wrong, she knows she could lose her toddler, Annet. The thought of it makes her feel sick.

Yesterday, when she was out shopping, one of her neighbours had seen Evi, noticed how strange and on edge she'd looked. Her neighbour had gone home and told her husband, completely unaware he was a

Stasi spy, codenamed 'Walter'. Walter had noted this nugget of information, added it to a list of things to pass on to his Stasi handler.

Back at the house they get ready: Peter puts on thick underpants to keep him warm in prison if he's arrested, Evi bundles Annet into her best outfit, then dresses herself in her green dress-suit and burgundy heels. It's the only outfit she'll have with her if she makes it into West Berlin; she might as well make it a nice one. Then Evi stuffs nappies and money into her white handbag. Finally, she walks through the house, making sure the shutters and windows are open. She doesn't want anyone noticing anything unusual: they're a family out for the afternoon, nothing more.

Then, for the second time in a month, Peter and Evi leave the house with Annet, hoping never to see it again. As they walk away, Peter throws the key into a ditch and Evi turns back for a final glance: she sees two nappies hanging on the washing line, the mattress they would lie on together when the sun was out, and Annet's baby clothes soaking in a bowl. A snapshot of their old life frozen in time.

NBC

On the balcony of a building overlooking the Wall, an NBC cameraman, Harry Thoess, is setting up. Five stories high, on Wolgaster Strasse, he has a perfect vantage point. From the window, Harry can see over the Wall straight into Schönholzer Strasse. It's such a good position that the diggers ask if they can use it to give the final signal to Ellen: a white sheet draped out of the window. That'll mean they've broken through into the cellar, that they're ready for the escapees. Reuven Frank agrees, but reluctantly, for he is breaking his own rule: that NBC film but never help. Yes, he's funded the tunnel, but until now, no one from NBC has directly assisted the diggers. But somehow, he can't bring himself to say no.

Harry looks through the camera, zooms in over the death strip, over the triangular tank traps, over the Wall, towards the building with the tunnel underneath. It's tall, once grand, but the front is now covered in holes and cracks, shrapnel damage from the war. There's an arched doorway under which sits a small white ceramic plate decorated with a blue pattern and the number seven. A man on a bike cycles by, two women and a child walk slowly down the street, a gang of school-aged kids push babies in prams. Then you see the VoPos: one stands on a guard-tower smoking a cigarette, two are chatting to a group of boys, and a couple of VoPos stroll down Schönholzer Strasse, glancing into the doorway of number seven before moving on.

Evi, Peter and Annet

Walking out of the S-Bahn, Evi, Peter and Annet (and Peter's mother, who wants to escape with them) head to the pub. When they get there, panic: the place is rammed with workers, out spending their end-of-week pay, and here they are, a smartly dressed family, completely out of place. Weaving their way through the drinkers and the smoke, they make for a table in the corner, where they sit, shrinking back into the wall, hoping no one notices them.

The cellar in West Berlin

It's the biggest argument they've had. Everyone's shouting, they're angry and scared. Uli and some of the diggers had arrived for what they thought was just an ordinary digging shift, only to be told the escape would happen that evening. Then they'd seen Peter and Klaus standing there with their camera and lights. What on earth was happening? That's when Mimmo and Gigi finally told them about the American TV crew. Reeling, confused, some of the diggers threaten to leave. If an American TV network knows about the tunnel, who else does? We're out, they say, we've been lied to. Mimmo and Gigi try to reassure them – it's safe, you can trust them – but the argument goes on for almost an hour until Mimmo finally persuades the diggers to set their fears aside and do the job. They'll discuss it all after.

Peter and Klaus film the final preparations. Joachim crawls through the tunnel, checks the earth is holding firm, the electric lights all working. The tunnel is dark, muddy, but also, somehow, a thing of beauty; its lights gently illuminate the shaft, all the wires are neatly held back, the border sign still swings halfway down to mark the point where West becomes East. It's not just the longest tunnel dug under the Wall so far, but the most high-tech and lovingly constructed.

Now they have to decide who will crawl down the tunnel and break into the cellar. Hasso steps forward. 'I'll do it,' he says, and he looks at Joachim and Uli. But Uli says he can't go with Hasso, his mother has told him not to risk his life again – he can help, just not go into the East.

Everyone looks at Joachim. There's a pause. Unlike most of the diggers, Joachim has no one he's trying to rescue, no one he's risking his life for. He could walk away now, he's done so much already, and leave someone else to do it, someone who's rescuing their wife or brother, someone with skin in the game. No one would ask questions or berate him. But in that moment, none of that occurs to Joachim. Somehow, everything in his life has led to this moment – that first escape on the horse and cart where his father was taken, his smuggling trips to West Berlin, the hours experimenting with coils and wire and circuit boards, that newspaper article naming and shaming students in Dresden, his escape to West Berlin, all the months digging the tunnel, the escape that went wrong – and he finds himself nodding, saying, 'Yes, I'll do it.' And of course he will; he'll do it because he's done it once before, he'll do it because the sequence of decisions he's made has brought him to this point and this is simply the next step; he'll do it because he's learnt that life is a series of problems – you just have to find the solution.

Ellen

She sits on a bench in a playground. It's sparse, just a couple of swings and a slide. Holding a newspaper in front of her, the East Berlin tabloid B.Z., Ellen pretends to read, darting her eyes now and then to that fifth-floor window over the wall, willing the white sheet to appear.

She'd crossed the border faster than she'd expected, just half an hour, then taken a taxi to a street near Schönholzer Strasse. It felt strange to be here, in East Berlin, for the first time. She'd never seen anywhere so bleak: derelict buildings, run-down shops and hardly anyone around. She watches two elderly women cross the road leaning on walking sticks, she glances up at some kids at a window, who peer blankly down at her, and then, for the first time that day, she remembers it's her birthday. She thinks of her mother, remembering a prayer she used to whisper over her when she was a little girl, and Ellen murmurs it softly now, the swing next to her creaking in the breeze.

Evi, Peter and Annet

An hour later, Ellen still hasn't arrived at the pub. Nursing their drinks, Evi and Peter look down, desperate not to attract attention. It's likely there are Stasi informants here at the pub and they know there are VoPos just outside. The door opens and Evi feels a pulse of adrenaline, as she has every time someone walks in, but it's not Ellen. It's a woman in a Dior dress and heels, with a man and a child. They must be escapees too. It makes Evi more nervous; they all look conspicuous and out of place.

The afternoon darkens, a cool September night setting in. Evi watches the steady stream of men arriving at the pub, then, with a shudder, notices a strange warmth spreading on her thighs and realises that Annet's nappy is so full it's leaking onto her dress. If anyone sees the wet patch, they'll know something's up, so she presses Annet closer to hide the stain and eyes the door.

Watching. Waiting.

The tunnel

Hasso and Joachim (and another digger – Joachim Neumann) grab their duffel bags, heavy with drills, screwdrivers, hammers and guns. Ducking down into the tunnel, they start crawling. The wet clay squelches under the weight of their hands and knees as they scrabble under Bernauer Strasse, the death strip and the Wall, the sounds from the street receding as they crawl further into the East. At the end of the tunnel, they unfold, standing tall in the shaft they've dug out over the past few days, looking up at the ceiling that slopes into the cellar. Banging on it with hammers, the sounds returns to them, hard and flat. Brick, they guess.

Hasso climbs on top of Joachim's shoulders and drills into the ceiling, pink pieces of brick flaking down until a tiny hole appears and they hear a whistle of wind. Heartened, Hasso drills harder, shattering the brick, widening the hole, realising too late that the whistle wasn't wind, but water, which is now spurting onto his face. Joachim and Hasso recoil, remembering the stories – how the Stasi flood the cellars of basements along the border to stop escapes – and they know that if the water carries on like this, they could drown. But it calms to a dribble and Hasso steadies his hand, tightening his grip on the drill as he smashes the brick. Eventually, the hole is big enough to climb through, and they squeeze into the cellar.

It's large. Dark. There's an unidentifiable smell and in front of them, a door. Standing there, they size it up, but they know they don't have much time, the water in the tunnel is rising, and so Hasso runs forward, throwing the full weight of his body against the door, and it bursts open.

Then: another door. Stronger locks. Joachim pulls out two sets of skeleton keys – borrowed from a friend – and he kneels, trying each key until he finds one that fits the lock and turns. So far, so good. Just one final thing to do before they can give Ellen the signal: check the building number. They must be sure they've broken into the right apartment. One misread of the theodolite and they could be under number eight or six, then when the escapees arrive at number seven, the operation would unravel.

Rustling in his duffel bag, Joachim pulls out a blue coat and throws it on, hoping he looks like a workman. That will be his story if the VoPos catch him. If they don't believe him, there's the gun in his pocket.

At the door he pauses, listening through the keyhole, for it's now late afternoon. People are returning from work and he must wait until the hallway is clear.

Eventually, silence.

Joachim opens the door, slips out into the apartment and checks the hall for the *Stiller Träger* – the 'Silent Porter' – the board listing the names of the people living there, and, he hopes, the address. He finds the board, sees the names, but no building number. Only one thing for it. Joachim creeps towards the door, the door that opens onto a street full of VoPos. For a brief moment, he hesitates. Of everything he's done so far, this is the most dangerous. He has no idea what is waiting behind this door. For all he knows, a VoPo could be standing there, but he can't let himself think about that, he needs to carry on. Just another problem to solve.

He pushes the door. There's a sudden rush of street noise. Kids playing. Two women pushing prams. Then, the VoPos. They're distracted, talking to people in their hut, and so Joachim snatches his chance, runs across the street, looks back at the apartment, and there it is: a big number seven above the door. He almost laughs with relief.

Back in the tunnel, he picks up one end of the telephone and rings back to the cellar, telling the other diggers they're in the right place. And so the messages bounces from phone, to walkie-talkie, to phone, eventually reaching Harry Thoess, the NBC cameraman in the building high above the Wall, who reaches for the white sheet, and flings it out of the window, hoping that Ellen is somewhere below and that she'll see it and remember what it means.

Ellen

She sees it. A flash of white tumbling out of the window, the outline of a figure behind it. The sheet kick-starts Ellen's memory and the map flashes up in her mind, her fear lifting, replaced by the strong sense that she knows exactly what to do. Walk straight ahead. Turn right. Cross the road. Right again. Following the lines in her head, Ellen steers herself through the streets effortlessly, confident at each turning that she's remembered it right.

Fifteen minutes later, Ellen is at the first pub. She swallows. Dry tongue, heart pounding, she pushes the door open. A wave of noise hits her. She's never been into a pub, let alone one like this, and she feels the eyes of a hundred men as she walks between them, scanning the room for the escapees. She wonders how she'll spot them, but then, to the right of the bar, she sees them: children, two couples, eyes fixed on her, and she knows she's in the right place.

Matches, she remembers, that's the signal in pub number one, and she strides up to the counter and in a loud voice asks for some from the barman. He frowns, puzzled by someone in a pub not asking for a drink, but he turns to get some and Ellen risks another glance at the families behind her. She sees Peter and Evi, notices the stain on Evi's skirt. To her relief they're watching, eyes fixed, breath held. The barman returns with her matches, she pays him, slowly, purposefully, wishes him a good evening and leaves.

All Ellen can do now is hope they've seen the signal, and she walks back to her bench at the playground to check the sheet is still there. It is. She lights a cigarette, and perhaps it's the nicotine buzzing through her blood, or perhaps it's the high from having given the first signal, but she finds herself standing up and walking towards Schönholzer Strasse.

She's curious to see what the street looks like. Closing her eyes for a second, she pulls up the image of the map and follows the lines again, this time heading towards the Wall, then turning left into the street with the tunnel underneath.

There she sees it: number seven. Ellen has now gone completely off script, deviating from the instructions given to her by Mimmo, and as the adrenaline from today's mission flows through her, she forgets to be afraid, forgets about the VoPos, and all she can think about is wanting to see inside the building. Like a blinkered horse, Ellen strides down the street towards the apartment, oblivious to what's either side of her. The women with their prams. The children playing. The VoPos.

On the other side of the Wall, Harry Thoess, the NBC cameraman is watching Ellen through his lens, baffled and terrified she's about to get caught, and he radios to Mimmo in the tunnel and tells him that Ellen is standing in front of the door. Mimmo is shocked, can't understand what she's doing, but all he can do is listen, helplessly, as Harry tells him, in a terrified whisper, that he's just seen Ellen push the door open and disappear inside.

The cellar in East Berlin

Joachim, Hasso and some of the other diggers are hovering by the cellar door, listening to the sounds in the hall. It's six in the evening and the escape is meant to have started. Each time the door to the building opens, their stomachs lurch, hoping it's people on their list, but they can tell from the whistling, the loud footsteps, that it's just residents returning home. They can't understand what's happening. *Why aren't people here yet? Has Ellen passed on the signals? Have the escapees got lost?* Joachim and Hasso pull out their guns, fingers on triggers as they stand there. Listening.

Ellen

She's in the hallway. Excited. Curious. She sees the cellar door, tiptoes past, and sneaks upstairs. First floor. Second floor. Third floor. It's only when Ellen reaches the fourth floor that she stops, realises what she's doing, this insane risk that she's taking, and she darts downstairs, hurries through the hall and crashes out onto the street.

Idiot! She thinks. *What was I thinking?* Head down, Ellen walks past the VoPos, brings up her mental map and scurries towards the second pub.

There, Ellen orders a glass of water: the second secret signal. She drinks it and as she leaves, she sees them: a group of people sitting in a corner, hands gripping the table, looking stiff and pale.

Now, just one final pub. One final signal.

The last pub is more crowded than all the others; after all, it's now 6.30 and Friday night is in full swing. Ellen sits at a table, motions for a waiter and asks for coffee. He shakes his head, 'We don't have any', and her brain freezes. Ellen hadn't discussed this with Mimmo – what to do if the pub didn't have what she wanted – and suddenly the room feels very loud and the pain in her ears returns, the blood pumping loudly through them as she tries to think.

Think!

'Coffee!' she says to the barman again, very loudly, almost shouting, hoping the escapees in the pub will hear and get the message. 'Really, you don't have any coffee? Any at all?'

The waiter shakes his head again; her mind rattles and Ellen comes up with another idea.

'If you don't have coffee,' she says, 'then bring me a cognac.' At least they both begin with the same sound, she thinks. The barman leaves, returns with the cognac and she downs it, the first time she's tried it, the taste of vinegar lingering in her mouth. After a cigarette, Ellen walks to the toilet, takes out her notebook and shreds the paper with the addresses on, flushing them away. She's beginning to panic now, the nicotine and alcohol giving her the shakes, and she knows this is the moment she needs to leave, race to the checkpoint before the escape begins, because if anything goes wrong, they'll close the border. Ellen runs out of the pub, waves down a taxi and asks for Friedrichstrasse station.

Sitting in the taxi, she looks out of the window at the Trabis on the road – the tiny pastel cars that fill East Berlin's streets; she watches women on bikes weaving in and out of puddles, gangs of kids whooping and playing; and as she loses herself in it all, she forgets about the big wodge of money in her bag, the money she was meant to get rid of before arriving at the checkpoint, for if anyone finds it, they'll know she's up to something and so it will unravel.

Evi, Peter and Annet

They turn onto Schönholzer Strasse and see it: number seven. Just the VoPos to get past now. Squeezing Annet's hand, Peter, Evi and Peter's mother walk down the street, trying to look relaxed, keeping their eyes down – away from the men in uniforms, their Kalashnikovs tight against their chests. Finally, they arrive at the door. Peter pushes it open and they walk inside.

The cellar in East Berlin

Joachim can tell straight away, these footsteps are different. Tentative. No whistling or chatting. He hears whispering. A scuffle. The door handle wobbles and Joachim reaches forward, unlocks the door and pushes it open, sees them all standing there.

Relief flows through him as Peter gives the code: 'You busy handymen!' And they all fall into the cellar, Gigi pulling his friend Peter in to a bear hug. It's happening, but there's no time to be relieved or excited, as they know that at any time the VoPos could get suspicious about all the people wandering into the apartment. They have to move fast. It's dark, just one lamp by the entrance to the tunnel but there's no time for Evi's eyes to adjust.

Evi crouches, holding Annet in her arms. A digger motions for her to give Annet to him; she'll be too heavy for Evi to carry through the tunnel. Evi hesitates. Suddenly the weight of what they're about to do crashes down on her; images of Annet in the arms of a VoPo flash through her mind, and for a moment none of this feels worth that unthinkable risk.

But Evi's body moves and she finds herself handing Annet over and begins crawling. The tunnel is smaller than she'd imagined; her shoulders bash against the sides as she clambers through in the dark, and she gasps as the skin on her knees shreds against the gritty floor. She crawls for minute after minute, willing the tunnel to end, but it keeps going on and on. She breathes fast. 'Stay calm,' she hears from the digger behind, the one holding Annet, 'nothing's going to happen; keep going.'

Joachim watches them go, listens to the sound of their feet scudding against the clay. He can't follow. His job is to stay here, in the East, until everyone crawls through. As Evi and Annet disappear, all he remembers thinking is, how strange – the baby didn't cry once.

At the other end, in West Berlin, Peter and Klaus Dehmel are standing at the top of the shaft that leads down into the tunnel, camera pointing at the hole. It's dark. Nothing moves. Then—

A white handbag appears. Then a hand. An arm. Then a woman in a dark dress crawls out of the tunnel. Covered in mud, Evi's feet are bare; she's lost her shoes somewhere in the tunnel. It's taken her twelve minutes to crawl through the dirt and water. She looks up towards the camera, shrinking from the light, then starts climbing the ladder, dress laden with water, hands shaking with exhaustion. She's almost at the top when she hears a loud ringing and she wonders if something's happened in the tunnel, if it's a warning, an alarm, but just as she realises it's coming from her ears, she faints, Klaus, the NBC lighting guy running forward to catch her. He lowers Evi onto a bench and she sits there, eyes fixed on the tunnel as Mimmo appears, holding Annet. Evi bundles her child into her arms, rocking her back and forth, nuzzling the nape of her neck.

Ellen

Opening her purse to pay the driver, the glass walls of Friedrichstrasse station looming over the taxi, Ellen sees the wodge of money and her stomach falls. So much of it, and she knows she has to get rid of it before she goes into the station in case border guards search her. She gives the driver his fare, then thrusts a bundle of notes into his hand. He's speechless, his mouth open but silent as Ellen leaves the car and runs to the station. Too much still, she has too much money, and she scans the ground, eyes lighting on a drain. She kneels down, wraps the money in a handkerchief and stuffs it in.

Walking up the stairs to the station, Ellen calms herself – *there is nothing suspicious on me; you've done everything you need to do* – and she joins the queue of people, waiting to cross to the platform where trains will take them to West Berlin. As Ellen stands there, thinking back to that taxi driver, her breath catches as she realises what a stupid mistake it was to give him all that money. *What if he's working for the Stasi? And he tells someone all about a strange woman giving him money at the border?* But there's little time to dwell on it as a policewoman has stopped in front of her.

'*Folgen Sie mir,*' she says. 'Follow me.'

The cellar in West Berlin

The cellar of the factory is crammed. People sit, huddled together, catching their breath after the long, wet crawl, warming their sodden knees in front of electric heaters. Some are already leaving the cellar, Wolf Schroedter walking them out of the factory and into his VW van, driving them to friend's houses where they can spend their first night in West Berlin – before registering at Marienfelde Refugee Camp.

Since Evi, Peter and Annet crawled through, there's been a steady stream of escapees, including Hasso's sister, Anita, who'd arrived in a short black Dior dress and white high heels, clambering through the tunnel with her husband and toddler. Up in the cellar, Anita sits next to Evi on a bench, the camera filming the mothers as they wash their muddy legs in a bucket, then gently clean their toddlers with rags, changing them into clean white cloth nappies. Anita's toddler's clothes are so wet that she dresses her in one of Joachim's jumpers, her daughter's legs sticking through the arm sleeves.

Peter and Klaus film everyone who crawls through: eight-year-olds, eighteen-year-olds, eighty-year-olds. Each is wetter than the last; the water is now halfway up the tunnel.

On the other side, in East Berlin, Joachim waits by the door. He can't leave till everyone is here and he's jumpy. They've been lucky to get this far, to get so many people through, and each hour he waits, the greater the chance of being discovered. Buggies are now piling up conspicuously in the apartment outside the cellar – one of those problems no one foresaw. Outside, on Schönholzer Strasse, with darkness setting in, the VoPos have turned on their searchlights, the street now washed in pools of white.

Around eight, Joachim hears a noise at the door, sees the handle slip down, and there in the doorway is a giant of a man in a long dark leather coat and hat. One hand in his pocket.

Stasi. That's Joachim's first thought, and as he panics, trying to work out what to do, behind him, Hasso pulls his gun out of his pocket. 'Hands up, now!' he says, voice trembling.

Though the man obeys, lifting his hands from his pockets, Hasso's finger feels for the trigger and pulls.

Ellen

Ellen sits uncomfortably in a small room at the train station. The room is bare, just a few chairs and a square table at which the policewoman is standing, rummaging through her bag. The policewoman empties everything out and runs her fingers along the lining. Ellen watches, mind racing: *Have the Stasi discovered the tunnel? Did someone notice me in the pub? Did the taxi driver tell someone about the money?*

The policewoman looks at her. 'What were you doing in East Berlin?'

'A friend, I was here to see an old school friend.'

Policewoman's face is blank.

'Undress. Put your clothes on the table.'

Ellen removes her headscarf, her blouse and skirt, nylons, pants and bra. Policewoman searches. Everywhere. Nothing like this has ever happened to Ellen before and she feels sick. Humiliated.

'Okay,' says the policewoman eventually, having found nothing. 'You can go.'

Ellen dresses, leaves the room and walks to passport control, feeling as though she's holding something combustible inside that could erupt at any moment. At the platform there's a train waiting and she runs onto it. She sits down. A rigid statue. The train shudders into motion, and Ellen hears the announcement, the most comforting sequence of words she's heard in a long time: 'You are now leaving East Berlin.'

Yet as the train moves, Ellen barely breathes: instead, she contains all the emotions from that day – her fear of getting the signals wrong, or getting lost or caught, her regret about going into the building, panic over the lack of coffee, the money in her bag, the humiliating strip-search – and it's only once the train reaches Lehrter Bahnhof, the first stop in West Berlin, that her body crumples and she looks down at her knees, now shaking uncontrollably, wondering how she, Ellen Schau, just a twenty-one-year-old from Düsseldorf, no experience of anything like this, how she held it together this long.

The cellar in East Berlin

Instead of a bang there's a metallic click and Hasso's gasp of surprise as he realises he didn't pull the trigger but the safety catch. That's when he sees them: the woman and boy standing behind the man in the coat. The man isn't a Stasi agent; it's just a young couple with their son.

Hasso and Joachim pull them into the cellar; they're all laughing nervously with relief. If Hasso's gun had fired, the VoPos outside would have heard, run in, everything unravelled. It's a narrow escape that puts everyone on edge. But the next families come to the cellar and crawl through. No drama.

Claus the butcher is now the only digger left waiting for someone, his wife Inge, the pregnant woman thrown in a communist prison after she was caught escaping. Claus hasn't seen Inge since then, and because of the diggers' suspicions about him he'd only found out about the escape at the last minute. He'd asked someone to smuggle a message to Inge that day, desperately hoping she'd find out in time and come.

As Joachim and Hasso wait by the door for the final people on the list, something happens that no one predicted: the caretaker of the building locks the main door to the street. Until now, the escapees could open the door to the building themselves. Now they can't get in.

Automatically, Joachim reaches for his blue workman's coat, barely thinks about it. Creeping into the dark hall, he kneels at the door, fiddling with his skeleton keys. His chest is constricting, but his mind is calm. He's done it before; he can do it again. He finds the right key, unlocks the door, creeps back into the cellar. The next group of people come through, but ten minutes later, another resident comes home for the night and locks the door again. Out goes Joachim to unlock it. He goes out again and again, unlocking this door that leads to a street patrolled by VoPos until around eleven in the evening when a woman appears with two children. He lets them in, knowing they'll be the last.

In the cellar in West Berlin, the camera is still focused on the tunnel. Claus is standing there, losing hope that Inge will come. Then he hears a noise. A hand emerges from the tunnel, then a woman. It's dark, everyone is covered in mud, and the woman barely glances at Claus as she squeezes past. She climbs the ladder, looking confused, tired. Then Claus hears another noise coming from the tunnel. A digger appears, something white in his arms, and Claus's heart jumps as he realises it's a baby – tiny, just four months old – and at that moment Claus knows, somehow, that the child is his. He bends down and gently takes the bundle, delivering the baby from the tunnel.

It's a boy. His son. It's the first time he's seen him, the first time he's touched him, held him, and as Claus cradles his child, Inge looks back, sees this mud-covered man holding her baby, looks down, and later she'll say that it was by his bare feet that she knew him – her husband. Claus and Inge go towards each other, out of the eye of the camera.

Joachim

Joachim stands in the cellar in East Berlin alone. He's stayed there, at the most dangerous place, till the very end, shepherding everyone through, risking his life as he creeped out into the apartment, again and again to unlock the door. Counting them, he realises twenty-nine people have crawled through the tunnel. With the water up to his knees, he knows that's it. Time to go.

As he looks at the tunnel, the sides beginning to fall in, Joachim's mind races, snapshot-memories of the last four months appearing in his head like frames on a film-reel. The leaks. The electric shocks. The mud, so much mud. The blisters. The Stasi soldier under the window. The people who came tonight. Knowing they're all safe in West Berlin, he feels the most intense happiness he's ever experienced. More exquisite than his own escape.

Then, for a reason he can't explain, he thinks of his father, the last time he saw him, when he was just six, sitting on his lap, looking up at his face before soldiers took him away. Joachim holds on to the memory, the feeling of being held, the fearless problem-solver suddenly a child. Perhaps if you lose someone in an escape that goes wrong, the only thing that can heal you is an escape that goes right. Or perhaps he feels what every child craves: the pride of a parent.

There's a final piece of footage from that night. Klaus and Peter are filming the escapees gathering their things. The camera tracks each one in their mud-stained, ripped clothes as they walk towards the door, the door that leads to West Berlin, the other half of their city that somehow became a different country. As the last person walks through it, they look back and the door closes softly behind them.

58

Walter and Wilhelm

———◦———

T HREE DAYS AFTER the escape, on 17 September, Stasi Second
Lieutenant Horn receives a phone call from one of his informants,
a man he calls 'Walter'. Walter wants to meet; says he has something
important to tell him. They meet and Horn is glad Walter called: it
seems Walter's neighbours have committed one of the most serious crimes
of East Germany – they have escaped. Following the meeting, Horn
writes a report:

> 17th Sept, 1962
> Main division II/5
> - Operative group -
> BStU
> [Federal Commissioner for the Records of the State Security
> Service of the former German Democratic Republic]
> 0228
> Berlin, 17.09.1962
> Meeting with Contact Person (CP) 'Walter'
> Employee: Second lieutenant Horn
> Meeting Report
>
> 'Walter' called today and asked to meet because he had some
> important news. As a result, a meeting was held with him in which he
> reported the following:
>   On Saturday 15 September, when he came to his weekend property
> in Wilhelmshagen with his family, he learnt from his wife that young
> Evi Schmidt seemed very strange to her when shopping on Thursday
> and the young couple have not been seen since Thursday 13
> September. It is curious because everything looks as if they are not

gone . . . two nappies are still hanging on the washing line and the mattress is still laying where they always sunbathe in the garden. Likewise, the windows are not closed and nor are the window shutters, which they usually closed when they were not at home.

'Walter' then saw the same thing and it also seemed strange to him because they always left their property differently if they were away for a few days. They were not seen for the entire weekend and Peter Schmidt's other neighbour named [---] expressed their concerns to 'Walter' as to whether the Schmidt family could be deserters from the republic, particularly as Eveline Schmidt's grandfather came to the property multiple times on Saturday and Sunday without knowing that they were not there or where they could be.

Measures:
Make contact with Secret Informant 'Wilhelm' and get further details from him. If it is established by these measures that they are not back yet and there are no known reasons for them being gone, contact will be made with the section commissioner (ABV).

Signed, Second lieutenant Horn

* * *

20th Sept 1962
Main division II/5
- Operative group -
BStU
[Federal Commissioner for the Records of the State Security Service of the former German Democratic Republic]
0232
Berlin-Wilhelmshagen, 20.09.62

Transcript from meeting with 'Wilhelm'

On Thursday to Friday 13th–14th, I noticed that my neighbour had vacated his home. Peter Schmidt's mother has also not been seen since then. On the day after the disappearance, the grandfather, who is named Sperling and resides in Neu-Venedig, came and wanted to gain entrance but he was not able to get in. He came back to check several times.

The disappearance must have been very sudden as I saw Annet running excitedly through the woods in the morning the day before. A car with the registration number B – DA 466 came by with two men days before the disappearance. They took pictures of the whole family . . . and handed over a bag with contents . . . I do not know what was in the bag. I have not seen the men again since then.

Peter Schmidt himself left by bicycle every morning at around 8.30 hrs. He returned home in the evening between 4.30 and 5 hrs. He was supposedly working. I heard someone shouting 'Evelin' near the fence on the morning after the disappearance, which is Mrs Schmidt's first name. I could not see anyone when I came out.

Peter Schmidt's chimney was smoking fiercely on the day before the disappearance. I said to my wife: 'They are filling the whole area with smoke.' They were presumably burning something unpleasant. The disappearance must have been very sudden because there are still nappies hanging on the washing line. Furthermore, he put up a new fence and spread weed killer. I suspect that he suddenly received a message and then disappeared.

Signed 'Wilhelm'

59

The Search

A FTER THE STASI Section Commissioner reads those reports from
Walter and Wilhelm, he sends a small team to Evi and Peter's
house. Inside, everything looks as it should: the furniture is there, as are
clothes, toiletries and food, and the windows are open. It looks as though
the family are out on a day-trip, yet they know from their informants
that Evi and Peter haven't been here for three days.

Then one of the officers notices that some things are missing: there's
no handbag, no ID cards. They conclude that Peter, Evi and Annet must
have 'left democratic Berlin illegally'. Then they seal off the house.

Now they are certain that the Schmidt family has escaped, committing the serious crime of *Republikflucht*; it's time to find someone to
blame. It's the usual Stasi response: when someone escapes, find a relative or friend who knew about the escape plan and punish them.

At first they struggle to find anyone connected to Peter and Evi. The
Stasi discover that Evi's mother is dead, that her father lives in West
Germany. No siblings. Then – a lead. They hear that her grandparents
live nearby. And that's when they call Evi's grandfather, Rudolph Sperling,
and tell him to come to the police station. They will interrogate him,
and once he's admitted to being part of it, they can arrest him.

60

Film-reel

REUVEN FRANK KNEELS on the floor, covering a piece of cardboard in white paint. It'll work well enough – a makeshift projector screen for the footage. He's been awake most of the night, desperate to see it. While Evi, Peter, Annet and the others were crawling through the tunnel, Reuven was waiting at the NBC bureau. Told it would all be over by nine in the evening, he'd sat there, hour after hour, hoping Peter and Klaus would arrive and tell him everyone was safe.

Around ten, Reuven had ordered an expensive meal. It sat in front of him, uneaten. Just before midnight he couldn't wait any longer and he'd asked Gary Stindt to drive him past the factory. It was a risk, but they were careful, not stopping the car or slowing down as they drove by. Peering out of the window, Reuven could see the street was quiet, no police cars, no searchlights from the East, nothing to indicate the escape was blown. Back at the bureau he'd sat there again, startling at every noise, looking up to see if the Dehmel brothers were here.

Eventually, at two in the morning, Peter and Klaus arrived. Their faces said it all: it had happened. No shootings. No arrests. They'd left the film at a friend's lab, told the technician to develop it quickly, ask no questions. And now, at noon the day after the escape, they're about to watch it.

Peter inserts the film into the projector. It whirrs into life, and Reuven watches as a shot of the tunnel appears on the cardboard. Then a shot of the ladder leaning against the shaft. Reuven's eyes widen as he sees a hand appear in the tunnel. The hand pauses, draws back, then a head emerges and a whole person crawls out and stands in the shaft. Evi. The footage is silent, and in that silence, Reuven barely breathes. He's mesmerised, eyes glistening as he watches person after person crawl into West Berlin. For he knows what it's taken to get this far; he's watched hours of footage of digging; he's seen, on film, their tired faces, the sweat dripping down their arms; he's seen glimpses of the escape that went wrong; and he knows that no one has ever made a film like this, where cameras have been there all the way through, a film that shows the terrifying, exhausting reality of pulling off such an escape. Reality TV they might call it.

Reuven sits, motionless, as he watches people crawl through – women in high heels, young men in smart suits, frail grandparents – all the way till he sees Claus holding his son for the first time, and his heart swells. There's a final shot of the basement, then a click as the films runs out and the cardboard becomes lifeless once more.

He takes a moment to think, then Reuven the TV producer comes to life, his brain spilling out ideas about how to edit the film. He begins working on it that day with his editor, carries on into the next and the day after that. Editing the film is unlike anything he's ever done. There's no sound, no interviews, just action. He sorts through it chronologically, deciding which character to focus on, which diggers and escapees to make the most of. He wants it to be exciting, gripping, but also to show the hourly, daily, weekly monotonous grind of pushing spade into earth, the relentlessness of it all. As well as the film from the tunnel, he has home-movies, shot by Mimmo during his visits to Peter and Evi's house in East Berlin, as well as stilted footage from the early stages of the escape. Because they only started filming one month after the digging began, Peter and Klaus had asked Mimmo, Gigi and Wolf to re-enact some of the early scenes: their search for the tunnel site, their meetings over maps. In their sunglasses and hats, cigarettes held loosely between their fingers, they'd wandered around the border, peering into bushes, looking unconvincing as they re-created those early days.

Reuven also has footage from over the Wall of life in East Berlin – long queues outside shops, desolate streets. They work long into each night. Reuven wants to finish editing the film in Berlin, wants to keep NBC's involvement in the tunnel secret until he's ready to explain it to the world. He knows it's controversial.

A week into the edit, as he reaches the footage from the escape, Reuven realises the film is missing something – an ending. He doesn't want the escape to be the last scene; he knows his audience will want a final chapter. And so, like a twenty-first-century TV producer who blurs the line between filming and contriving, he decides to throw a party. NBC will provide food and whiskey, and in return, all the characters in this film – the diggers, the escapees, the messengers – will agree to be filmed.

One last time.

61

The Bug

THE STASI AGENT presses his headphones closer to his ears, moves the dial on his radio to get a better signal, hovering over 162.5 MHz. There. He can hear perfectly. Two people are talking. West Berliners. He doesn't know their names, but that's okay, he can just use letters. He begins typing:

> **A:** Have you heard that at 5 p.m. a press conference will take place with Bahr?
> **B:** Who is Bahr?
> **A:** Bahr is the spokesperson of the Senate. Apparently at the weekend, twenty-five East Berliners came to West Berlin via a tunnel.
> **B:** No I haven't heard.
> **A:** So X told me there was a news report by Associated Press – what can I do to find out more about it?
> **B:** Call the press office of the Senate. The number is in the telephone directory and then ask for Mr X . . .

The Stasi agent sits back. This is big. A tunnel. Around twenty-five East Berliners escaped through it. He must tell his senior officer right away. But by the time he tells him, the secret is out and the Stasi are among the last to know.

62

The Pushchair

———•———

S IEGFRIED HEARS ABOUT the escape four days after it happens: on
18 September. *Twenty-nine people into West Berlin.* He was right inside
the escape network, yet he'd failed to stop it.

There's no indication in the Stasi files as to what Siegfried feels, no
recorded meeting with his handler to discuss it. His only mention around
that time is his certificate – his Silver Medal. Erich Mielke, head of the
Stasi, signed it himself – on 15 *September.* As Mielke sat there, uniform
on, pen in hand, honouring one of his most productive spies, twenty-nine
escapees were celebrating their first day in West Berlin.

You can sense the Stasi's disappointment about the operation, their
humiliation. In their first report, they note that 'the flight from the
GDR of the twenty-nine through the tunnel supposedly has really taken
place'. In a second humiliation, they only hear about the tunnel from
an announcement in West Berlin's Senate. The West Berlin press had
been ordered to stay silent about the tunnel until they were sure there'd
be no risk to the diggers. It was only on 18 September, four days after
the escape, that the press chief in West Berlin's Senate gave the go-ahead.
The story splashed onto the front pages of newspapers in West Berlin,
in capitals across Europe, then into America, in the *New York Times:*

TWENTY-NINE EAST BERLINERS FLEE
THROUGH 400-FOOT TUNNEL

The journalists are well briefed, the articles include details about the
leak, the help of the authorities in West Berlin and the distance: at 120
metres, it's the longest tunnel dug under the Wall so far.

Humiliated about the largest single escape since building the Wall,
the Stasi scramble to take control of the story. They start with the tunnel.

Desperate to find it, they comb the streets near the border. For two days, nothing. Then, at eight in the evening, on 20 September, a VoPo takes a look inside number seven Schönholzer Strasse and notices a tattered pushchair in the cellar. He moves it and discovers what it was concealing: a small passage, and there, in all its washed-out, muddy glory, is the tunnel.

Within hours the cellar is crawling with Stasi officers. They measure the tunnel — width, depth — then try to crawl in, but it's full of water. Undeterred, they dig another tunnel to access it further back, but it collapses. They dig another. It collapses too. They send a guard regiment platoon with six pressure hoses to suck the water out, but they don't get much. In a final desperate and expensive attempt, they begin backfilling the tunnel with pumped concrete, until they discover that the walls of the tunnel — all the way back to the border — have fallen in.

Determined to do something, anything, they draw a map of the tunnel route, mostly using guesswork. In a neat hand, a Stasi officer draws a map of the surrounding area along with street names, house numbers, the presumed route; then — with exquisite and unnecessary detail — he adds the details of locations, silt areas, even cracks on the pavement.

There are practical reasons for wanting to know all this — the Stasi learn about the expertise of the tunnel diggers, the methods they used — but it's also the knee-jerk reaction of an organisation that is dedicated to chronicling everything: the emotions of its prison inmates, the lives of its citizens, the facial characteristics of escapees, and now this — the physical detritus of an escape it failed to stop.

Once they've done as much as they can at the tunnel, they turn to the next stage of the investigation. They want to know who they've lost, the names of every single person who crawled through the tunnel. Because there is always someone they've left behind. Someone to punish.

63

The Party

———◆———

A T A RESTAURANT in West Berlin, Joachim sits at an oval white-clothed table wearing a suit and tie, chatting conspiratorially to the people around him: tunnellers, refugees and the NBC camera-crew. It looks like a wedding party; the tables are crammed with wine bottles, half-eaten food, and the air hazes with smoke.

As the camera pans the room, you see Anita laughing as she picks at her brother Hasso's beard, you see Piers Anderton draining his tumbler; everyone is locked into conversation – Claus and his wife Inge, Mimmo and Ellen, all of them with sparkling eyes, cigarettes wedged between fingers. The women have bought or borrowed glamorous dresses, they've bee-hived their hair, and the men wear dark suits and ties. This time, Peter and Klaus have brought a microphone, and you hear everyone talking and laughing while a jazz brass band plays in the background. Evi sits in the corner wearing a black dress with white spots and a pearl necklace, her hair up, looking distractingly beautiful.

But amid the laughter, when you look closer, every now and then you see their faces flicker from joy to something else. There's sadness: some of the diggers had hoped that they could get additional friends or family members out through the tunnel the following day, but it flooded. Claus had even returned to the tunnel with scuba-diving gear, but eventually they'd had to let the tunnel go. There's anger too, about the NBC film, and there are rumours that some of the diggers have ended up with a lot of money. And there's fear. Like refugees the world over, having dreamt about West Berlin for so long, they're experi-encing the crash, where the promised land doesn't match the dream. In East Berlin, though they felt trapped, were terrified of being drafted into the army, there was free healthcare and education, cheap food and rent. They've all spent the last few days exploring West Berlin, discovering that food and clothes are expensive, and finding jobs won't be easy. Apart from the clothes they're wearing, they have nothing. But tonight, they put all that aside. They drink, dance and laugh about making it into the newspapers.

At his table, Joachim puts down his drink and looks around the room at everyone, all these people he helped rescue. He'd gone back to the tunnel a few days ago to collect some tools and say goodbye before the water took it. It was a strange feeling. For the past four months, he had spent most of his waking hours there – the digging shifts had shaped his days, the escape the goal to which everything in his life had been directed – and now he was watching the tunnel disintegrate. Crawling down it one last time, past his stove pipes, electric cables, telephone, his eyes had caught on something: a pair of shoes. Tiny, just the size of his hand, they were wet, covered in mud. He'd picked them up, taken them home. Sitting there now, at the party, he remembers those shoes, makes a mental note to find out which child they belong to.

Towards the end of the night, Peter stands up; everyone wants him to sing a song accompanied by his guitar. With the confidence of someone who's drunk too much whiskey, he stumbles to the front of the room, grinning. Thanking Mimmo and Gigi for rescuing him and his family, he begins an Italian song, an old Neapolitan ballad, romantic, over-the-top; some of the people in the room recognise it from versions sung by Frank Sinatra, Elvis Presley and Pavarotti, and Peter seems to summon them all as he sings, face contorting emotion, eyes beseeching his audience, wallowing in the attention.

Watching Peter sing, Reuven knows he has it now: his ending. Just one final scene to record: a piece to camera from his correspondent, Piers Anderton. Standing outside the restaurant in a long, beige trench coat, looking into the lens, Piers takes a deep breath and begins. He talks about the Wall, the people who escaped East Berlin over the last year, the people who died trying. He ends with this:

'Twenty-one [men] gave half a year of their lives to dig this tunnel. But there will be other young men. And other tunnels.'

64

The Canoe

———•◆•———

To know about a planned escape and not to tell the authorities is a crime, punishable with time in prison. So as Evi's grandfather, Rudolf Sperling, sits in Köpenick police station, he knows that whatever he says during this interrogation will either mean he's free to go home, or he'll be arrested. He needs to choose his words carefully.

Rudolf's interrogator starts by saying that Evi has committed the crime of *Republikflucht* – escaping from East Germany. If Rudolf knew about it and didn't tell anyone, his interrogator says, he could go to prison. If Rudolf lies about anything, he could go to prison. Then the questions begin.

His interrogator asks Rudolf about Evi's early life. Rudolf tells him about their family, how he and his wife had looked after Evi since she was six after her mother died. Rudolf tells him how Evi met Peter, how Peter had struggled since the Wall went up – how he'd given him odd-jobs now and then. And he talks about the 'two Italians' (Mimmo and Gigi) who occasionally visited.

After a few hours, Rudolf comes to Friday 14 September, the day of the escape. He describes how Evi rushed into his house and left straight away with Peter. He was worried, he says, when Peter didn't return the next day, so he'd walked to their house, where he saw baby clothes sitting in a bowl of water in the garden. He'd wrung them out to dry and put them on the lawn.

His interrogator listens. Takes notes. 'Have you heard from them since then?'

'No,' Rudolf says, 'no letter or postcard. I don't know where they are.' Then he adds: 'But I assume they went to West Berlin.'

Rudolf's interrogation is typed up – dates, names, everything. His interrogator sits back, trying to work out if Evi's grandfather is telling the truth. Luckily for him, he is. Like most who planned to escape, Evi didn't tell anyone about her plan, not even her grandparents – her surrogate parents. She'd had to leave without saying goodbye, no idea if they'd ever see each other again. Evi's grandfather is grateful he didn't know. It's much easier to be convincing if you're not lying.

At the end of his interrogation, Evi's grandfather mentions something random, seemingly unrelated to anything. He mentions the canoe he once gave Evi as a present. Maybe it's only natural, at the moment when he realises he may never see his granddaughter again, to think of it. He knows he has joined the ranks of those in East Berlin who are left behind, those too old, too young or too scared to escape, those who wake up one morning to realise that the people they love have gone and they may never see them again.

And perhaps it's these details – the canoe, the clothes in the bowl, the steady voice – whatever it is, Rudolf passes the test. He's allowed to leave the police station and he returns home to the place where he'd watched Evi grow up, where she'd learnt to read, ride a bike, and where she'd paddled on the water in her canoe. Now, just a memento, the canoe is moored up at the house, never to be used again, soon to be hidden by the long grass.

65

The Plane

———◆———

REUVEN FRANK WALKS onto the plane. Finally, after two weeks in West Berlin, he's finished editing the film and he's flying back to New York. He can't believe he's got this far, never thought the escape would work, let alone the documentary, and now he's shepherding the cut film back home.

Scared about losing it in the hold, Reuven had put the film-reel – all 12,000 feet of it – in a cabin bag. He pulls it close. A heavy secret. Newspapers all over the world have the story of the twenty-nine escapees, but only a few people know it's been captured on film. It needs to stay that way until he's ready to write a press release, spin a narrative. Reuven Frank the storyteller knows how important that is.

The line into the plane moves and Reuven takes his seat in the first-class cabin. He puts his bag underneath it, hidden from prying eyes. Sitting back, his eyes close just as he feels the gentle pressure of a hand on his shoulder.

Excuse me sir, a man is saying, we have Willy Brandt on board; could you swap so we can all sit together?

Of all the things Reuven thought might go wrong between Berlin and New York, this wasn't one of them. He pauses. He can't say no to a request from the mayor of West Berlin, so he smiles and walks to a different seat, realising as he sits down that he's left the film under Willy Brandt's seat. At any moment, the mayor of West Berlin could look down, find it, and who knows – perhaps even confiscate it. And he doesn't want to draw attention to the film by going back to retrieve it. In the belly of Reuven Frank, an unease sets in: there's always something you can't predict.

As the plane arcs away from Germany, underneath it, now a tiny speck, is the factory. Though the tunnel has collapsed, the cellar is intact, full of the detritus of the escape: spades, clothes, shovels, picks, trainers, electric cables. The diggers left it all there, knowing that as word spreads about the tunnel, reporters will want to come and see the cellar, take photos at the shrine of this spectacular escape. But there are some things they removed: all traces of NBC. Before Peter and Klaus left for the last time, they'd combed the cellar, picking up anything that could lead to the American TV network, following Reuven Frank's orders that no one should know.

They thought they'd taken everything, but sitting in the corner of the cellar, as Reuven's plane wheels over the Atlantic is a small cardboard box. Inside, a reel of film.

66

The Second Party

JOACHIM'S EYES FLIT round the room. Another party, but this one feels different. Unhinged. Earlier, Hasso had thrown a glass against the wall – part celebration, part release. They're all still feeling it, the after-effects of taking a risk that could have lost them everything.

A few days ago, Evi had sat at the kitchen table in the flat she was renting with her husband, Peter, and started screaming, then found she couldn't stop. She'd clung to the table, scared that if she didn't hold tightly enough she might jump through the window. Memories scrolled through her mind: crawling through the tunnel, her toddler Annet in the arms of a digger behind Evi, terrified that the Stasi might catch them and take Annet, and she might never see her again. Though it didn't happen, something had taken Evi's mind back there, to that memory. Perhaps only now, in the safety of West Berlin, could she express the most animalistic terror she'd ever felt, in a scream that came from the bottom of her belly and threatened to never end.

But tonight, Evi is composed, alcohol bubbling through her as she sits at a table in a short black dress. They're all high on whiskey and wine and the dancing has begun. Looking round the room, she sees Joachim, his eyes resting on her.

Evi blushes. She's intrigued by Joachim, the man who dug the tunnel but had no one to rescue. The man who carried out the most dangerous parts of the operation – going outside to check the apartment number, unlocking the apartment door again and again. She can't understand how anyone can be that brave when for as long as she can remember, she's been afraid. A memory flashes up: Evi aged six in a chicken coop with her mother, hiding from Russian soldiers in those horrific final days of the war. Her mother had died from TB a few months later, leaving Evi to figure out so many things on her own. There is something

238

in Joachim — in his courage, his steadiness — that she admires, that she wants.

Joachim stands up, finds himself walking towards Evi, doesn't know what he'll say when he gets there, but the words spill out of his mouth. 'Do you want to dance?'

Evi laughs and they move to the centre of the room, Joachim wondering why on earth he asked her to dance when he's always hated dancing, never got the hang of it. The music is sexy, a rhythm that speaks to the hips, and he starts swaying, relaxing into the sixties twist that everyone is dancing. Evi shakes her head, laughing. 'I can't do it,' she says.

Joachim looks back at her. Holds her gaze. 'I'll teach you.'

As they move to the same rhythm, everyone around them fades into the background until suddenly, behind Evi, Joachim sees movement — a flash of someone walking fast, and he realises it's Peter, her husband. He's leaving, and Evi sees it too and runs and follows, leaving Joachim, alone, in the middle of the room.

67

The Press Conference

R EUVEN FRANK LOOKS at the sea of cameras and journalists in front of him. Over a hundred people in the room, all looking at him, expecting answers. It was never meant to come out like this.

A few days ago, some journalists had gone to the cellar in West Berlin to take photos. Looking around, one had seen the cardboard box of film, 'DuPont' written on the outside. They all knew NBC was the only network to use that brand of film. 'NBC was here!' he'd shouted. *Time* magazine broke the story, revealing in an article called 'Tunnels Inc.' that NBC had funded the tunnel in return for film rights. After that, things had gone crazy.

CBS (who were fuming that they'd dropped *their* tunnel story and NBC hadn't) wrote to the State Department, complaining that in ditching their own film when NBC had carried on, they'd been left in the cold. The State Department had cabled the American Embassy in West Berlin, asking whether they'd given NBC their approval. No, they replied, they hadn't.

For a few days, NBC kept quiet, hoped the story would go away. But as the storm grew, they knew they had to get out in front and they organised a press conference for Thursday 11 October 1962, which is why Reuven Frank and Piers Anderton were now sitting on stage at NBC headquarters in New York.

Looking at the journalists, Reuven Frank thinks carefully about his answers. They've scheduled the film for 31 October, just three weeks away. If he messes up now, they'll cancel it.

It begins. The journalists ask about the money. How much did NBC pay the diggers?

The real answer is $12,000, which paid for five tonnes of steel for the rail in the tunnel, a VW van, electric cables and bulbs, pumps to suck out water, compressors and pipes to bring fresh air in, pulleys, ropes and motors for the cart, and lastly, several months' worth of tea, coffee and sandwiches.

To the journalists, Reuven gives a shorter answer. 'Not much in TV terms,' he says. 'And the tunnel would have been built without it,' he adds.

Someone asks when NBC got involved.

In the summer, he replies, only after the students had been digging for a few weeks. He wants the journalists to understand that the tunnel would have been built anyway, even if NBC hadn't funded it. 'We were not going around recruiting tunnel builders.'

Then he tells the press about the mechanics of filming the escape, the long hours in the tunnel, all the safety precautions to protect the diggers and keep the tunnel secret, and then it's done. Reuven Frank and Piers Anderton leave the stage, hoping this will put an end to it.

But the next day the story catches fire.

The *New York Times* runs an article claiming that NBC helped *build* the tunnel, and newspaper stories appear with interviews from diggers in West Berlin who feel angry about the film, saying they should have got a cut of the money. Some are calling for the film to be banned.

West Berlin's Senate then puts out a statement saying the film should be dropped. The East German government writes a letter, describing the film as an 'attack', complaining that escape tunnels cause damage to 'gas mains and electricity lines' and demanding that the US government 'inflict severe penalties' on the NBC journalists. Even a state-run news service in Moscow gets involved, claiming that NBC had hired the diggers, that the refugees were played by actors, and that if the film went ahead it would inflame the situation in Berlin. As a journalist for the *New York Times* put it, the issue had become 'a minor international incident'. And all this in the autumn of 1962, when Americans were so terrified about an accidental nuclear war between the US and the Soviet Union that fallout shelters were sprouting up all over the country.

But Reuven Frank still hopes things will calm down. He hunkers down in his office with Piers Anderton and the two of them sit next to each other, working on the film. They're making good progress. Because most of the footage is silent, Reuven has commissioned jazz bassist Eddie Safranski to write a score. Give me a hint of Kurt Weill, says Reuven, but not too much that it's a cliché. Reuven and Piers are now working on the narration. Sitting at typewriters, they spend hours each day on the script, paring it down, ridding the sentences of phrases like *'free world'* that Reuven knows can numb an audience. The words they reach for aren't the words of politics and ideology, but the language of the tunnel: mud, dirt, pulleys, blisters, carts. They want those who are watching to know what it's like, what it's *really* like, to spend four months of your life digging a tunnel; what the people who crawl through it are risking, what horrors they must be leaving to make those decisions. They want this to be a story not for the mind, but for the heart and the gut.

As they write, every so often Reuven's door flings open and someone tells them about the latest developments in the film-saga, but they ignore them, burrowing deeper in their work, spending hours in the studio, marrying footage of digging and crawling to music and words. On 16 October, they've almost finished and they know that what they've made is special, not like anything they've seen before.

That afternoon, as they tweak the final section of the film, the door opens: it's an NBC staffer with something to tell them. Reuven tries to wave him away, but the man says it's important. There was a press conference a few hours ago, he says; a State Department spokesman said that the NBC film is 'not in the national interest', that it's 'risky, irresponsible, undesirable and contrary to the best interests of the United States'.

He leaves the room, and as Reuven Frank looks back at the film, ready to go, he knows that apart from him and Piers, no one will ever see it.

68

The Library

EVI WALKS INTO her office at the library. It's been a long morning, padding around the shelves, replacing books read by students at the Technical University: politics tomes, maths books, poetry, music – and of course – the engineering manuals that the diggers used while digging the tunnel.

She feels grateful to be here, to have found a job, just two months after arriving in West Berlin. It hadn't been easy. First, there was the search for a place to live – Evi and Peter had found a one-bed apartment in a student hall in Grunewald, not far from the CIA villa where Joachim first tasted pineapple marmalade. It was tiny, the three of them stuffed into one room, and they knew they would need somewhere bigger soon. So Evi had started looking for work.

One crisp November morning, walking down Hardenbergstrasse, Evi heard her name ring out: 'Frau Schmidt?' It was her old boss from the library in East Berlin. She was looking for someone to work with her at the university library. Was Evi interested?

Evi started working there a few weeks later, cataloguing books, just as she'd done back home. It was calming. She loved being around the musty smell of paper as she brought order to all the knowledge in the library. It was also a welcome break from Peter. Since arriving in West Berlin, things hadn't gone well. Without the Wall to push against, they were pushing against each other, feeling their differences more acutely. While Evi was out working, Peter would hang out at home, looking out of the window, strumming his guitar. Always the dreamer. Evi used to love that in him, but now, things had changed. As Peter put it, they were like a 'flock of birds who move together until they reach their goal and then everything falls apart'.

Sometimes at the university Evi would bump into Joachim, they'd eat lunch together in the canteen and she'd feel drawn to him, just as she had been that night when they danced together, but Evi had her family to think about, her daughter. One day she'd decided she couldn't risk it all by seeing Joachim, and now she kept her distance.

Then a few weeks ago, Evi had found a larger apartment for the family, and she and Peter made plans for the move. But then, Peter had flown to Holland for a lithography course, leaving Evi to move house on her own.

Walking into her office today, Evi feels exhausted by the thought of moving house, feels abandoned by her husband and defeated by everything. Then the door opens, a librarian walks in and says: 'Frau Schmidt, there's a phone call for you.'

It's Joachim. He says he'd heard that she was moving house on her own; would she like some help? Evi's stomach lurches and she thanks him, tells him her address.

Later that week, Joachim goes to her flat to help Evi pack up the house. As they put clothes and pans in boxes, they talk and Joachim discovers that he feels safe with Evi, feels as though she understands all the different pieces of him. Living in West Berlin is still strange for someone who'd spent all their life on the other side of the border, and Evi is the umbilical cord that reconnects Joachim with the parts of him he might forget. Joachim discovers that, like him, Evi had a tough childhood, growing up without her father, and without her mother too. There's a shyness to her, but a resilience that he's drawn to as she tells him about getting her first job aged fourteen, finding her way in the world.

By the time Joachim has helped Evi move house, he realises he is falling for her, but Joachim, the man-who-rescued-strangers, knows he is not the kind of man who will meddle in a marriage, and he pushes these feelings to the back of his mind.

69

A Message

———◦•◦———

REUVEN FRANK IS back in Berlin. It's December 1962, and he's
given up on the film ever being shown. A few weeks after his
press conference the world had changed: an American spy plane flying
over Cuba had brought back photos of missiles on the island – medium-
range, nuclear-capable, they had been sent there by Khrushchev. The
Soviet president now had nuclear weapons that could reach American
cities.

President Kennedy had to respond, but how? Discussions in the White
House had run long into the night, Kennedy's yellow doodle-pad filling
with black scrawls. Some advisors wanted air-strikes on Cuba, but
Kennedy talked them down, decided he would give Khrushchev an
ultimatum: if the Soviet leader didn't remove these missiles, the US
would begin a blockade of Cuba. Behind the scenes, diplomats prepared
for war: American embassy staff in Berlin evacuated wives and children,
and Kennedy sent forty American ships ready to impose the blockade.
At 7 p.m. on 22 October, Kennedy appeared on TV, told the country
what was going on. That day, NBC announced it would postpone the
film.

Then the world held its breath.

If Kennedy had misjudged Khrushchev, they could be moments away
from nuclear war. But five days later, Khrushchev caved in, agreeing to
dismantle every single one of his missiles in Cuba. It was a victory for
Kennedy, the man who'd done so little when the Berlin Wall was built.
The 'boy in short pants' had learnt from that experience, shown he could
stand up to Khrushchev.

The press soon moved on to other things and the controversy about
the NBC film died down. NBC gave money to some of the aggrieved
diggers, West Berlin's Senate was no longer calling for the film to be

banned and, most importantly, after NBC reassured the State Department that the film wouldn't endanger the lives of the diggers, and that they had sought permission from anyone who appeared in the documentary, the State Department softened its position.

Still, it was made clear to Frank that the film would never air – NBC managers were worried about blowback from the White House. Reuven was devastated. He knew he was too deeply involved, cared too much, but that was because he'd seen the finished film and knew that, unlike anything else about Berlin, it would explain to audiences across America why the city mattered, why the US should never leave it to fester on its own.

One night, in a moment of despair, Reuven talked to his wife and decided to resign. NBC accepted, but asked him to wait out the year – and now he had flown to West Berlin to work on a final documentary for NBC, something unrelated to the tunnel.

Arriving at Hotel Kempinski, Reuven asks for his key and the receptionist tells him he has two messages in his box. Opening it, he finds a tiny pick and shovel, along with a message from Peter and Klaus Dehmel. 'In memory of what we went through together', it says.

Smiling, he turns to the second message: it's a telegram from New York. He reads it once. Then again, barely daring to believe it. It's from his boss at NBC. He says they have scheduled the film for Monday 10 December at 8.30 in the evening.

70

The Film

———

I T'S EARLY EVENING on Monday 10 December and across the US, TV
dinners are being prepared, baths hastily finished, curtains pulled against
the winter cold in preparation for tonight's TV. Usually, on Monday
nights, most American homes tuned into CBS, watching prime-time
tuxedoed-comedians performing overly rehearsed routines, but tonight,
hardly anyone is watching CBS. Instead, just before 8.30 p.m., people
turn on NBC for a long-awaited film: *The Tunnel*. With all the controversy surrounding the documentary – the articles, the criticisms – the
publicity for the film couldn't have been better.

At 8.30 p.m. exactly, there's a short announcement, then the film
begins, opening with this written statement:

*The program you are about to see is a document on human courage in seeking
freedom. It is a first-hand report – filmed as the event took place – of the digging
of a tunnel, and an escape, under the Wall that divides Berlin.*

Then up flashes apartment number seven Schönholzer Strasse. An oboe
plays a mournful tune, the camera zooms in towards the flat, over the
Wall, and Piers Anderton begins his narration.

*That is number seven Schönholzer Strasse, a narrow tenement one-city block
inside Communist East Berlin . . .*

You see a couple of women stroll by in long coats, a man on a bicycle,
and the pockmarked walls of number seven Schönholzer Strasse. Piers
Anderton continues his narration, describing how people had come to
this apartment on Friday 14 September.

247

Some had come two hundred miles. All were strangers to this place. They came here past the . . . armed People's Policemen on patrol . . . they went quietly down these cellar stairs by ladder down a shaft and stood fifteen feet below the surface of Schönholzer Strasse. There was a tunnel there, less than three-feet wide and three-feet high. Through this, they crawled . . . one hundred and forty yards to West Berlin and a free future. I'm Piers Anderton, NBC News Berlin. And this is the story of those people and that tunnel.

Over the next seventy-eight minutes, in eighteen million homes, people who so far have only seen short news reports about the Berlin Wall, people who had little understanding of what was happening in the city, watch the story unfold. They see the Wall, the death strip, the tank traps and the VoPos up close, and listen as Piers Anderton explains how the students were planning 'the most daring refugee rescue operation in Berlin's history'. They watch the diggers smash through the concrete at the factory, they watch them lying on their backs in the tunnel, digging, covered in mud, then they see the flood of water that almost destroyed it, the floorboards floating; they see Joachim with his inventions – the lights, the stove pipes, the telephone – and then from over the Wall, they watch the home videos of Evi and Peter in East Berlin, preparing to leave everything behind. They see the photo of Peter Fechter lying dead, they watch Ellen disappear into the East, then finally, they watch as Evi climbs out of the tunnel, up the ladder, followed by twenty-eight others. At that point, Piers Anderton reflects on it all:

To escape through a tunnel is as risky as to build one. What lies ahead is unknown. The couriers were strangers. The rendezvous could have been a trap. Death was not the greatest danger. Prison camps can be worse. These are ordinary people, not trained or accustomed to risk. What must they be leaving to risk this?

Then finally, the American viewers watch Inge crawl through the tunnel with her baby, and the camera freezes on Claus's face as he bundles his son into his arms, holding him for the first time.

The next day, the reviews appear. Reuven Frank is nervous, has no idea what to expect after all the controversy about the film, but the response is unlike anything he'd imagined.

The *LA Times* describes the film as 'one of the most profound and inspiring human documents in the history of the medium'. The *Boston Globe* writes that it is 'probably without parallel in the brief history of television'.

One journalist points out that in the run-up to that year's Senate elections, Republicans in Washington had accused Kennedy of doing almost nothing to tell the world about Berlin's 'Wall of Shame'. The journalist suggests that *The Tunnel* should now 'head the list of government films and be telecast in all free countries and across as many communist borders as possible. For, if the Wall symbolises "the failure of Communism," the tunnel symbolises man's incessant drive for freedom.' And perhaps the government was listening, for The United States Information Agency (run by Edward R. Murrow) buys hundreds of copies of *The Tunnel* and screens them around the world. Foreign broadcasters all over the world buy copies of the film and screen it (except, of course, in communist countries.) And so the government that once threatened to ban Reuven Frank's film is now firmly behind it. There's even a rumour that President Kennedy watches *The Tunnel* and is moved to tears.

A few months later, on 26 June 1963, Kennedy flies to West Berlin, his first visit as president. At City Hall, he walks on to a large wooden platform. In front of him, in the square and stuffed onto balconies, half a million Berliners cheering and screaming.

Kennedy had been apprehensive about coming to West Berlin, worried that people might still be angry about his anaemic response to the Wall, but on the thirty-five-mile drive from Tegel airport, millions of West Berliners had lined the streets in the June sun, hanging from trees, lamp-posts, traffic lights, standing on rooftops waving scarves and handkerchiefs. As Kennedy stood in his open-top limousine waving to them and laughing in disbelief, people screamed until they were hoarse: 'Ken-ne-dy! Ken-ne-dy! Ken-ne-dy!' They threw flowers at him, his driver leaning over to wipe confetti off the windshield so he could see the route.

If he'd come in the months after the Wall was built, Kennedy might have been heckled. But he is now the hero of the tank stand-off at the border and the hero of the Cuban Missile Crisis, the man who stood up to the Soviets.

People watched as Kennedy visited Checkpoint Charlie, then Bernauer

Strasse, walking down the street that Joachim and the others had tunnelled under, into the East. Climbing a platform overlooking the Wall, Kennedy had gazed at it, seemingly unprepared for the sight of the barbed wire, the watch-towers and the grey concrete stretching into the distance. A few brave women in East Berlin waved at him from their windows, VoPos looking on. Walking back down, a journalist from *Time* magazine (one of 1,500 reporters covering the visit) said that 'Kennedy looks like a man who just glimpsed hell.'

Now, standing on a stage overlooking the square at City Hall, Kennedy is about to make his speech. He'd drafted it back in Washington, filled it with meaningless phrases intended not to provoke the Soviets. All morning it had been bothering him, the mismatch between his sterile words and the unfettered emotion in West Berlin. On the drive to City Hall, Kennedy had redrafted his speech, throwing away the notes he'd brought with him. He knew that West Berliners needed to hear something different from the man who'd done so little to prevent the Wall.

Standing in front of them all now, he begins. Slowly and steadily at first.

'I am proud to come to this city as the guest of your distinguished mayor, who has symbolized throughout the world the fighting spirit of West Berlin.'

The crowd is quiet. Expectant.

Kennedy looks straight ahead. 'There are many people in the world who really don't understand . . . what is the great issue between the free world and the Communist world,' he continues. 'Let them come to Berlin.'

A cheer.

'There are some who say that communism is the way of the future. Let them come to Berlin.'

A bigger cheer.

Then Kennedy talks about the spirit of West Berlin, how he knows of no town or city that has been besieged for eighteen years that still lives with the force, hope and determination of West Berlin. He describes the Wall as the 'most obvious and vivid demonstration of the failures of the Communist system' and as an 'offence against history, separating families, dividing husbands and wives and brothers and sisters and dividing a people who wish to be joined together'. He says that one day, 'this city will be joined as one' and then, in a line he'd been practising, knowing it all depends on getting the pronunciation right, he says:

'All free men, wherever they may live, are citizens of Berlin and therefore, as a free man, I take pride in the words *Ich bin ein Berliner* ["I am a Berliner"].'

The people in front of him and on balconies surrounding the square go wild, screaming, crying, 'Ken-ne-dy! Ken-ne-dy! Ken-ne-dy!' Two years ago, Kennedy didn't care much about Berlin, just wanted the problem to go away, and Berliners felt abandoned. Now, emboldened after his handling of the Cuban Missile Crisis, Kennedy had shown he'd stand by them. Later that evening, as Kennedy sits on Air Force One, he tells an advisor: 'We'll never have another day like this as long as we live.'

Back in West Berlin, the streets are speckled with confetti, cleared away over the following week by street cleaners. On the other side of the Wall, two days after Kennedy's visit, Nikita Khrushchev arrives from Moscow. Not wanting to be outdone by Kennedy, he tours East Berlin in an open car with a handful of party functionaries lining the route. At East Berlin's City Hall, Khrushchev gives a speech that he hopes will rival Kennedy's: just as Kennedy delivered a line in German, Khrushchev decides he will too, and at the end of his speech, he shouts *Ich liebe die Mauer* – 'I love the Wall!' This time there are no cheers and screams, just a few polite claps. Then Khrushchev flies home to Moscow, leaving the divided city.

Across the Wall, in West Berlin that same month, on the Ku-damm, women in flimsy dresses and men in T-shirts sit outside at street cafes, cigarettes glowing in the night, bright neon signs advertising coke and burgers and films, radios playing American rock and roll. The air is thick with the promise of summer. Through half-open windows in the flats around them, there's the flicker and murmur of televisions, turned on for a special film.

A few streets away, Joachim, Wolf and some of the other diggers are sitting in one of their university dorm rooms. Cross-legged on the floor, beers in their hands, they wait. They never thought they'd get a chance to see it, this film they were part of – some unwittingly. But now, for the first time, it is to be broadcast in West Berlin, and, inevitably, through antennae turned to the West, East Berliners will watch it too.

As the film plays across Berlin, Piers Anderton's deep, serious voice spills through open windows into the streets that line the Wall. On Bernauer Strasse, the collection of makeshift wooden memorials has grown; at the top of each, the name of the latest person killed escaping: Otfried Reck. Hans Rawel. Horst Kutscher. Peter Kreitlow. Some of the memorials are festooned with spring flowers, placed there by grieving relatives in West Berlin. Occasionally, the Wall-tourists stop to take photos as they walk the length of the Wall in their summer shorts and sunglasses.

As they walk, under their feet, through the concrete, under the screed and clay, down in the dark and silence, there are new hollow chutes running between East and West Berlin. Inside, men and women are pushing spades with their feet and hands and pulling out clumps of earth. In escape circles, everyone has heard of the magic clay that holds firm under this street and soon there will be dozens of tunnels, most never reaching their destination, but occasionally, part inspired by the film they watch tonight, one succeeds and, like the twenty-nine people who crawled through the tunnel in September 1962, others, too, will escape.

But tonight, it's a film for Joachim, Hasso, Uli, Wolf, Mimmo, Gigi, Ellen, Evi, Peter, all the tunnellers, messengers, escapees who can lose themselves in their own story. When it ends, they switch off their TVs, and drink and talk into the night. At one of the parties, a Stasi informant lurks in the corner, listening.

New stories are beginning. New plans. New betrayals.

71

The Letter

———◆———

June 1963

WOLFDIETER SITS ON a wooden stool in his prison cell writing a letter to Renate. It's cramped, there are three other prisoners in there with him, but they give him space as he sits at a small table.

He'd spent the morning in the prison-factory building furniture, an eight-hour shift beginning at six. Eighteen months into his sentence and he's figuring out how to survive prison, working longer shifts for extra money that he spends in the prison tuckshop on biscuits and jam. The guards barely give prisoners enough food to live off, so these extra titbits keep him going. Most of his dreams are about food, nearly always the same dish: spaghetti, tomato sauce and schnitzel – his favourite meal as a child.

Sitting at the table, Wolfdieter tries to work out what to write. It's not easy: there are strict rules about letters, only twenty sentences allowed, nothing political or it will be blacked out by the guards. But all he can think about as he sits there, pencil hovering, are the things he can't write.

He wants to tell Renate about the prison choir he'd joined, fifty men in a small room, belting out Russian songs, practising for a concert they would give soldiers in the nearby Soviet barracks. (Like the Nazis, the Stasi liked to give their prisons an air of civility.) A few weeks into rehearsals, when the men had come to trust Wolfdieter, he'd discovered what was really going on during choir rehearsals: this was the Brandenburg Prison resistance. He wants to tell Renate how his time in prison had changed since then, how the group did remarkable things like ensuring prisoners returning from solitary got extra food and blankets, and smuggling messages from prisoners to family and friends. Wolfdieter never thought that in the horrors of Brandenburg Prison, where men lost limbs in factory accidents, went mad in solitary, or even killed themselves, that he would find this kind of hope. This solidarity.

He wants to tell Renate about the Catholic priest in the next-door cell who's been in solitary for nine months, how they talk through the sewage pipe that connects their cells, the priest whispering mass for Wolfdieter with lit candles.

And he wants to tell Renate how good it feels when he's allowed outside in the yard now and then, how he looks up at planes on their flight path west, dreaming about one day sitting in one, flying home to his mother and father.

As he writes the first sentences, an anaemic few platitudes about life in prison, he thinks about Renate, wonders whether she's coping, whether she has found a resistance group that has lifted her soul as his has been lifted. He hates not knowing what she's feeling and he wants, somehow, to give her what these men have given him: to lift her, send her strength and hope. And then it comes to him, a line in *Hamlet*, that he wants to share. But he knows he cannot write it in full – it will be crossed out in thick black ink – and so instead, he simply writes that he's been thinking of *Hamlet*, particularly Act One, Scene Three, and he hopes, somehow, Renate can find out what he means.

Later that day, when the guard comes to his cell, Wolfdieter hands him the letter hoping he has found the right words.

72

Hamlet

———•———

RENATE IS WALKING in the prison yard. It's small, concrete walls stretching high into the sky. Around her, women pace the perimeter in a circle, one behind the other, shoulders hunched, eyes down. Caged animals repeating the same steps they took the day before and the day before that. But today, something – *someone* – is different: Renate. She is walking taller, her chest lifted; even the women behind her notice and they know something must have happened.

That morning, Renate had received a letter from Wolfdieter. It was short, but she didn't mind. It was *his* handwriting, *his* words, none blacked out. Already, she knew it off by heart, the brief note about how he was doing okay in prison, then at the end, this strange line about Hamlet. It made her laugh. The stuff Wolfdieter read was always so weighty, intense: Dostoevsky. Shakespeare. Wolfdieter mentioned a particular scene in *Hamlet*, but it didn't mean anything to Renate; she decided she would ask the prison warder for a copy of the play later. There was a library in prison, all part of their re-education, and there was a chance they might have the play.

Until now, Renate hadn't read much in prison; reading a book felt like an act of hope and she didn't have much of that. Five months in solitary had almost destroyed her; she had found nothing to cling to. Then there was the day she had sat on her loo in her cell, picked up the newspaper that masqueraded as loo-roll, and discovered the news story about Wolfdieter's trial. She saw his sentence: seven years. She'd be out long before him and they'd be separated again. Sitting in her cell, all alone, day after day, week after week, she had wept. And wept. There were so many tears that at one point a prison guard had opened the door, told her to stop crying as she would need some tears for life after prison. Something in that advice had touched her and she'd stopped crying and started singing instead, mostly 'Die Gedanken Sind Frei', a resistance song sung by prisoners who'd stood up to the Nazis: 'Our thoughts are free . . . no one can guess them . . .' Renate sang the song loudly in her cell, again and again until the guards banged on her door.

After five months, Renate was eventually allowed out of solitary and put to work in a prison-factory making dresses, which felt like bliss as she was among people again. She made friends with her cell-mates, most of them prostitutes, taught them maths, helped them write letters home. But there was no women's choir. No resistance group. This letter was the first thing to give her hope.

That day, Renate asks a guard if she can request a copy of Hamlet. She knows it will take a while; she has to be patient. She waits weeks, months, almost a year. Then one day, a guard brings the play to her cell. Hands shaking, Renate flicks the pages until she finds the right scene, runs her eyes across the words until she sees the lines that she knows Wolfdieter meant for her.

> This above all – to thine own self be true,
> And it must follow, as the night the day,
> Thou canst not then be false to any man.
> Farewell. My blessing season this in thee!

She knows immediately what he means: trust no one, remain true to yourself. The words lift her, and so the lovers, the pen-pals who were once separated by the Wall, became pen-pals once again, from prison cell to prison cell, counting down the days till they can see each other again.

73

The Gold Mercedes

August 1964

W OLFDIETER KNOWS SOMETHING is up when the guard, the one they call 'Leg-of-a-Stool' (because that's what he beats people with), walks into his cell and tells him not to go to his shift. Wolfdieter panics: *Am I going to solitary? Another interrogation? Another prison?*

Ten minutes later, another guard enters and takes Wolfdieter to a different cell. Inside – his old clothes, the ones he came to prison in that night, almost exactly two years ago. The guard motions for Wolfdieter to get changed, and Wolfdieter puts the clothes back on; they flap around his stick-limbs. Then yet another guard arrives, takes him to yet another cell.

Wolfdieter knows what this room is: it's a holding cell for people who are about to leave prison. But he's only two years into his seven-year sentence, his time isn't up, so he is now terrified that they've found something else on him, an extra charge. Perhaps he's off to court right now. Through the window, Wolfdieter sees two friends on laundry shift. He waves to them; he wants them to know where he is in case some-thing terrible is about to happen.

A few minutes later, Wolfdieter is brought downstairs, the door opened and he finds himself standing outside the prison, a Stasi officer in front of him holding a pistol. Wolfdieter's mouth goes dry as he follows the Stasi officer to a car and sits inside. As he is driven out of the prison complex, Wolfdieter finds himself thinking of Renate. She is now out of prison, waiting for him. His nails dig into his hands: *Please don't let my prison sentence be extended.*

Two hours later, the car parks outside a vast concrete building in East

Berlin, hundreds of windows reaching high into the sky. Climbing out of the car, he sees the street sign, Magdelanenstrasse, and his legs go weak. Everyone knows the address; it's one of the most notorious Stasi prisons, this one, right in the heart of the Stasi's headquarters, in the same building as Erich Mielke himself. Wolfdieter is taken to a cell and he sits on the bed, the light darkening around him.

That night he doesn't sleep. He's scared of what might come through the door, and animal-like, he wants to be prepared to meet it. Every fifteen minutes a bell tolls from a nearby church, and he listens to each chime as night eventually turns to dawn. When the sun rises, he's exhausted and hungry, eyeing the door until, finally, it opens. A guard walks in with a tray, and when Wolfdieter sees what's on it, his mouth fills with saliva. It's a piece of bread with butter. Next to it, a sausage. He's not eaten anything like this for two years and he gulps the food down, now completely confused.

Next, Wolfdieter is taken into a room where a senior Stasi officer sits behind a large desk, his shoulders decorated with badges. 'Wolfdieter Sternheimer, you are being released early on the generosity of Walter Ulbricht following paragraph 346 of criminal law which states that a prisoner can leave early for good behaviour.'

Wolfdieter looks at him blankly. He doesn't dare believe it. *Good behaviour?* Maybe they'd found out about the prison resistance group and this was all a trick.

Following the man outside the cell, Wolfdieter sees two other prisoners: a skinny man with grey skin and a small, pale girl. Behind them, a good-looking man in a sharp suit and tie. The man in the suit motions for the three prisoners to follow and walks them out of the building towards a gold Mercedes. The three prisoners climb inside, sitting in silence as the man drives them to his office, where he introduces himself: 'I'm Dr Wolfgang Vogel,' he says, 'a lawyer.'

Later, they'll discover that Dr Vogel works for the East German government, arranging prisoner releases like this. One day his name will be famous for the extraordinary number of swaps and releases he organises, but right now, Wolfdieter isn't interested in him, he just wants to get over the border, as until he's in West Berlin, none of this will feel real.

Soon, another lawyer arrives – from West Berlin – and he walks the prisoners to his car – another Mercedes. Wolfdieter sits inside, looking out of the window as the car weaves through East Berlin, and it's then that he realises, his legs beginning to shake, that the car is heading to the same checkpoint where he was caught two years ago, trying to return to West Berlin the night the escape went wrong. Now, he is sitting in a Mercedes, the barrier effortlessly pinging up, the car driving Wolfdieter over the border and into West Berlin, where it parks at the lawyer's office, and that's when Wolfdieter sees her, his mother, and he runs to her, wrapping his bony body into hers, crying and shouting, 'Those damned pigs! Those damned pigs!' as all the anger and terror and lone-liness of the past two years rises and spills out.

A few hours later, Wolfdieter is on a plane. He is with his mother, flying home to southern Germany. The lawyer told Wolfdieter he couldn't stay in West Berlin, he didn't want anyone finding out about the prisoner release; this was the first they'd organised and if journalists got hold of the story, it might scupper the next one. For this is a controversial busi-ness. Wolfdieter's release had come at a price: 40,000DM (£3,500), paid for by the West German government. Eight hundred and sixty other prisoners were also on the list, a similar price paid for each. Wolfdieter was shocked, shocked that the West German government would pay for people like this, giving money to its enemy, East Germany.

'And why was I chosen?' Wolfdieter had asked.

And that's when the lawyer told him all about a secret list, smuggled out of Brandenburg Prison by a Catholic priest, concealed within a candle, covered in wax. The hairs on Wolfdieter's neck had risen as he realised this was his cell-neighbour, the priest who'd whispered mass with him. It was all part of a secret plan, dreamt up by the Brandenburg Prison resistance, to draw up a list of prisoners who should be released in case a swap was ever agreed. They knew lawyers from West Germany would negotiate with lawyers from East Germany, but they didn't want the Stasi to choose which prisoners would be released. There were 12,000 political prisoners in East German prisons and they wanted the right people to get out: people who'd been stuck in solitary for years, who might go mad if they weren't let out early; people who hadn't become prison informants. And one of the names on the list was Wolfdieter. After the Catholic priest smuggled the list out of prison, he had taken it to the lawyer in West Berlin. *What he'd risked*, thinks Wolfdieter. If the prison guards had found it, they would have sent the priest back to prison, perhaps another five years. Perhaps all of them in solitary.

Now, as the plane arcs south-west over Germany, Wolfdieter looks out of the window and his stomach plunges as he sees it below him.

The prison. *His* prison. Brandenburg.

And it's only now, looking down at the prison, that he realises in his bones that he is free, and as he pictures his cell-mates in the yard, knowing that they will be looking up at the plane, he wishes he could somehow tell them to hold on; that one day, sooner than they think, they, too, might be free.

74

Final Report

—•—

November 1976

SIEGFRIED SITS IN front of his latest handler. It's fifteen years since he was recruited by the Stasi. Now, they want to know if they should still trust him. They've got a bad feeling about him, something they can't pin down.

The Stasi can't fault Siegfried's record: eighty-nine arrests, including thirteen escape-helpers in West Germany. Forty of those arrests were from that first tunnel, the rest in other escapes he'd betrayed since – other tunnels, passport schemes, an escape on a beer lorry. The irony was that because Siegfried hadn't betrayed the escape tunnel under Bernauer Strasse, no one suspected he was a spy. After all, he'd been inside the escape network, yet the Stasi hadn't found out about the tunnel. No one guessed that it was because Siegfried didn't have enough information to betray it.

And so Siegfried had become bolder. He'd invite Bodo Köhler round for dinner at his flat and pump him for information over cognac; he'd cut Wolf Schroedter's hair in his salon while asking about his latest tunnel plans; he even told his Stasi handler that Bodo Köhler lived alone, said no one would notice if he was hit over the head, or kidnapped and taken to East Berlin. Siegfried became one of the most productive spies the Stasi had in West Berlin, but in the end, he was too good. He betrayed so many of the Girrmann Group's operations that they disbanded in 1963. They knew they'd been infiltrated, never worked out who. The West Berlin intelligence agencies once called Siegfried in for questioning, but didn't find anything incriminating.

The Stasi thought it was only a matter of time before someone in

West Berlin discovered he was a spy, and so they trained Siegfried in one-way radio communication and cipher and sent him to Baden-Baden in West Germany under instructions to infiltrate French occupation circles. Siegfried arrived, then—

Nothing. Over the next few years, Siegfried went from star-recruit to wash-out. He rarely made contact with his handlers, gave them no information, and they were worried. When the Stasi called Siegfried to East Berlin for a meeting, Siegfried said he was trying his best, but no one in Baden-Baden would give him work as they'd heard about his conviction for homosexuality all those years ago. They wanted to keep their distance. The Stasi didn't believe Siegfried, accused him of being 'highly unreliable in all matters', and, like a disappointed teacher, told him to go away and think about how to change the situation. Unhappy in Baden-Baden, Siegfried had moved back to West Berlin, said he would try harder, promised the Stasi 'he was game for everything', but then he went quiet again, started refusing to do things.

It's hard to know why Siegfried was behaving like this. There are no letters or diaries of his to draw on. But when you look at what he did next, it seems he was having regrets. In the late sixties, Siegfried did some voluntary work for Amnesty International, joining campaigns to get people out of East German prisons, one of them a prisoner called Günter, who Siegfried had betrayed. But the campaign had no effect – after all, East Germany viewed Amnesty as an extremist organisation. Instead, when Günter was eventually released, Siegfried looked after him, even helped set up a group within Amnesty to take care of former prisoners. When the Stasi discovered that Siegfried was working at Amnesty, 'the left-wing extremist group', they were delighted, instructing him to infiltrate their operations and tell them everything he discovered. Siegfried agreed, but then missed three meetings with the Stasi, and now, four years later, on 27 November 1976, they want to know what is really going on.

The meeting is short. Siegfried gives his usual answer: of course I'll carry on helping you, whatever you want. But each time his handler asks him to do something specific, he comes up with a reason for saying no.

Like a sleepwalker jolted awake, it's as though Siegfried had looked back at everything he'd done and didn't like what he'd seen. His trajectory had been steep: from the lowest of informants, in just a few years he'd risen fast, busting escape operations, earning bonuses and medals. He was the kind of person the Stasi loved recruiting: someone who got a taste for informing, who went further than they ever imagined; someone who discovered too late that they didn't have to do everything the Stasi asked.

Despite the reams of Stasi reports about Siegfried Uhse, it will be impossible to fully understand why he carried on spying for so long. Perhaps it was even unclear in his own mind. Siegfried talked often about his ideological belief in East Germany, but his handlers never quite believed him. The threat of a Stasi prison on account of his homosexuality always hovered in the background, right from that first interrogation, yet many informants who were blackmailed by the Stasi found ways of being less productive than he was. And now, it seems, Siegfried was looking for a way out. Perhaps, even, to atone.

After the meeting is over, Siegfried's handler writes a long report, describing the good work Siegfried has done, as well as the frustration of the last ten years. As with a bereft lover, there's a lot of introspection about what went wrong, why Siegfried pulled away. Eventually, his handler concludes that he must have been turned by the West Berlin intelligence services when they interrogated him. The Stasi officer ends this report, the final file written about Siegfried Uhse, with this sentence: 'It is . . . proposed that the connection to the unofficial collaborator should be terminated and the material should be archived in division XII.'

And so, fifteen years after they'd reeled him in, finally, the Stasi let Siegfried Uhse go. Like a pencil sharpened too many times, there was not much they could do with the stub, except throw it away.

75

Airborne

JOACHIM SITS ON the plane. It's small, wobbling as it leaves the tarmac and lifts into the sky, high above Germany. Joachim looks at the needle on the altimeter.

One thousand metres.

Two thousand metres.

And there it is: that familiar knot of adrenaline that always kicks in around now.

Two thousand seven hundred metres.

Three thousand.

Joachim may not have achieved his boyhood dream of being an astronaut, but this is close enough. It's time. The window is open; Joachim checks his straps, takes a deep breath and jumps.

This is his favourite part.

Free fall.

After almost one hundred jumps, Joachim has worked out how to control his body. As he somersaults through the ice-cold air, he twists one hip, arches his back until he finds the perfect position, arms stretched out in front, legs behind, falling through the air-stream towards earth.

Joachim checks the altitude. Two thousand metres. Not time to pull the parachute yet.

It had all started with an advert he'd seen in a newspaper for a parachute club. He didn't know why, but he was drawn to it. He'd gone to the club, practised jumping and rolling from gym vaults until he could do it effortlessly, then a few months later, he'd flown to Hanover for his first jump. That first time he'd felt it – a feeling so intoxicating he knew he'd have to return. And so he'd come back, again and again, to get that hit, the feeling he's about to experience as he plunges towards the fields and trees and tractors and cows of West Germany, as he hits 1,000 metres, then 800, then 600, his target altitude. And it's this moment that he does it all for, knowing that what he does right now will determine whether he lives or dies – Joachim who'd been forced out of his home and lost his father; Joachim who'd always felt trapped in East Berlin; Joachim who'd spent months underground, feeling compelled to help others escape – and now, at 600 metres, he feels his freedom more intensely than at any other moment in his life, an exquisite undiluted sensation of total control as he looks up, reaches for the straps on his shoulders and pulls.

Epilogue

1989

O N 9 OCTOBER 1989, rumours spread through the city like wildfire. Tonight is the night, they say.

Six months earlier, a small group of people had started protesting every Monday outside a church in the East German city of Leipzig. There were only a handful at first, calling for free elections, but every week, more turned up: a hundred, five hundred, a thousand, two thousand, ten thousand, twenty thousand, until tonight, when it seems as though everyone in Leipzig is planning on protesting, and all over the city, teenagers, mothers, students, teachers, doctors, bus drivers and grandparents are crouched over paper and cardboard, making posters and putting on layers of warm clothes in case they're arrested. People are feeling bolder, not because of anything that's happened in East Germany, but because of what had happened in the country theirs was modelled on: the Soviet Union.

After a succession of elderly leaders who'd either died on the job or were about to, the Soviet Union was now led by spring chicken (fifty-four-year-old) Mikhail Gorbachev. For the first time, communist Russia was ruled by someone born *after* the 1917 revolution, and it showed. Gorbachev turned his back on Stalinism, reforming Russia through his twin policies of *glasnost* (opening society) and *perestroika* (economic reform). This wasn't so much idealism as pragmatism – the Soviet Union was in the middle of an economic crisis and this was Gorbachev's way out. The previous year, in 1988, President Reagan had visited Gorbachev in Moscow, where the two men announced they were now 'friends', despite Reagan's visit to Berlin, where he'd called on Mr Gorbachev to 'tear down this Wall!'

266

Then a few months ago, in July 1989, Mikhail Gorbachev had announced that his army would no longer prop up communist governments in Eastern Europe; people could choose their own rulers. The 'Sinatra doctrine', he jokingly called it – people could now do things 'their way'. And within weeks, they were all doing just that.

In Hungary, people voted for a new reformist government, which pulled down its barbed-wire fence on the border of Austria. In Poland, semi-free elections were held, the communists losing hundreds of seats. And across Estonia, Latvia and Lithuania, two million people formed the longest human chain in history, demanding independence from the Soviet Union. One by one, Eastern countries were turning their backs on Stalinism. Only one country remained resolutely, stubbornly Stalinist: East Germany. A country that – despite a secret economy in arms-trading and prisoner-trading (by 1989, East Germany had sold 34,000 prisoners to the West, making 3.4 billion DM) was now heavily in debt and almost bankrupt. Its new leader, seventy-seven-year-old Erich Honecker, was determined to keep it going at all costs. A crazed doctor trying to keep a dying patient alive.

As well as the stiff prison sentences for dissidents, there were the sweeteners that Honecker hoped would win people's loyalty – big events that he thought might keep young people distracted from revolution. He put on a succession of rock concerts – Bob Dylan, Depeche Mode, Bryan Adams, Joe Cocker – and then, in 1988, Bruce Springsteen and his E Street Band walked on stage at a disused cycling track and played for 300,000 East Germans, who swayed and sang along to 'Badlands', 'War' and 'Born to Run', waving hand-stitched American flags. Give people enough of these moments and maybe they would come to love the country – that was Honecker's thinking. Instead, when the concerts were over and people returned home, back to their mundane reality, most felt even more hungry for something different. But they were stuck, stuck behind the one thing that Erick Honecker knew was keeping East Germany alive: the Wall.

Now, almost thirty years after it was built, the Wall was almost unbreachable, with every inch of it patrolled by border guards – 320 metres between them during the day, 260 metres at night. They were equipped with 2,295 vehicles, 10,726 submachine-guns, 600 light and heavy machine-guns, 2,753 pistols, 992 tracker dogs, 48 mortars, 48 anti-tank guns, 114 flame-throwers, 682 anti-tank rifles and 156 armoured cars. It's partly why East Germany was bankrupt: Wall security cost the country 1 billion DM each year.

But still, the Wall wasn't perfect. Despite the VoPos and the machine-guns, every year, people managed to escape. Not many, only a few hundred, but enough to spur Erich Honecker into making a secret plan to extend the life of the Wall for another hundred years, modernising it into a more high-tech version, with electric sensors and cameras alerting VoPos to escapees before they even got close to the Wall, preventing the brutal deaths that still occasionally made the news, embarrassing the government.

Also protecting the border was the Stasi. Back in the 1960s there were a few thousand employees, but now, by 1989, it had swelled to 274,000. One of the Stasi's main objectives was preventing escapes, which is why 90 per cent of escape plans were betrayed during the planning stage – most people never got close to the Wall.

Tunnels were now out of fashion; over seventy had been dug in the early sixties, but only nineteen were ever finished and succeeded – including a 'senior citizens' tunnel, dug by twelve elderly people from a chicken coop. Most tunnels were betrayed before they were finished, or collapsed, or the diggers ran out of money. Instead, people resorted to ever more imaginative attempts, like Winfried Freudenberg, a baby-faced thirty-two-year-old engineer who built a thirteen-metre-high hot-air balloon from polyethylene sheets, climbed in on 8 March 1989, flew over the Wall, but lost control, rising 2,000 metres into the freezing air, where he hovered for five hours before crashing to the ground and breaking every bone in his body, dying instantly. He would be the last person to die in Berlin trying to escape.

By now, most accepted the Wall as a fact of life. Despite Kennedy's speech back in 1963, it had outlasted him and five other American presidents. West Berliners mostly ignored it and were sick of the tourists who still came to see it in their thousands, taking photographs of the vast concrete slabs covered in rose bushes, clematis, murals and graffiti.

But while the Wall stood strong, a new escape hatch had emerged – the back-door route. With the border between Hungary and Austria now open, East Germans were driving to Hungary in their Trabis and streaming over the border into the West. And by the late 1980s, hundreds of thousands were also applying to leave through exit permits, Honecker allowing a certain number of people to go each year, thinking that it was better to let his opponents leave, rather than stay and cause trouble.

People who left East Germany often felt smug about getting out. *Der Doofe Rest* – 'the stupid leftovers' – is how some described those who stayed. But over the past few months, as those 'stupid leftovers' saw the world changing around them, instead of demanding to leave, they had a new demand that was more worrying for the government: they wanted to *stay*. They wanted the government to leave instead.

The pace of change had taken everyone by surprise, but the party was fighting back. Only two days ago, on 7 October 1989, East Germany had celebrated its fortieth anniversary with a huge military parade through East Berlin. Tanks. Red flags. A torchlit procession. And tonight, as the country prepares for the protest, the Stasi is strategising about how to defeat this movement. By now, over thirty years after its creation, the Stasi is a small army with its own aircraft and personnel carriers as well as thousands of anti-tank missiles and machine-guns. And the man still in charge of it is Erich Mielke. Eighty-one-years-old, he's as belligerent as ever and plans to keep fighting. But like an injured dog that lashes out as it nears the end, he's becoming more unpredictable. More dangerous.

Last night, Mielke had issued a code-red alert, giving his Stasi soldiers licence to kill on the streets. He'd seen earlier that year how Chinese soldiers had shot hundreds of protesters in Tiananmen Square and he told his Stasi commanders to take note. Then Erich Mielke activated his secret plan for '*Day X*', the day of crisis that he knew had arrived. He ordered commanders in Stasi branches all over the country to open secret envelopes, inside which were orders to arrest and imprison 85,939 East Germans. Mielke had drawn up a timetable for those arrests so they would be neatly staggered: 840 people every two hours. They were to be put in prisons, concentration camps, factories, schools, hospitals, each prisoner given two pairs of socks, two towels, a toothbrush and – for women – a supply of sanitary towels. Mielke had done everything he could.

Now, as dusk falls on 9 October, he waits. Inside the Stasi headquarters in Leipzig, soldiers stand at windows with loaded pistols, rifles and hand grenades, waiting.

All over the city, people are making calculations. They know what they're up against: they've seen the riot police with shields blocking the main roads, they've seen the soldiers with machine-guns slung across their chests, and there's talk already that this will be East Germany's Tiananmen Square. Hospitals are on standby for mass casualties and they've brought in extra supplies of blood. People know that if they come out tonight, they might not return.

Then, one by one, flickers of light pop up all over Leipzig. People carrying candles emerge into the dark streets and start walking to the main square. First, there's just a few; then, looking out of their windows, seeing the torchlit procession, others feel braver and they throw on warm coats, light candles, say goodbye and leave. Soon there are thousands, then tens of thousands, until 70,000 people are filling the streets, singing hymns, chanting for elections, freedom, democracy, until one chant dominates the others and the crowd shout it again and again:

WIR SIND DAS VOLK! – WE ARE THE PEOPLE!

As the crowd swells, people look around, barely believing what's happening, catching each other's eyes in disbelief, watching the police who surround them, terrified about what they might do. The last time there was a protest like this was 1953 when Joachim and his friends had marched in the streets and teenagers were crushed under Russian tanks.

Through secret cameras on street corners, the Stasi watch as the protest builds, trying to work out how to respond. They watch the singing. The chanting. They watch as a handful of police officers join in. And it sinks in that what they're witnessing is the most terrifying thing they've ever seen, the loss of the one thing that was keeping people loyal: fear.

The commander of the Stasi headquarters in Leipzig knows he has to make a decision. Fast. He has Mielke's backing to start shooting, but with so many protesters, he knows a single shot could start civil war, and as he looks at his soldiers, standing at the doors and windows of the Stasi headquarters, loaded pistols and machine-guns in their hands, finally, he decides what to do.

He locks the door.

That night there is no shooting. No tanks. No dead bodies. And the next day, everything is different. People who understood what the rules were, understood the limits of their power, know things have changed. It is a new time, one for taking risks, testing boundaries, seeing how far you can push things. New parties and trade unions are created, demonstrations spread through East Germany, to Potsdam, Dresden, Rostock, Halle, Magdeburg, and in each city, the protesters target the same place: the local Stasi headquarters. As the protesters chant, sing and shout, inside, Stasi officers do what they do best: they write detailed reports about everything they can see and hear.

Meanwhile, the party panics. They sack their leader, Erich Honecker, hoping that will be enough.

It isn't.

Still the protests grow.

The party announce a new leader, a man with an equine face and long teeth – Egon Krenz – who promises reform.

Three hundred thousand people gather in Leipzig with posters mocking Krenz and his 'horse-face', calling for him to go too.

Then, on 4 November, there's a protest that's different to all the others. So far, it's only in cities outside East Berlin that people have had the courage to march on the streets. In East Berlin, where people feel the eyes of Mielke from the House of One Hundred Eyes, few have been brave enough. But that night, and over the following week, tens of thousands gather outside the Stasi headquarters, the place where so many have been interrogated and imprisoned. Inside, Erich Mielke sits at his desk, typing the chants he hears through the windows: 'Burn the buildings down, out with the Stasi swine, kill them!'

On 9 November, the Politburo meet. They need to do something big to save the country, and eventually they come up with a plan, a gesture that they hope will extinguish the protests. They will relax travel restrictions, allowing anyone to leave the country if they apply for a permit, only refusing people in special circumstances. After they make their decision, they tell Günter Schabowski, one of their members, to speak to the press. Schabowski is nervous. He wasn't in the meeting, doesn't really know the details, but he prepares to wing it.

Just before six in the evening, Günter walks into the International Press Centre in Mohrenstrasse and sits at a long table in front of TV and print journalists from all over the world. There are other items on the agenda; his announcement comes an hour later, right at the end of the press conference when half the journalists in the room are asleep. Literally. Looking exhausted, Günter Schabowski reads out the note he was given, telling the journalists about the new regulations.

There are confused faces. Murmuring. One journalist asks if this is a mistake. Schabowski confirms that it isn't. Then another question: 'When will this new provision come into force?'

In a flush of embarrassment, Schabowski realises he doesn't know. He looks down, turns his piece of paper over, looking for an answer, but finds none. He looks at the journalists. 'It will come into force . . . uh . . . to my knowledge . . . immediately.'

The journalists leave, still confused, begin filing reports. Then at five past seven, Associated Press condense Schabowski's lengthy statement into one powerful sentence: 'According to information supplied by SED Politburo member Günter Schabowski, the GDR is opening its borders.'

The TV networks pick it up and, within an hour, around a hundred people have arrived at various checkpoints, asking to go to West Berlin.

Border guards tell them to return tomorrow.

Then more people arrive – two hundred, four hundred, until there are thousands standing at checkpoints demanding to leave, pushing against the screens at the checkpoint. It is the beginning of a stampede.

Schabowski had messed up. The new provisions were only meant to take effect the next day, and even then, people were meant to apply to leave, not just turn up, but now there are tens of thousands of people swarming the checkpoints.

Erich Mielke calls Krenz, the new horse-faced leader of East Germany; tells him what's going on. The two men talk, briefly discuss shutting the border completely, enforcing it with tanks, but they know it's too late. And so, finally, Erich Mielke gives up his fight and can only watch as the country that he spent his life building and defending rapidly falls apart.

At the checkpoints, commanders realise things are becoming dangerous – soon hundreds could be killed in a stampede – and eventually, one commander makes a decision.

He opens the border and lets people through.

And so they stream in: mothers who haven't seen their children in years, teenagers in pyjamas who race through holding hands, old men in warm coats who stumble across with walking sticks, hands shaking with excitement, crumpling into the arms of West Berliners there to greet them, everyone laughing, weeping, whooping as they watch people clamber to the top of the wall, and dance and scream and sing in the glare of searchlights, looking down at the city that was divided in a single night, had remained so for half-a-lifetime and is now, finally, reunited.

Afterword

·—◆—·

I N JOACHIM'S FLAT, he asks if we can pause the interview for some
water.

Evi brings some, a plate of biscuits too, then she sits down to show
me photographs from their life together. There's a photo from their
wedding day, Joachim in a dark suit and red tie, Evi with her hair in a
bob, wearing a short white dress and heels. Joachim stands just behind,
her back-stop; Evi looks so happy she could float. They married in 1971,
six years after Evi and Peter divorced.

Along with the photos, Evi shows me her Stasi file. She only found
out a few years ago, in 2017, that she had one. She'd been wandering
around a museum a few years earlier, reading about all the files that were
uncovered and she'd submitted a request, not expecting to hear anything.
Then one day a letter arrived, inviting her to the Stasi Archives at
Alexanderplatz, where Evi discovered her own file, seventy pages long,
and realised that two of her neighbours – 'Walter' and 'Wilhelm' – had
been spying on her and her family for years.

Those files – along with millions of others – were found in Stasi
offices after they were stormed by protesters who smashed their way
through steel doors with bricks and discovered secret cellars stuffed with
champagne, pineapple and peaches, along with tens of thousands of sacks
of paper. Some of the files were intact, hundreds of thousands shredded.

And so began the process of *Aufarbeitung der Vergangenheit* – 'working
through the past'. As the files were puzzled back together, the extent to
which the Stasi had manipulated and controlled the lives of people in
the East was revealed, to the shock of those who'd lived through it: the
microphones, the cameras, the nepotism, the mistreatment; then the
more gruesome and bizarre discoveries like the radioactive tags the Stasi
inserted into people's clothes to keep track of them, no consideration
for their long-term health.

In 1991, the German parliament passed a law allowing the files to be searched to uncover Stasi perpetrators and informants. Within a few years, over three million had asked to see their files, discovering what had really happened to friends or family who'd gone missing or were killed at the Wall. Like Evi, many only found out then that friends, brothers, sisters, even parents and children, had betrayed them, and relationships all over the country were destroyed. There was shock in West Germany too, about the thousands of spies the Stasi ran there, infiltrating its intelligence services, newspapers, businesses, police force, politics.

The irony was that since the Stasi had been so meticulous in recording details about life in the East, these files were used to help build cases against those responsible for the worst violence. While the number of people killed at the Wall was relatively low (around 140), the number of people who died at the hands of the state since its earliest days is estimated by some to be as high as 100,000.

The most high-profile trial was that involving Erich Mielke, the head of the Stasi, the longest-serving secret police chief in the Eastern bloc. It began when he was called to the new parliament a few days after the Wall fell. Like the Wizard of Oz in denial about the collapse of his kingdom, Mielke puffed up his chest and made a speech saying everything was under control; that the Stasi were the best guardians of East Germany. As the new parliamentarians booed and hissed, Erich Mielke recoiled, stammering and stuttering, unused to this feeling of rejection, eventually raising his arms and shouting, on the verge of tears, 'But I love you all! I love all human beings!' The most feared man in all of East Germany, a man who'd lived in a palatial home with an indoor pool, was arrested, placed in solitary confinement and, in 1993, sentenced to six years in prison for the murders of two police officers in 1931, the only charges they had enough evidence for. Mielke was released early on health grounds in 1995 and died five years later. Before he died, he made a final request, asking for access to his own Stasi file, correctly guessing that there would be one on him.

There was a smattering of other well-publicised trials involving border guards who'd killed escapees at the Wall, but the few found guilty were given short or suspended sentences. And then there were the Stasi employees who tried to atone; around a hundred who spoke publicly about their work, expressed regrets. But most slid into the background and hoped no one would ever find out what they'd done.

Meanwhile, their victims often remained stuck in the past, obsessed with trying to find those who betrayed them. At one point, two of Siegfried Uhse's victims who spent years in prison tracked him down, asking the authorities to bring him to trial, but they said it was too late, his crimes were too long ago. When I interviewed Wolfdieter, the only time he became emotional was when he talked about Siegfried Uhse: he told me he'd spent years looking for him, showed me a folder full of photos, convinced he was alive somewhere, yet he wasn't sure what he would do if he ever found him.

When you talk to people who lived behind the Wall, it's these personal betrayals that seem to have caused the deepest hurt: children betrayed by parents, parents betrayed by children, friend betrayed by friend. They want to know why, how someone could do it, yet I wonder what Siegfried would say; whether there is any answer he could give that would explain the decision he made in that interrogation room aged twenty-two: a decision that would shape and define the rest of his life.

At Joachim's flat, it is now dusk and night has fallen around us. We stand up and stretch our legs, wander to the windows, where the lights of Berlin twinkle below us, a city that still owes much of its identity to the Wall, though there's not much of it left. Joachim tells me how he used to go to the Wall in the days after the border was opened. Standing under an umbrella in the November rain, he watched the Wall come down, piece by piece. Sections of it would soon be sold to museums and private buyers all over the world, to the relief of many who lived near it who wanted to forget it ever existed. Now, apart from a few sections here and there, there's almost no sign of it; just a strip of granite, dark grey, running along the ground, and the words 'Berliner Mauer 1961–1989'.

Joachim and I talk about what happened in the years after the Wall came down, after die Wende – 'the turning point': the techno activists who streamed over the border into East Berlin, creating a raver's paradise in abandoned power plants and bunkers, dancing in places where only a few years ago they would have been shot. The hundreds of thousands of East German workers who went the other way, desperate for a taste of life in West Germany, buying shiny Toyotas for their shiny new lives, flying off on package holidays to Majorca before finding that they missed their old life in the East – the free healthcare and education and sense of solidarity – and a wave of *Ostalgie*, a nostalgia for life in the East swept in. For by 1989, many of those in East Germany had only known life behind the Wall, and that life, to them, was normal. Now, suddenly, they were exotic oddities; the world they'd known, they were told, belonged to the past.

We talk about the towns and cities in East Germany that lost their purpose, their rusting polluting factories closed down, thousands made redundant, many of them flocking to the hard-right in search of something new to believe in.

And we talk about the so-called *Mauer im Kopf* – 'Wall in the head' – referring to the psychological Wall that lives on, with many in Germany still thinking of themselves as *Ossis* (people from the East) or *Wessis* (people from the West). Joachim tells me how whenever he meets people from his generation, he always knows whether they're an *Ossi* or a *Wessi* because, after all, they've lived entirely different lives; the East is still much poorer than the West and it will take years for the two Germanys to feel like one.

Just as we're about to finish the interview, Joachim asks if I want to see them: the shoes he'd found back in the tunnel moments before it collapsed. He disappears into his bedroom and returns with them, nestled into the palm of his hand. They're beige leather, once soft on top but, with age, they've hardened. I turn them over and there on the soles I see them – flakes of mud from the tunnel, still there after sixty years.

I return the shoes to Joachim and he cradles them protectively. They're special to him, something to remind him of the time he gave half a year of his life to dig a tunnel and rescue twenty-nine strangers. But they're special too, for another reason: for the shoes were kicked off in the tunnel by Evi's daughter Annet, now Joachim's step-daughter. Joachim and Evi keep them in their bedroom, a homage to the tunnel that brought twenty-nine strangers into the West and brought Joachim a family.

Before I leave, I ask Joachim what he thinks about the other walls in the world right now, for the world is riddled with walls like never before: there's the wall on the American–Mexican border, the barrier separating

Israel from the West Bank and from Gaza, the wall separating Egypt from Israel, Syria from Israel, Jordan from Syria, Turkey from Syria, Greece from Macedonia, Macedonia from Serbia, Serbia from Hungary, Kuwait from Iraq, Iran from Pakistan, Malaysia from Thailand, Pakistan from India, India from Bangladesh, China from North Korea, Botswana from Zimbabwe, Zimbabwe from South Africa – thousands upon thousands of kilometres of wall separating countries all over the world, often accompanied by watch-towers, mines, electric fences, armoured vehicles, night-vision cameras, dogs, just like the Berlin Wall.

Then there are the walls *within* countries – the so-called peace walls that divide Protestant and Catholic areas in Northern Ireland, the walls that separate communities from one another in Cape Town, Lima and São Paulo, the blast walls that surround neighbourhoods in Baghdad and Damascus. There are walls that run through desert (such as the 1,700-mile Moroccan wall) and even plans for a floating barrier on the sea, off the island of Lesbos to stop people crossing by boat from Turkey.

As usual, Joachim is thoughtful. He talks about how the politics behind many of these walls are different: after all, some walls are built to keep people in, others to keep people out; some are built to contain violence and have done so successfully, others are built to give a country a sense of identity.

Then a thought occurs to him. 'There is one thing they all have in common,' he says. Holding the shoes in his hands, he continues: 'Wherever there's a wall, people will try to get over it.' Then he laughs. 'Or under it.'

What They Did Next

—◆—

Piers Anderton left NBC in 1964 and worked for two other broadcasters (ABC and KNBC) before leaving journalism in 1971 and moving to Sussex, England. He died of cancer in 2004.

Reuven Frank became president of NBC in 1968, serving for two terms. *The Tunnel* was his proudest achievement. It won three Emmys at the 1963 awards, including the most coveted award, Program of the Year, never before (or since) won by a news organisation. On stage at the award ceremony, Reuven Frank addressed the 50 million TV viewers, criticising the State Department for interfering with the film, before dedicating the awards to the tunnellers. In a *New York Times* obituary after his death in 2006, Reuven Frank was described as a 'founding father of broadcast journalism'.

Joan Glenn continued working for the Girrmann Group as an escape-helper, even after the American Embassy in West Berlin called her in to warn her that the Stasi were on to her. After Joan eventually left West Berlin's escape network, she remained in West Germany, working as an occasional translator.

Hasso Herschel dug more tunnels – some were betrayed by spies, others succeeded. Along with another digger, Burkhart Veigel, Hasso invented a new escape scheme, sneaking thousands across the border, hidden in a Cadillac. Hasso went on to run clubs and restaurants, and now lives on a sheep farm just outside Berlin.

Erich Honecker, leader of East Germany when the Wall fell, was arrested in 1990 on suspicion of corruption and high treason. While on remand, Honecker fled to Moscow but two years later he was extradited to Berlin to face trial. The trial was suspended due to Honecker's terminal liver cancer and he died in Chile in 1994.

President Kennedy was shot five months after his visit to West Berlin by an assassin in Dallas, Texas. Tens of thousands of West Berliners returned to the square at City Hall, holding torches as they mourned Kennedy's death. Though the Wall outlived Kennedy and five other American presidents, none of his successors ever backed away from Kennedy's promise in his speech in Berlin to stand by the city, and Khrushchev never meddled again in West Berlin.

Uli Pfeifer helped dig three other tunnels, though none succeeded. In the late sixties, he drove across Africa with Hasso Herschel in a Land Rover and when he returned to Germany, Uli set up his own engineering company. After his girlfriend, Christine, was released from prison, she was forced to become a Stasi informant, though, unlike Siegfried Uhse, Christine never gave the Stasi information they could use, and two years later the Stasi dropped her. Christine married and had children, as did Uli. They met on 9 November 1989, and ate dinner together, a few hours before the Wall fell. Widowed in 2015, Uli lives in West Berlin, and now and then he still sees Christine.

Evi Rudolph worked as a librarian until she retired in 1992. When West Berliners were finally allowed to visit family and friends in East Berlin in 1972, Evi applied for a permit so that she could see her grandparents. By then, her grandfather had died and her grandmother had dementia and no longer recognised her. Her daughter, Annet, became a teacher and has two sons.

Joachim Rudolph finished his degree in communications engineering in 1971, despite losing so much study time to the tunnel. After university, he worked as a sound man with the Dehmel brothers, then became a maths and physics teacher and taught in a school in Nigeria. In 2012 he was given one of Germany's most prestigious awards, the Federal Cross of Merit, for his bravery in digging the tunnel. Joachim lives in Berlin with his wife, Evi.

Wolf Schroedter helped dig more tunnels using some of the NBC money. He abandoned one after he heard noises underground and real-ised the Stasi were digging towards his tunnel to cut it off. Wolf lives in the middle of a forest, just outside Berlin, with his wife and a beau-tiful Rhodesian ridgeback.

Hans Conrad Schumann, the border guard who leapt to West Berlin over the barbed wire, the subject of that famous photograph, married and worked in a car factory in West Germany. After the Wall fell, Schumann visited his family in East Germany, where he discovered that many thought he was a traitor. Depressed and turning to alcohol, Hans Conrad Schumann hanged himself.

Ellen Sesta wrote a book about her involvement in Tunnel 29 called *Der Tunnel in die Freiheit* (The Tunnel to Freedom). It was published shortly after Mimmo died.

Luigi Spina and Mimmo Sesta flew to Paris, Rome, Vienna and Zurich, selling photographs and footage of the escape to magazines and broadcasters. Mimmo used some of the money to fund his wedding to Ellen at the end of 1963. Mimmo Sesta died of a heart attack in 2002.

Renate and Wolfdieter Sternheimer remained separated by the Wall for a year after Wolfdieter's release from prison, deciding it was too risky to attempt another escape. Wolfdieter visited Renate in East Berlin at weekends, but they never felt safe and were convinced that Renate's flat was bugged. One night, Renate told Wolfdieter they should split up; he should find someone in West Berlin to be with. But, secretly, Wolfdieter had enlisted the help of lawyers to negotiate Renate's release from East Berlin. In September 1965, Renate crossed the border at Friedrichstrasse with Wolfdieter and they married a few years later. Every year, on 8 August, the day they were arrested, Wolfdieter and Renate eat at a restaurant and celebrate their life together, their two beautiful sons, and the fact that they didn't let the Stasi destroy their lives. At the end of the night, they raise their glasses and say: '*Ätsch!*' ('Up Yours!')

Claus Stürmer wanted to help dig more tunnels, but his wife, Inge, said no more. Enough drama.

Siegfried Uhse never worked for the Stasi again after that meeting in 1977. Very little is known about Siegfried after he stopped working for the Stasi. Reports suggest that he died in 2007 from liver disease in Thailand.

Joachim and Evi's wedding day, 7th June, 1971.

Joachim and Evi in their apartment in Berlin, standing beneath the original ceramic number 7 from Schonholzer Strasse.

Interviewing Joachim Rudolph at his apartment in November 2018.

The shoes that Joachim rescued from the tunnel, belonging to Annet, his future step-daughter. You can still see traces of mud from the tunnel on the soles.

Renate and Wolfdieter Sternheimer with a photo from their wedding day back in January 1966.

Number 7 Schönholzer Strasse today. To the left of the entrance,
a plaque commemorates Tunnel 29. The inscription reads: In the basement of this
house ended a 135-metre-long tunnel, which was dug from West Berlin, through
which 29 people on the 14th and 15 September 1962 succeeded in escaping to the
West. Dug by brave men, who chose this dangerous way so they could hold their
wives, children and loved ones in their arms, this [tunnel] achieved worldwide fame
as 'Tunnel 29'. In the area of Bernauer Strasse at least twelve tunnels were started, of
which only three were successful. The other projects failed – mostly after being
betrayed. These escape tunnels demonstrate the despair people had after the building
of the Berlin Wall and their longing to find, across the inhumane border, a way to
freedom.

Locations

After the release of the BBC podcast series, many listeners got in touch through social media, asking if I could send details of addresses in Berlin relating to the events of *Tunnel 29*. Below is a list of locations in Berlin. A few buildings have changed beyond recognition, but most are still intact, many of them now museums dedicated to preserving memories from the days of the Berlin Wall.

For an interactive, searchable map, click on: bit.ly/Tunnel29Map.

FORMER WEST BERLIN

- *Haus der Zukunft* – House of the Future: This was the headquarters of the Girrmann Group, West Berlin's largest escape network: Goethestrasse 37, Zehlendorf.
- Siegfried Uhse's flat in West Berlin: Augsburger Strasse 21, Schöneberg.
- Marienfelde Refugee Centre: Now a museum at Marienfelder Allee 66/80.
- Cellar in West Berlin from where Joachim and the others dug the main tunnel under the cocktail-straw factory: Wolgaster Strasse (the building itself no longer exists).
- Flat overlooking the wall where Harry Thoess set up the NBC camera to film the escape: Ruppiner Strasse.
- Replica of Tunnel 29: This is at the Berliner Unterwelten-Museum in the district of Wedding. The museum runs tours of Berlin's history below ground, from bunkers to escape tunnels. Brunnenstrasse 105.
- CIA house where Mimmo told the Americans about the leak. P9: Podbielskiallee 9.
- Checkpoint Charlie: This is where Mimmo and Gigi crossed into East Berlin when they visited Peter and Evi. Friedrichstrasse 43–45.
- Berlin Wall Memorial: From a special viewing platform you can see a 70-metre stretch of the original Berlin Wall along with a watch-tower. The site also contains the moving 'Window of Remembrance', a collection of photographs of those who died at the Berlin Wall. Bernauer Strasse 111.
- RIAS radio: This was on Hans-Rosenthal-Platz, Schöneberg. It is now the site of Deutschlandfunk, one of Germany's most popular national broadcasters.
- John-F-Kennedy-Platz: The square where John F. Kennedy gave his famous 1963 speech. District of Rathaus Schöneberg.

FORMER EAST BERLIN

- Friedrichstrasse station: The train station where Siegfried Uhse was caught smuggling cigarettes into East Berlin and the main crossing point between East and West Berlin.
- Heinrich-Heine-Strasse 46: The checkpoint where Wolfdieter Sternheimer was arrested.
- East German Police Headquarters: Wolfdieter Sternheimer was brought here after being arrested. Keibelstrasse 36, Mitte.
- Tränenpalast – 'The Palace of Tears': The glass and steel departure hall next to Friedrichstrasse, where Wolfdieter said goodbye to Renate after visiting her in East Berlin. Now a museum at Reichstagufer 17, Mitte.
- Sendler's house, where the betrayed tunnel broke through: Puderstrasse 7, Treptow.
- Corner of Puderstrasse and Herkomerstrasse: This is where the Stasi arrested many of those hoping to escape through the betrayed tunnel.
- Breakthrough site of the second, successful tunnel: Schönholzer Strasse 7, Prenzlauer Berg. A plaque on the wall next to the apartment marks the spot.
- 'Orient': The safe house where Siegfried Uhse met his handler the day he betrayed the escape operation. During the days of the GDR, this street was renamed Wilhelm-Pieck-Strasse, after a communist politician. Since then, the name has reverted back. Torstrasse 72, Mitte.
- Stasi headquarters: Now a museum that has preserved the offices of Erich Mielke in their original condition. Over 800 million pages of Stasi files are stored here. Normannenstrasse 20, Lichtenberg.
- The Agency of the Federal Commissioner for the Stasi Records (BStU): This is where Stasi files are brought when requests are made to see them. Karl-Liebknecht-Strasse 31–33, Mitte. Runs occasional exhibitions.
- Hohenschönhausen Prison: Wolfdieter Sternheimer was confined here while in remand: Genslerstrasse 66, district of Hohenschönhausen. Now a museum.

OUTSIDE BERLIN

- Brandenburg Prison: Anton-Saefkow-Allee 38, in the Görden quarter of Brandenburg an der Havel. Now a museum.

Notes

FOREWORD

xiv, over seventy countries: This figure comes from Elisabeth Vallet, Director of the Center for Geopolitical Studies, Université du Québec à Montréal (UQAM).

1, 'The first thing': Author interview with Joachim Rudolph.

CHAPTER 1

3, Joachim pulls his: Author interview with Joachim Rudolph.

4, 'Das Ministerium des': Recording of the announcement by the GDR Interior Ministry about the closure of the sector border, 13 August 1961. Source: The German Broadcasting Archive (Deutsches Rundfunkarchiv).

4, 'Wollankstrasse, Bornholmer': Ibid.

CHAPTER 2

6, Joachim wakes to: Author interview with Joachim Rudolph.

7, six million soldiers: Beevor, *Berlin*, 11.

8, millions of refugees: In *Berlin*, Anthony Beevor says that around 8.5 million Germans fled their homes in the East between 12 January and mid-February 1945.

CHAPTER 3

11, They'd arrived back: Author interview with Joachim Rudolph.

11, Red Cross: Beevor, *Berlin*, 339.

12, raping over a hundred thousand: Beevor, *Berlin*, 410.

12, unearthed by Russian soldiers: Richie, *Faust's Metropolis*, 594.

CHAPTER 4

14, coating him in: Author interview with Joachim Rudolph.

17, prisoner-of-war camps: Epstein, *The Last Revolutionaries: German Communists and their Century*, 83.

17, known as socialists: Richie, *Faust's Metropolis*, 620.

17, 'It has to look democratic': Cited by Wolfgang Leonhard, one of the ten German Communists who returned with Ulbricht in an interview with *Der Spiegel*, 18 April 2005; https://www.spiegel.de/spiegel/print/d-40077646.html.

CHAPTER 5

18, 'Get over here!': Author interview with Joachim Rudolph.

19, 'beautiful horses': Quoted in Kempe, *Berlin 1961*, 109.

20, a hundred and fifty thousand people to Bautzen: Taylor, *The Berlin Wall*, 47.

21, 'Hurrah! We're still alive': Richie, *Faust's Metropolis*, 672.

CHAPTER 6

23, 'High on the Yellow Wagon': Author interview with Joachim Rudolph.

25, one of the most powerful weapons: General Clay, quoted in Richie, *Faust's Metropolis*, 669.

26, Joachim and his mother: Author interview with Joachim Rudolph.

CHAPTER 7

28, 'Brothers, to the sun': Richie, *Faust's Metropolis*, 684.

CHAPTER 8

30, Joachim is on the train: Author interview with Joachim Rudolph.

32, 'Tausend kleine dinge': Jampol, *The East German Handbook*, 147.

CHAPTER 9

34, closely guarded secret: Koehler, *Stasi*, 49.

35, thousands of helium balloons: Koehler, *Stasi*, 130. KgU stands for *Kampfgruppe gegen Unmenschlichkeit*.

36, his police would come: As the Stasi put it: 'The Ministry of State Security is entrusted with the task of preventing or throttling at the earliest stages – using whatever means and methods may be necessary – all attempts to delay or hinder the victory of socialism.' Stasi guidelines from 1958, cited in Fulbrook, *Anatomy of a Dictatorship*, 47.

37, Hundekeller: Koehler, *Stasi*, 108.

37, Sixteen thousand died: Koehler, *Stasi*, 109.

38, 330,000 people left: Hertle, *The Berlin Wall Story*, 34.

38, 'Failed to stop': 'Universal Appeal', *Time*, 28 July 1961.

CHAPTER 10

40, open sealed envelopes: Taylor, *The Berlin Wall*, 161.

40, hosting a garden party: Chronik der Mauer website.

40, soldiers skulking: Taylor, *The Berlin Wall*, 160.

41, 12,000 members: Kempe, *Berlin 1961*, 326.

41, bought secretly: Kempe, *Berlin 1961*, 324.

41, twenty-seven-mile-long internal border: Kempe, *Berlin 1961*, 325.

CHAPTER 11

43, 'That is all over now': Robert Lochner interview recorded in the US National Archives.

44, 'Ulbricht! Murderer!': Taylor, *The Berlin Wall*, 183.

CHAPTER 13

46, 800 people escaped: Richie, *Faust's Metropolis*, 720.

47, sixty-seven more: Taylor, *The Berlin Wall*, 265.

CHAPTER 14

48, 350,000 Soviet soldiers: They were stationed in East Germany and in other parts of Soviet territory nearby. Kempe, *Berlin 1961*, 56.

49, sidle up to European diplomats: *Financial Times*, 25 August 1991, IX.

49, 'like sausages on an assembly line: Taylor, *The Berlin Wall*, 116.

49, 'chronic opportunist': Wedge, 'Khrushchev at a Distance: A Study of Public Personality', *Society* 5, 24–8 (1968).

50, 'went berserk': O'Donnell, *Johnny, We Hardly Knew Ye*, 295.

50, wasn't going to be constrained: Smyser, *Kennedy and the Berlin Wall*, 67.

50, 'roughest thing in my life': Harrison, *After the Berlin Wall*, 152.

50, wept on his brother Bobby's shoulder: Hersh, *The Dark Side of Camelot*, 383.

50, doodled the word 'Berlin': O'Donnell, *Johnny We Hardly Knew Ye*, 306.

50, 'I think they have the right': Reeves, *President Kennedy: Profile of Power*, 204.

52, 'A wall is a hell of': Smyser, *Kennedy and the Berlin Wall*, 106.

52, 'Why,' President Kennedy asks: Ausland and Richardson, 'Crisis Management: Berlin, Cyprus, Laos', *Foreign Affairs* 44 (2 January 1966), 301.

53, 'Look how slowly I'm working': As recounted by US Army First Lieutenant Vern Pike, quoted in Kempe, *Berlin 1961*, 473.

53, Walter Ulbricht had broken: The agreement stipulated that East Germany was not allowed to restrict movement in Berlin. By building the barbed-wire fence, Ulbricht had done just that.

53, tens of thousands of concrete slabs: Taylor, *The Berlin Wall*, 241.

54, 'we could have moved': *Foreign Relations of the United States, 1961–1963*, Vol. XIV, *Berlin Crisis, 1961–2*, Doc. 181, Letter from the President's Special Representative in Berlin (Clay) to President Kennedy, Berlin, 18 October 1961.

54, 'a band of stonemasons': quoted in *Die Mauer*, *New Yorker* article, 20 October 1962.

CHAPTER 15

55, wasn't allowed to study: Author interview with Joachim Rudolph.

55, the party sent Grenzgänger: Taylor, *The Berlin Wall*, 191.

56, quadrupled to 7,200: Dennis, *The Rise and Fall of the German Democratic Republic 1945–1990*, 102.

56, 'anti-fascist protection barrier': Walter Ulbricht, *Neues Deutschland*, 28 August 1961.

57, *The Black Channel*: *The Black Channel* ran on East German TV every week for thirty years.

CHAPTER 16

59, decided to escape: Author interview with Joachim Rudolph.

59, seven-tonne dump truck: Kempe, *Berlin 1961*, 405.

61, one day before her birthday: Hertle and Nooke, *The Victims at the Berlin Wall*, 37.

61, 'the blood stain': PdVP-Rapport Nr 234, 23.8.1961 in PHS, Bestand PdVP-Rapporte, Archive-No. 8037, Bl. 8.

61, 'violating the laws': Hertle, *The Berlin Wall Story*, 53.

62, 'ULBRICHT'S HUMAN HUNTERS': *BZ* newspaper, 25 August 1961.

62, one last time: Kempe, *Berlin 1961*, 366.

62, making notes of future trouble-makers: Hertle and Nooke, *The Victims at the Berlin Wall*, 25.

CHAPTER 17

65, 'Oh man. The clouds': Author interview with Joachim Rudolph.

CHAPTER 18

68, a stone has fallen: In my interview with Joachim, he used a beautiful German expression to describe this moment: '*Mir fällt ein Stein vom Herzen*', which means 'a stone fell from my heart'.

68, 'the Free World': Richie, *Faust's Metropolis*, 715.

69, For Berlin is: One of the spies working in West Berlin when Joachim and Manfred arrived was David Cornwall, an intelligence officer who was writing his first book under his pseudonym, John le Carré. As George Smiley, his best-loved character, described Berlin: 'the place is a total minefield . . . even the damn cats are wired'.

CHAPTER 19

71, Siegfried clutches his bag: Stasi report, 29 September 1961, BStU / MfS AIM 13337/00016.

72, recruit twenty-five new informants: Richie, *Faust's Metropolis*, 763.

72, 'breathing organs': Ernst Wollweber, 'Schlusswort auf der Dienstkanferenz in der Bezirksverwaltung Halle am 15.5.1957', cited in Müller-Enbergs, *Die Inoffiziellen Mitarbeiter* (MfS-Handbuch) (Berlin, 2008), 5.

72, 65 per cent of church leaders: Interview with former Stasi official, quoted in Funder, *Stasiland*, 197.

72, into the ZAIG: Richie, *Faust's Metropolis*, 764.

73, one informant per: Koehler, *Stasi*, 9.

CHAPTER 20

75, over two hundred kilometres: BStU / MfS (Stasi Archives)

75, the first report: Stasi report, 2 October 1961, BStU / MfS AIM 13337/00016.

76, '101-point system': Richie, *Faust's Metropolis*, 763.

78, letter of commitment: Stasi report, 30 September 1961, BStU / MfS AIM 133347 / 64.

79, 'I, Siegfried Uhse': Ibid.

79, A few days later: Stasi report, 13 November 1961, BStU / MfS AIM 13337/64.

CHAPTER 21

80, Evi and Peter Schmidt sit: Details of this meeting from author interview with Evi Rudolph.

80, like a caged animal: From interview with Mimmo Sesta in *Der Tunnel*, dir. Marcus Vetter, 1999.

81, felt the Wall looming: From author interview with Evi Rudolph.

81, over eight thousand had escaped: Hertle, *The Berlin Wall Story*, 106.

82, Walter and Wilhelm: Stasi file on Evelin Rudolph, BStU / MfS 0202. Hauptabteilung II/5.

82, 'friends visiting': Ibid.

CHAPTER 22

83, glad of the coat: Author interview with Joachim Rudolph.

84 lowest birth rates: Taylor, *The Berlin Wall*, 357.

86, Eventually, after an hour: Hertle and Nooke, *The Victims at the Berlin Wall*, 63.

CHAPTER 23

87, stands in front: The details of this meeting with Bodo Köhler come from Siegfried Uhse's Stasi report dated 19 March 1962, BStU / MfS AIM 13337 / 64.

87 escape networks in *West* Berlin: Anweisung Nr 1/60 des Ministers für Staatssicherheit v. 4.5.1960; BStU, MfS, MdL/Dok., Nr 3499, documented in Damian von Melis and Henrik Bispinck (eds), *Republikflucht: Flucht und Abwanderung aus der SBZ/DDR 1945 bis 1961* (Munich, 2006) 215.

87, Two hundred Stasi officers: Koehler, *Stasi*, 148.

88, In the morning: Details from interview with Joan Glenn in the *Stanford Daily*, 10 October 1962.

89, Yet Joan kept going: As Joan would later say in an interview, 'We were a little blind to any danger. We wanted to help. I know this sounds naïve but when you are asked for help by one of the East Germans it is impossible to say no.'

90, the Stasi report: Stasi report dated 19 March 1962, BStU / MfS AIM 13337 / 64.

CHAPTER 24

91, Wolf gets hold of some: Author interview with Wolf Schroedter.

93, Just as it sinks in: Ibid.

93–4, tidy up after themselves: Luigi Spina interview in *Der Tunnel*, dir. Marcus Vetter, 1999.

94, Mimmo who has the idea: Interview with Mimmo Sesta and Luigi Spina in *Der Tunnel*, dir. Marcus Vetter, 1999.

CHAPTER 25

94, Arriving at the factory: Author interview with Joachim Rudolph.

96, taking it in turns: Author interview with Joachim Rudolph; Wolf Schroedter in NBC Film *The Tunnel*, broadcast 10 December 1962.

CHAPTER 26

97, hundreds of gravestones: Author interview with Joachim Rudolph and Uli Pfeifer.

97, he was arrested: Profile on Berlin Wall Memorial Site: www.berliner-mauer-gedenkstaette.de/en/hasso-herschel-789.html.

97, 'One of these days': Interview with Hasso Herschel in *Der Tunnel*, dir. Marcus Vetter, 1999.

98, Uli was born in Berlin: Author interview with Ulrich (Uli) Pfeifer.

99, '*All the cells in the human body*': Author interview with Ulrich (Uli) Pfeifer.

CHAPTER 27

101, revealing sticks of dynamite: Interview with Hasso Herschel in *Der Tunnel*, dir. Marcus Vetter, 1999.

CHAPTER 28

103, looks across the table: Stasi report dated 22 May 1962, BStU / MfS AIM 13337/64 (000152).

103–4, 'He is a very friendly': Stasi report dated 5 April 1962, BStU / MfS AIM 13337/64 (000091).

104, 'he has an open mind': Stasi report dated 10 April 1962, BStU / MfS AIM 13337/64 Part II/1 (000118).

105, Siegfried tells Lehmann: Stasi report dated 22 May 1962, BStU / MfS AIM 13337/64 (000152).

106, 'It was the right thing': Ibid.

CHAPTER 29

107, 'Four Blasts in 15 Minutes': *New York Times*, 27 May 1962.

108, along with sandbags: Mitchell, *The Tunnels*, 65.

108, 'I intended this signal': Hertle, *The Berlin Wall Story*, 80.

CHAPTER 31

111, Reuven Frank took his seat: Frank, *Out of Thin Air*, 172.

112, 'Open with a shot': Frank, *Out of Thin Air*, 30.

112, 'What a wonderful way': Frank, *Out of Thin Air*, 30.

113, 'transmission of experience': Frank, *Out of Thin Air*, 181.

114, 9 per cent of American households: 'Number of TV Households in America: 1950–1978'; http://www.tvhistory.tv/Annual_TV_Households_50-78.JPG, '2021, https://americancentury.omeka.wlu.edu/items/show/136.

114, **'They've closed the border':** Frank, *Out of Thin Air*, 172.

115, **'Every news story should':** Frank, *Out of Thin Air*, 182.

116, **'If you find something interesting':** Frank, *Out of Thin Air*, 173.

CHAPTER 32

117, **every time they heard:** Letter from Piers Anderton in Reuven Frank Papers, Tufts University.

118, **'Those swine shot me':** This was twenty-seven-year-old Heinz Jercha – a butcher and father. Details from Hertle and Nooke, *The Victims at the Berlin Wall*, 74.

118, **they could smoke away:** Wolf Schroedter interview, as well as Sesta, *Der Tunnel in die Freiheit*, 43–7.

118, **front-page scoop:** *Der Spiegel*, 'Escape Through the Wall', March 1962.

119, **stick a sign on it:** Associated Press article, 12 May 1962.

119, **'Talk about realism':** *LA Times* article, 21 May 1962.

119, **impressed but scared:** Author interview with Wolf Schroedter.

119, **fiddling with the bolt:** Piers Anderton letter dated 24 July 1988 in Reuven Frank Papers, Tufts University.

CHAPTER 33

121, **'I've got to talk':** Frank, *Out of Thin Air*, 193, and Piers Anderton letter in Reuven Frank Papers, Tufts University.

121, **'That's crazy!':** Interview with Reuven Frank, Newseum.

CHAPTER 34

122, **a small fibreboard case:** Letter from NBC Chief, Robert Kintner, to Dean Rusk, 20 November 1962 (Reuven Frank Papers).

122, **lies on his stomach:** Piers Anderton letter to Reuven Frank, 24 July 1988, Reuven Frank Papers.

123, **film the rest of the operation:** Frank, *Out of Thin Air*, 195.

CHAPTER 35

124, **Siegfried closes the door:** Stasi report, 25 June 1962, BStU / MfS AIM 13337/64 Part II/1.

125, **Siegfried gets a phone call:** Stasi report, 30 June 1962, BStU / MfS AIM 13337/64 Part II/1.

125, **'the Secret Collaborator':** Stasi report, 30 June 1962, BStU / MfS AIM 13337/64 Part II/1.

126, **They shot him:** This was twenty-two-year-old Siegfried Noffke.

CHAPTER 36

127, **hundreds of stove pipes:** Author interview with Joachim Rudolph.

127, **$7,500 down his trousers:** Piers Anderton letter in Reuven Frank Papers, Tufts University.

CHAPTER 37

130, 'Report on the Schmidt family': Stasi report, 20 June 1962, BStU / MfS 0202 Hauptabteilung II/5.

CHAPTER 38

131, Piers Anderton is lying in: Piers Anderton letter, 24 July 1988, in Reuven Frank Papers, Tufts University.

131, 'The East Germans are swines': *The Tunnel*, NBC, broadcast 10 December 1962.

132, 'only a fool': Frank, *The Making of the Tunnel*, 14.

132, would never meet any diggers: Letter from NBC Chief Robert Kintner to Dean Rusk, 20 November 1962.

CHAPTER 39

133, Joachim is soaked: Details in this chapter are drawn from author interviews with Joachim Rudolph, Uli Pfeifer and Wolf Schroedter.

135, smuggling them over: Munkel, *State Security*, 144.

135, 'We've seen water': Mimmo Sesta interview in *Der Tunnel*, dir. Marcus Vetter, 1999.

136, 'the Wall of Shit': Interview with Deutschlandfunk Radio on 20 August 2015.

136, Mimmo and Gigi: Interview with Luigi Sesta in *Der Tunnel*, dir. Marcus Vetter, 1999.

CHAPTER 40

139, blotted out West Berlin: Richie, *Faust's Metropolis*, 727.

CHAPTER 41

142, Wolfdieter lies on her bed: Details in this chapter drawn from author interviews with Wolfdieter and Renate Sternheimer.

CHAPTER 42

145, Renate leaves Ostkreuz: Author interview with Renate Sternheimer.

146, A few streets away: Author interview with Wolfdieter Sternheimer.

146, 'Joan seemed emotionally cold': Siegfried Uhse handwritten letter, 20 July 1962 BStU / MfS (000174).

146, Siegfried had even been asked: Stasi Meeting Report, 27 July 1962, BStU / MfS AIM 13337/64 Part II/1 (000177).

147, buzzes at a tall, brown door: Stasi Meeting Report, 6 August 1962, BStU / MfS AIM 13337/64 Part II/I (000186).

CHAPTER 43

148, Renate sits in her bathroom: Author interview with Renate Sternheimer.

149, Siegfried's head is full: Stasi Meeting Report, 7 August at 1 p.m., BStU / MfS Abteilung II/3 (0054).

150, Wolfdieter stands at the meeting point: Author interview with Wolfdieter Sternheimer.

151, in an abandoned building: Mitchell, *The Tunnels*, 134.

151, his second bag: Author interview with Joachim Rudolph.

152, Eighty metres to: Measurement taken from Stasi Report on Kiefholzstrasse tunnel, 10 August 1962, BStU / MfS 0018.

153, waited in a bush: Stasi report, 7 August 1962, BStU / MfS Department VII / 1553 (0057).

153, one man approaches: Stasi Report on Kiefholzstrasse tunnel, 8 August 1962, Department II, 0064.

153, Evi, Peter and their toddler: Author interview with Evi Schmidt.

154, The Stasi follow them: Stasi Report on Kiefholzstrasse tunnel, 7 August 1962, Department XIII, BStU / MfS (0062).

155, 'I feel sick': Stasi Report on Kiefholzstrasse tunnel, 7 August 1962, Department XIII, BStU / MfS (0066).

155, From over the Wall: Letter from Robert Kintner to Dean Rusk, 20 November 1962, Reuven Frank Papers.

156, hacking into the floorboards: Author interview with Joachim Rudolph.

157, At precisely this moment: Author interview with Wolfdieter Sternheimer.

156, Back at the house: Stasi Report on Kiefholzstrasse tunnel, 7 August 1962, Department XIII, BStU / MfS (0066).

159, In his brightly lit cell: Author interview with Wolfdieter Sternheimer.

CHAPTER 44

160, Wolfdieter sits in the van: The information in this chapter comes from my interviews with Wolfdieter Sternheimer as well as from the excellent Hohenschönhausen Memorial, both its online site and the museum in the former prison.

162, A Stasi file: Stasi report, 8 August 1962, BStU / MfS AIM 13337/64 Part II/I (000196).

163, It starts with: Wolfdieter Sternheimer interrogation, August 1962, BStU / MfS, 13337/64 part II/1 (000203).

164, they sent a dog: Stasi report, 8 August 1962, BStU / MfS AIM 13337/64 Part II/I (000098).

164, They noted the tools: Stasi report, 8 August 1962, BStU / MfS AIM 13337/64 Part II/I (0075).

165, spread false rumours: Munkel, *State Security*, 128.

166, no idea if: Author interview with Wolfdieter Sternheimer.

166, 'Your statements are': Edith Sendler interrogation, August 1962, BStU / MfS, 13337/64 part II/1 (000216).

CHAPTER 45

169, Siegfried is nervous: Stasi report, 12 August 1962, BStU / MfS, 13337/64 part II/1 (000214).

CHAPTER 46

172, looks at his watch: Author interview with Joachim Rudolph.

CHAPTER 47

174, Wolfdieter lies in bed: Author interview with Wolfdieter Sternheimer.
177, single shot to the neck: Koehler, *Stasi*, 18–19.
177, sells products made in its prisons: Munkel, *State Security*, 128.
177, 'Red light radiation': Munkel, *State Security*, 124.
179, Renate has never forgotten that: Author interview with Renate Sternheimer.

CHAPTER 48

181, Joachim lies back: Author interview with Joachim Rudolph.
181, They would talk politics: Frank, *Out of Thin Air*, 194.
182, scrambling over the: Hertle and Nooke, *The Victims at the Berlin Wall*, 102.
183, 'Mr President': Wyden, *Wall*, 273.
183, 'He is dead': Ahonen, *Death at the Berlin Wall*, 55.
183, 'The matter has': Wyden, *Wall*, 273.
184, 'PROTECTING POWER': Ahonen, *Death at the Berlin Wall*, 56.
184, they knew that: Hertle, *The Berlin Wall Story*, 83.
184, monitor everyone: Ahonen, *Death at the Berlin Wall*, 60.
185, 'The life of each': Schwarzer Kanal, DDR-Fernsehen, 27 August 1962.

CHAPTER 49

187, Claus went to the border: From Claus and Inge Stürmer interviews in *Der Tunnel*, dir. Marcus Vetter, 1999.
189, Wolf is on the road: Author interview with Wolf Schroedter.

CHAPTER 50

192, 'Remember,' says Reuven: Frank, Reuven, *Into Thin Air*, 195.
193, General Clay thought Kennedy: Smyser, *Kennedy and the Berlin Wall*, 128.
194, 'SHELTERS: HOW SOON': *Time* magazine, 20 October 1961.
194, the Americans switched on: Cate, *The Ides of August*, 482.
194, ordering four submarines: Taylor, *The Berlin Wall*, 283.
194, most dangerous moment: William Kaufman, a Kennedy administration strategist who advised on both Berlin and Cuba said: 'Berlin was the worst moment of the Cold War . . . although I was deeply involved in the Cuban Missile Crisis, I personally thought that the Berlin confrontation . . . where you had Soviet and US tanks literally facing one another with guns pointed was a more dangerous

situation.' Interview with Professor William Kaufmann, National Security Archive, George Washington University.

195, Neither wanted the situation: General Clay's analysis as quoted in Smyser, *Kennedy and the Berlin Wall*, 142.

CHAPTER 51

197, a forty-year-old: Hertle and Nooke, *The Victims at the Berlin Wall*, 110.

CHAPTER 52

198, the Stasi informant: Stasi report from 'Wilhelm', 20 September 1962, BStU / MfS 0232.

CHAPTER 53

199, she feels safe: Author interview with Ellen Sesta.

CHAPTER 54

201, they're learning more: Stasi report, 13 August 1962, BStU / MfS, Division II (000214).

CHAPTER 55

202, corner of Café Bristol: Author interview with Ellen Sesta; see also Sesta, *Der Tunnel in die Freiheit*, 180.

CHAPTER 56

203, a coded message: Frank, *Into Thin Air*, 196.
204, Ellen lies in bed: Author interview with Ellen Sesta.

CHAPTER 57

205, She wakes with: Author interview with Ellen Sesta.
206, Evi comes running: Author interview with Eveline Rudolph and Evi's grandfather's interrogation in Stasi report, 27 September 1962, BStU / MfS 0264.
206, noticed how strange: Stasi report, 17 September 1962, BStU / MfS 0228.
207, Peter puts on thick underpants: Interview with Peter Schmidt in *Der Tunnel*, dir. Marcus Vetter, 1999.
207, zooms in over: *The Tunnel*, NBC, broadcast 10 December 1962.
208, threaten to leave: Author interview with Uli Pfeifer.
209, Uli says no: Author interview with Uli Pfeifer.
209, But in that moment: Author interview with Joachim Rudolph.
209, Holding a newspaper: Author interview with Ellen Sesta; see also Sesta, *Der Tunnel in die Freiheit*, 200.
210, An hour later: Author interview with Evi Rudolph.

210, **Ducking down into the tunnel:** Author interview with Joachim Rudolph.

211, **Hasso steadies his hand:** Interview with Hasso Herschel in *Der Tunnel*, dir. Marcus Vetter, 1999.

215, **Evi crouches:** Author interview with Evi Rudolph.

216, **her stomach falls:** Author interview with Ellen Sesta.

217, **People sit:** NBC Film *The Tunnel*, broadcast 10 December 1962.

217, **Buggies are now piling up:** Piers Anderton letter to Reuven Frank, 24 July 1988 in Reuven Frank Papers.

218, **Ellen sits uncomfortably:** Author interview with Ellen Sesta.

220, **Then Claus hears:** Interview with Claus and Inge Stürmer in *Der Tunnel*, dir. Marcus Vetter, 1999.

220, **later she'll say:** Interview with Inge Stürmer in *Der Tunnel*, dir. Marcus Vetter, 1999.

220, **thinks of his father:** Author interview with Joachim Rudolph.

CHAPTER 58

220, **Three days after:** BStU / MfS, Stasi report from meeting with Contact Person 'Walter', 17 September 1962, 0228.

CHAPTER 59

225, **then they seal off:** Stasi fax to Köpenick People's Police Station, 25 September 1962, BStU / MfS, 0253.

CHAPTER 60

226, **Reuven Frank kneels:** Frank, *Into Thin Air* 199, and Frank, *The Making of Tunnel 29*.

227, **wandered around the border:** *The Tunnel*, NBC, broadcast 10 December 1962.

CHAPTER 61

229, **The Stasi agent:** Stasi report, 18 September 1962, BStU / MfS 000015.

CHAPTER 62

229, **'the flight from':** Stasi report BStU / MfS, 2743 / 69 189.

230, **'TWENTY-NINE':** *New York Times*, 18 September 1962.

231, **Then, at eight:** Stasi tunnel report from 26 September 1962, BStU / MfS, 1962 000004.

231, **In a final:** Stasi tunnel report from 19 October 1962, BStU / MfS, 000035.

CHAPTER 63

232, **At a restaurant:** *The Tunnel*, NBC, broadcast 10 December 1962.

233, **He'd picked them up:** Author interview with Joachim Rudolph.

233, **'Twenty-one':** Piers Anderton in *The Tunnel*, NBC, broadcast 10 December 1962.

CHAPTER 64

234, Rudolf's interrogator starts: Stasi report on the interrogation of Rudolf Gottlieb, 27 September 1962, MfS / BStU 0265.

CHAPTER 65

236, Reuven Frank walks onto: Frank, *The Making of the Tunnel*, 20–1.

CHAPTER 66

238, She'd clung to the table: Author interview with Evi Rudolph.

CHAPTER 67

240, Reuven Frank looks at: Frank, *Into Thin Air*, 202, also *New York Times* article, 12 October 1962.
240, 'NBC was here!': Frank, *Into Thin Air*, 202.
240, *Time* magazine broke: *Time* magazine, 5 October 1962.
240, left in the cold: Cable from US State Department to American Embassy in West Berlin, 19 September 1962.
240, No, they replied: Cable from American Embassy in West Berlin to US State Department, 6 October 1962.
240, The real answer: Frank, *Into Thin Air*, 194.
241, West Berlin's Senate: *New York Times*, 14 October 1962 and cable from American Embassy in West Berlin to State Department, 16 October.
241, The East German government writes a letter: Letter from the Government of the German Democratic Republic to American Embassy in West Berlin, 18 October 1962. Since the US didn't recognise the East German government, there was no direct contact between East Germany and the US, so in a complicated piece of diplomacy, the East German government delivered the typewritten letter to the Czech Foreign Ministry in Prague, which passed it on to the American Embassy.
241, Even a state-run: Mitchell, *The Tunnels*, 252.
241, 'a minor international incident': *New York Times*, 22 October 1962.
242, something to tell them: Frank, *The Story of Tunnel 29*, 20–1, and *New York Times* article, 20 October 1962.

CHAPTER 68

243, One crisp November morning: Author interview with Evi Rudolph.
243, 'flock of birds': *Der Tunnel*, dir. Marcus Vetter, 1999.
244, Then the door opens: Author interview with Evi Rudolph.

CHAPTER 69

245, Khrushchev caved in: In return, President Kennedy would remove American missiles in Turkey – that part of the bargain was kept secret.
246, after NBC reassured: Letter from Robert Kinter (NBC) to Dean Rusk, 20 November 1962, Reuven Frank Papers.

246, unlike anything else: Frank, *Into Thin Air*, 206.

246, Arriving at Hotel Kempinski: Frank, *The Story of Tunnel 29*, 22.

CHAPTER 70

247, *the program you are about to see*: Placecard from start of film, Reuven Frank Papers, Tufts University.

249, One journalist points out: Rod Synnes in *The Milwaukee Journal Stations*, Friday 14 December 1962.

249, half a million Berliners: Smyser, *Kennedy and the Berlin Wall*, 4.

249, wipe confetti off: Smyser, *Kennedy and the Berlin Wall*, 4.

251, 'We'll never have': Sorensen, *Kennedy*, 61.

251, for the first time: The film shown in West Berlin was an edited version, broadcast by a German producer who had bought the one-time rights from Mimmo and Gigi.

252, a Stasi informant: Stasi report, BStU / MfS HAI 13256 47.

CHAPTER 71

253, Wolfdieter sits: Author interview with Wolfdieter Sternheimer.

CHAPTER 72

255, Renate is walking: Gerda, another escapee arrested at the tunnel, would later tell Renate that she could tell from the way Renate was holding herself that she was smiling.

CHAPTER 73

257, *Am I going to solitary*: Author interview with Wolfdieter Sternheimer.

259, There were 12,000: Hertle, *The Berlin Wall Story*, 99.

CHAPTER 74

261, Siegfried sits in: Stasi report, 4 November 1977, BStU / MfS AIM 13337/64 Part I/I (000269).

261, other escapes he'd betrayed: Stasi report, 4 June 1964, BStU / MfS AIM 13337/64 (000009).

262, 'highly unreliable': Stasi report, 2 July 1966, BStU / MfS 000245.

262, group within Amnesty: Veigel, *Wege durch die Maue*, 297.

263, 'It is . . . proposed': Stasi report, 23 November 1977, BStU / MfS 104 AIM 13337/64 (000269).

CHAPTER 75

264, Joachim sits on: Author interview with Joachim Rudolph.

EPILOGUE

267, on the border: Hertle, *The Berlin Wall Story*, 119.

268, 1 billion DM: Hertle, *The Berlin Wall Story*, 116.

268, swelled to 274,000: Koehler, *Stasi*, 8.

268, 90 per cent of escape plans: Hertle, *The Berlin Wall Story*, 161.

269, they were to be put: BStU / MfS *Vorbereitung auf den Tag X – Die geplanten Isolierungslager des MfS*, by Thomas Auerbach and Wolf-Dieter Sailer, 1995.

271, 'Burn the buildings down . . .': MfS, ZAIG, Nr 496/89 reprinted in *Mitter and Wolle, Ich lieb euch doch alle! Befehle und Lageberichte des MfS January–November 1989*, p. 250.

AFTERWORD

275, radioactive tags: Funder, *Stasiland*, 192.

276, thousands of spies: In *State Security and the Border*, Daniela Munkel writes that by the 1980s, approximately 3,000 West German citizens served as unofficial collaborators (IMs) for the Stasi and many had been active for decades. The espionage the Stasi carried out in West Berlin wasn't just about eliciting political, military and industrial secrets, but also involved spreading disinformation and revealing incriminating information to influence West German politics – the kind of disinformation campaigns we see around the world today. Munkel, *Stasi Reader*, 140.

276, high as 100,000: Richie, *Faust's Metropolis*, xlv.

276, the only charges: Koehler, *Stasi*, 410.

276, a final request: Funder, *Stasiland*, 254.

277, most slid into: Koehler, *Stasi*, 29.

277, soon be sold: One of the longest sections of the Berlin Wall anywhere in the world is in Los Angeles, running along Wiltshire Boulevard in the Miracle Mile district, erected as part of a commemoration project. These old pieces of the Berlin Wall have now become a site for protests against other walls, such as the Mexican–American wall.

WHAT THEY DID NEXT

280, 50 million TV viewers: *The International Newspaper of Radio and Television*, 27 May 1963.

280, 'founding father': Bill Carter in the *New York Times*.

283 died in 2007: From correspondence with Burkhart Veigel, one of the diggers, and author of *Wege durch die Mauer*.

Bibliography

ARCHIVES AND PAPERS

Chronik Der Mauer (Joint project of the Federal Agency for Civic Education with Deutschlandradio and the Center for Contemporary History Research Potsdam).

Der Bundesbeauftragte für die Unterlagen des Staatssicherheitsdienstes der ehemaligen Deutschen Demokratischen Republik (BStU): 'Stasi Archives', Berlin, Germany.

Deutsches Rundfunkarchiv, German Broadcasting Archive.

National Archives and Records Administration, College Park, Maryland.

Declassified CIA intelligence reports.

Declassified US State Department reports.

Internal letters and memos from NBC.

Telegrams and Cables from American Embassy in Berlin, 1962.

Berlin Brigade US Military Logs, 1962.

Reuven Frank Papers from Tufts University, Medford, Massachusetts.

Munkel, Daniela (ed.), *State Security: A Reader on the GDR Secret Police* (Department of Education and Research, Berlin 2015).

KEY ARTICLES

Bainbridge, John: 'Die Mauer: the early days of the Berlin Wall' (*The New Yorker*, 20 October 1962).

Frank, Reuven: 'The Making of the Tunnel' (Television Quarterly, 1963).

Films and documentaries
Der Tunnel, Documentary directed by Marcus Vetter, 1999.
The Tunnel, NBC documentary, broadcast on 10 December 1962 in the US.

Interviews (alphabetical)
Ulrich Pfeifer
Eveline (Schmidt) Rudolph
Joachim Rudolph
Wolf Schroedter
Ellen (Schau) Sesta
Renate Sternheimer
Wolfdieter Sternheimer

Books

Ahonen, Pertti, *Death at the Berlin Wall* (New York: Oxford University Press, 2011).

Beevor, Antony, *Berlin: The Downfall* (London: Penguin, 2002).

Cate, Curtis, *The Ides of August* (Berlin: Weidenfeld & Nicolson, 1978).

Clare, George, *Berlin Days 1946–47* (London: Papermac, 1994).

Dennis, J.M., *The Rise and Fall of the German Republic* (Routledge, 2000).

Epstein, C., *The Last Revolutionaries: German Communists and Their Century* (Cambridge, MA: Harvard University Press, 2003).

Frank, Reuven, *Out of Thin Air: The Brief Wonderful Life of Network News* (New York: Simon & Schuster, 1991).

Fulbrook, Mary, *Anatomy of a Dictatorship: Inside the GDR 1949–1989* (New York: Oxford University Press, 1995).

Funder, Anna, *Stasiland: Stories from Behind the Berlin Wall* (London: Granta, 2003).

Garton Ash, Timothy, *The File: A Personal History* (London: HarperCollins, 1997).

Harrison, Hope M., *After the Berlin Wall* (Cambridge University Press, 2019).

Hersh, Seymour, *The Dark Side of Camelot* (London: HarperCollins, 1997).

Hertle, Hans-Hermann, *The Berlin Wall Story: Biography of a Monument* (Berlin: Christoph Links Verlag, 2011).

Hertle, Hans-Herman and Maria Nooke (eds), *The Victims at the Berlin Wall, 1961–1989* (Berlin: Christoph Links Verlag, 2011).

Justinian Jampol (ed.), *The East German Handbook: Arts and Artifacts from the GDR* (Berlin: Taschen GmbH, 2017).

Kempe, Frederick, *Berlin 1961: Kennedy, Khrushchev and the Most Dangerous Place on Earth* (New York: Berkley Books, The Penguin Group, 2011).

Koehler, John O., *Stasi: The Untold Story of the East German Secret Police* (New York: Westview Press, 1999).

Leo, Maxim, *Red Love: The Story of an East German Family* (London: Pushkin Press, 2013).

Maclean, Rory, *Berlin: Imagine a City* (London: Weidenfeld & Nicolson, 2014).

Marshall, Tim, *Divided: Why We're Living in an Age of Walls* (London: Elliott & Thompson, 2018).

Mitchell, Greg, *The Tunnels: The Untold Story of the Escapes Under the Berlin Wall* (London: Transworld Publishers, 2017).

O'Donnell, Kenneth and Powers, David, *Johnny, We Hardly Knew Ye: Memories of John Fitzgerald Kennedy* (Boston: Little, Brown, 1983).

Preston, Diana, *Eight Days at Yalta: How Churchill, Roosevelt and Stalin Shaped the Post-War World* (London: Picador, 2019).

Reeves, Richard, *President Kennedy: Profile of Power* (New York: Simon & Schuster, 1993).

Richie, Alexandra, *Faust's Metropolis: A History of Berlin* (London: HarperCollins, 1999).

Schneider, Peter, *The Wall Jumper* (New York: Pantheon, 1983).

Sesta, Ellen, *Der Tunnel in die Freiheit* (Berlin: Ullstein, 2001).

Smyser, W.R., *Kennedy and the Berlin Wall* (Lanham: Rowman & Littlefield, 2010).

Taylor, Frederick, *The Berlin Wall: 13 August 1961 – 9 November 1989* (London: Bloomsbury, 2006).

Veigel, Burkhart, *Wege durch die Maue: Fluchthilfe und Stasi zwischen Ost und West* (Berlin: Bernliner Unterwelten, 2013).

Vogel, Steve, *Betrayal in Berlin: The True Story of the Cold War's Most Audacious Espionage Operation* (New York: HarperCollins, 2019).

Watson, Mary, *The Expanding Vista: American Television in the Kennedy Years* (New York: Oxford University Press, 1990).

Wyden, Peter, *Wall: The Inside Story of a Divided Berlin* (New York: Simon & Schuster, 1989).

Acknowledgements

T O JOACHIM RUDOLPH, the heart of this book: thank you for spending so many hours sharing your memories with me, in your flat in Berlin, and on the phone during lockdown. You put up with my endless questions in the hope that by telling your story, a new generation would understand the Berlin Wall and its consequences better. Without you, this book would not exist.

I am enormously grateful to the other diggers, messengers and escapees who spoke to me, and in some cases shared their own Stasi files, with information that has never before been public: Wolfdieter Sternheimer, Renate Sternheimer, Evi Rudolph, Uli Pfeifer, Wolf Schroedter and Ellen Sesta. And thanks to Dr Burkhart Veigel for your valuable insights.

To Sabine Schereck, thanks for your expert translation, your eagle-eyed comments on my first draft, and for remaining calm when I first drove on German speed-limitless autobahns. I'm also grateful to my other translators: Ute Krebs, Alexander and Beatrix Mett, and Laura Horsfall.

In Berlin, thanks to Gudrun Heuts at the Stasi Archives for trawling through reports, interrogations, photos and videos, and to Holger Happel at Berliner Unterwelten for indulging my requests to spend so much time underground, stuffed into the replica of Tunnel 29.

In the US, thanks to Pamela Hopkins at Tufts University for unearthing revelatory papers relating to Reuven Frank.

To my agent, Karolina Sutton, thank you for your full-throttled support right from the start, for your incisive feedback on my first chapters, and for the green tea that powered me through at the end. Thanks also to Caitlin Leydon, Joanna Lee and Anna Weguelin at Curtis Brown, and a bucketful of gratitude to the unstoppable Luke Speed for your energetic work on the film and TV side of things.

At Hodder, huge thanks to Rebecca Folland, Melis Dagoglu, Grace

McCrum, Cameron Myers, Lesley Hodgson, Ian Wong, Maria Garbutt-Lucero and Alice Morley for your imaginative work in bringing this book to life. And to my brilliant editor, Rupert Lancaster: thank you for seeing that there was a bigger story to be told and for finding so many ways to improve it. And I'm grateful to Nick Fawcett for his skilful copy-editing.

At Public Affairs, thanks to Colleen Lawrie, Melissa Raymond, Jaime Leifer and Miguel Cervantes for all their work on the American edition and their belief in the book.

At the BBC, special thanks to Mohit Bakaya for commissioning the podcast series and for the creative corridor-chats along the way; and to Richard Knight for your Midas-touch editing and to Eloise Whitmore for your sound wizardry. To my BBC buddies at Radio Current Affairs, thank you for the heady conversations in the studios once the faders are down, and for the after-work pub pep-talks. You are the most talented, creative journalists I've ever worked with and I've learnt so much from you all.

To my friends: deep love and a million thank-yous for cheering me on while I wrote this and for keeping me afloat during three lockdowns with early morning jogs, moonlit walks and long conversations into the night. You kept me sane and inspired me more than you know.

To Rosie, Livy and Sas: thank you for being there through absolutely everything with wisdom and silliness and for all those times when life unravelled and you put me back together. Thanks to Seb, who inspires us all by climbing mountains (despite your vertigo), and to Jon, Trewin and Amit for all your loving support. Thanks to my dad, whose insatiable curiosity sparked mine, and to my mum for reading to me every night when I was little and for your wise comments after going through this manuscript.

To Sukie and John, thank you for your long-standing encouragement and the stomach-expanding surprises that appeared through the letterbox. And to Bea, who was full of helpful advice at just the right time.

To my podcast listeners: I am hugely grateful for your emails and letters and for telling me you wanted more (I hope you haven't changed your mind after reading this). And to the schoolchildren who listened to the podcast: thank you for showing me that even nine-year-olds care about walls and refugees and war, and for sending me the Tunnel-29-inspired stories you wrote during lockdown.

Thank you to my wise seven-year-old Matilda, who adores books as much as her namesake, and who in asking the most simple of questions about this story helped me see things more clearly. And to my imaginative, whirlwind three-year-old, Sam, thank you for showing your enthusiasm by requesting tunnel-related bedtime stories most nights. I hope you enjoy this one when you're old enough to read it.

Finally, my most gut-felt thanks to my partner-in-everything: Henry. Writing my first book during three lockdowns with two children mostly off school wasn't ideal, and I would never have reached the end without you – my soul-mate and master of lockdown-nursery. You were the first to read this and found so many ways to improve it. I love the way you come at things, how you always see what's right with an idea before spotting what's wrong with it, and the way you laugh at me. I am unbelievably lucky to have you.

January 2021

Picture Acknowledgements

Text

Index

An invitation from the publisher

Join us at www.hodder.co.uk, or follow us
on Twitter @hodderbooks to be a part of
our community of people who love the very
best in books and reading.

Whether you want to discover more about a book
or an author, watch trailers and interviews, have the
chance to win early limited editions, or simply browse
our expert readers' selection of the very best books,
we think you'll find what you're looking for.

And if you don't, that's the place to tell us what's missing.

We love what we do, and we'd love you to be a part of it.

www.hodder.co.uk

@hodderbooks

HodderBooks

HodderBooks